# Going Virtual: Distributed Communities of Practice

Paul M. Hildreth
Independent Knowledge Management Consultant, UK

**IDEA GROUP PUBLISHING**
Hershey • London • Melbourne • Singapore

| | |
|---|---|
| Acquisition Editor: | Mehdi Khosrow-Pour |
| Senior Managing Editor: | Jan Travers |
| Managing Editor: | Amanda Appicello |
| Development Editor: | Michele Rossi |
| Copy Editor: | Jane Conley |
| Typesetter: | Jennifer Wetzel |
| Cover Design: | Michelle Waters |
| Printed at: | Integrated Book Technology |

Published in the United States of America by
   Idea Group Publishing (an imprint of Idea Group Inc.)
   701 E. Chocolate Avenue, Suite 200
   Hershey PA 17033
   Tel: 717-533-8845
   Fax: 717-533-8661
   E-mail: cust@idea-group.com
   Web site: http://www.idea-group.com

and in the United Kingdom by
   Idea Group Publishing (an imprint of Idea Group Inc.)
   3 Henrietta Street
   Covent Garden
   London WC2E 8LU
   Tel: 44 20 7240 0856
   Fax: 44 20 7379 3313
   Web site: http://www.eurospan.co.uk

Library of Congress Cataloging-in-Publication Data

Hildreth, Paul M., 1959-
  Going virtual : distributed communities of practice / Paul M.
Hildreth.
     p. cm.
Includes bibliographical references and index.
   ISBN 1-59140-164-X -- ISBN 1-59140-271-9 (s/c)
   1. Knowledge management. 2. Organizational learning. 3.
Interprofessional relations. 4. Virtual work teams 5. Information
technology--Management. 6. International business
enterprises--Communication systems--Case studies. I. Title.
   HD30.2.H55 2004
   658.4'038--dc21
                               2003008766

eISBN 1-59140-165-8

British Cataloguing in Publication Data
A Cataloguing in Publication record for this book is available from the British Library.

# Dedication

*For Maggie and Tom*

# Going Virtual: Distributed Communities of Practice

# Table of Contents

# Preface

As commercial organisations face up to modern commercial pressures and react with measures such as downsizing and outsourcing, they have come to realise that they lose a lot of knowledge as people leave the organisation and take their knowledge with them. Further pressure is being placed on organisations by the increased internationalisation of business, resulting in collaboration and cooperation becoming more distributed and international. This means knowledge has to be increasingly shared across time and distance.

The loss of knowledge and the need to share knowledge across different locations has led to an increased awareness of its importance as a vital resource, and organisations are taking steps to manage it. Knowledge Management (KM) is an approach that claims to deal with this; however, a lot of Knowledge Management deals with structured knowledge and emphasises a "capture, codify, store" approach. This is a major weakness of the current approach to KM, as a large part of it appears to equate more with Information Management. It is only very recently that there has been recognition and exploration of the importance of more subtle types of knowledge that need to be shared. Sharing such knowledge in a distributed environment has received even less attention, and there is a need for new ways of thinking about how knowledge is shared in distributed groups.

This recognition of the importance of the more subtle kinds of knowledge has caused even more debate. Many terms have been coined to describe the different types of knowledge — structured/unstructured, formal/informal, know what/know how and, the one which that appears to be most popular, Nonaka's (1991) explicit/tacit. They all, however, have the same approach and view different types of knowledge as opposites. An exception appears to be Leonard and Sensiper (1998) who prefer to view knowledge as a continuum, but even in this case the extremes (explicit at one end and tacit at the other) function as opposites.

These "less-structured" types of knowledge cannot easily be articulated and therefore cannot be as easily captured, codified, and stored. This poses further challenges as to how they should be shared. Currently, the main approach to this problem in KM appears to be to try to "convert" the less-structured knowledge into a form from which it can be captured, codified, and stored.

This approach would appear to be flawed in that it continues to fall into the same traps as existing KM approaches. Therefore, the approach described in this book moves away from regarding knowledge as made up of opposites, preferring to regard knowledge as a soft/hard duality where all knowledge is both soft and hard. It is simply the proportions that differ. This means that "converting" knowledge is an approach that cannot work, and another approach must be sought.

Lave and Wenger's (1991) Communities of Practice (CoPs) are identified as providing an environment that supports the sharing of the softer kinds of knowledge. Since Lave and Wenger introduced the term in 1991, CoPs have received a lot of attention and are currently the subject of much research and interest in both academia and commercial organisations. Initially a theory of learning, they are now firmly established as an organisational form in the commercial environment. They cannot be created or managed, as they are driven by an internal motivation and common purpose. Organisations that recognise their importance, look for them (as they are often unofficial and outside the formal structure of the company) and try to support, facilitate, and coach them as they evolve.

To date, CoPs have generally been co-located and studies of CoPs have taken place in co-located environments, but the pressures of globalisation are leading to an increasing need to share knowledge in a physically distributed environment. It is therefore important to explore how CoPs might function in such an environment and that is the subject of this book.

The book is organised in two parts:

The first sets the context for the book. It is an exploration of KM to date that explains the weaknesses of current KM approaches and introduces the notion of the soft/hard knowledge duality. The softer side of knowledge is examined from the point of view of three different approaches to knowledge at work:

- Common Ground (Clark, 1996);
- The theory of Distributed Cognition (Hutchins, 1995), and Boundary Objects (Star, 1989); and

- Communities of Practice (CoPs), which are identified as groups in which soft knowledge is created, sustained, and nurtured.

The second part is an in-depth study of the interactions and work of a distributed international CoP that has members in the UK, the US, and Japan. It covers electronic communication, face-to-face meetings, the problems experienced by the community, and how the members solve those problems. The method used to investigate the interactions of this CoP proved to be very useful for CoP work, and it is therefore described in some detail in the Appendices.

This book is presented in eight chapters to:

- discuss in detail the context of the subject;
- present the study of the CoP; and
- discuss the issues arising from the study and the implications for KM researchers and practitioners.

In Chapter I, we note that the pressures of downsizing, outsourcing, and globalisation have all contributed to the importance of knowledge and its recognition as an organisational resource. We also observe that, as a resource, knowledge needs to be managed. Knowledge Management is introduced as a field that is claimed to address this issue.

In Chapter II, we explore KM in greater detail. The notion of knowledge as a resource is taken further with a review of KM approaches that, up until recently, have tended to concentrate on the historical aspect, that is, sharing knowledge in a temporally distributed environment. We examine KM views of knowledge and see that there is a shift to recognising the importance of less structured knowledge that is difficult to abstract and capture. In this chapter, we make the distinction between "soft" and "hard" knowledge and argue that KM has gone through phases, managing hard knowledge by codifying and storing in order to share it, but that the present emphasis is on the sharing of soft knowledge. We raise the question as to what would be involved in sharing soft knowledge in a physically distributed environment.

Chapter III continues from Chapter II and further explores soft knowledge from three different perspectives, Common Ground (Clark, 1996), Distributed Cognition (Hutchins, 1995) including boundary objects (Star, 1989), and CoPs (Lave & Wenger, 1991). CoPs are identified as groups where soft knowledge is created, sustained, and nurtured. Different views of CoPs are taken and synthesised into a single view. We explore Wenger's (1998) recent work on CoPs to bring the notion of CoPs up- to-date. We note, however, that CoPs are regarded as an essentially co-located phenomenon, and therefore the problem facing the sharing of soft knowledge is how to facilitate their functioning in a distributed international environment.

In Chapter IV, we explore virtual teams and communities in order to highlight the issues that would face a CoP that has to operate in a distributed environment.

The study of the CoP itself is divided into two stages. The first is presented in Chapter V. We are introduced to the members of the community and spend a few days in the life of the community, covering interactions within the UK group, communication with the US side of the CoP, meetings, and media. We explore some initial insights from the first stage of the study and describe them in terms of the CoP characteristics and issues that are outlined in Chapter III. This helps us prepare for our participation in Stage Two.

In Stage Two of the Case Study, we travel with the UK members of the CoP to America and participate in one of their regular visits. This is covered in Chapter VI and covers their meetings, social events, collaboration, and planning. We also look at the issues and insights that arise from our time spent with the CoP in America.

In the case study, we have a detailed and interesting insight into the interactions and working of a distributed international CoP, but this is only one CoP. In Chapter VII, we talk to members of two other distributed international CoPs to see if what we have learned is true in other CoPs. The CoPs in this case are different from the main CoP in that the practice of the communities was extra to their normal work.

In Chapter VIII, we pull all the insights together in order to look at the lessons we have learned from the Case Study and to provide some answers to the questions and issues that were posed in Chapters III and IV. Key issues that are drawn out are the importance of both shared artefacts and the development of a strong relationship between the CoP members, often created in a face-to-face setting.

The method used for studying the CoP was an adaptation of the Contextual Design method (Beyer & Holtzblatt, 1998). It is a work analysis and redesign method, broadly ethnographic in approach, and it proved very useful for obtaining a detailed insight into the inner workings of a CoP. As it proved so useful in this area, a description and evaluation of the method is included in the appendices.

I hope that through the exploration of the CoP in the case study the issues that arise and the lessons that we learn will be of use to both academics and practitioners working in the field of CoPs. It raises the questions as to how CoPs and associated social issues should be managed, and demonstrates that it is essentially a human activity at the level of practice. The understanding that arises from the case studies should help practitioners be aware of problems and issues that are involved in supporting CoPs (especially those in a distributed environment). More importantly, it demonstrates that practitioners need to change their views of the organisation during the planning and implementation of KM projects. For example, practitioners need to explore where the social relationships are and how they can be supported rather than looking at the organisation in terms of where the information is and how it flows. Instead of simply looking for information flow and storage (the "hard" approach of capture/codify/store), it is essential to also consider and explore the social networks in the organisation (the "soft" side of the duality).

# REFERENCES

Beyer, H. & Holtzblatt, K. (1998). *Contextual design.* San Francisco, CA: Morgan Kaufmann.

Clark, H. (1996). *Using language.* Cambridge, UK: Cambridge University Press.

Hutchins, E. (1995). *Cognition in the wild.* Cambridge, MA: MIT Press.

Lave, J. & Wenger, E. (1991) *Situated learning. Legitimate peripheral participation.* Cambridge, UK: Cambridge University Press.

Leonard, D. & Sensiper, S. (1998). The role of tacit knowledge in group innovation. *California Management Review,* 40(3): 12-132.

Nonaka, I. (1991). The knowledge creating company. *Harvard Businesses Review,* (November/December): 96-104.

Star, S. L. (1989). The structure of ill-structured solutions: Boundary objects and heterogeneous distributed problem solving. *Distributed Artificial Intelligence,* 2: 37-54.

Wenger, E. (1998). *Communities of practice. Learning, meaning and identity.* Cambridge, UK: Cambridge University Press.

# Acknowledgments

This book is an adapted and shortened version of work that I undertook for my DPhil. The four years spent working on the research were stimulating, but difficult and exhausting. They were, however, not lonely years, for I had the support and encouragement of many people and the end would not have been reached without their help.

Grateful thanks are due to my supervisors at the University of York where this work was undertaken, Chris Kimble and Peter Wright, for the ready guidance, encouragement, and feedback that they provided over the four years. Sincere thanks must also go to Mike, Dave, and Stanley for giving so willingly of their time in the case study, and especially to Wayne for his help and support in organizing it.

The four years would have been much more difficult if it was not for the encouragement of my dear friends in the Management Information Systems Research Group who generated such a supportive, warm, and friendly atmosphere in the office.

I am also very grateful to the team at IGP who have been a big help in adapting the thesis, and then through the whole process of publication. They have all been most understanding of the difficulties and have been a great help in sorting out any problems and in keeping the whole process on track.

Of course, I must say a big thank you to my family, Maggie and Tom, my Mum and Dad, and my mother-in-law, for all the support, encouragement, and love that kept me going.

Finally, I must thank Trevor and Maggie, without whom I would not even have had the chance to embark on this fascinating path.

*Paul M. Hidreth*
*Independent Knowledge Management Consultant, UK*
*April 2003*

# SECTION I:

# BACKGROUND AND CONTEXT

# Chapter I

# Introduction

*The case study features a distributed international Community of Practice (CoP). CoPs are currently playing a major role in Knowledge Management (KM), and as organisations need to operate in a global economy, CoPs are having to function more and more in distributed environments. This chapter provides a context and background for the study by exploring the need for organisations to capitalise on their knowledge.*

## KNOWLEDGE IN THE MODERN ORGANISATION

Commercial organisations operating in the modern business environment face a range of pressures, of which globalisation, downsizing, and outsourcing are prime examples. These three pressures are each impacting on the knowledge of an organisation and have led to knowledge being recognised as a valuable resource that needs to be managed.

Downsizing and outsourcing mean a reduction in personnel. As people leave an organisation, it has been noticed that they take valuable knowledge with them. The organisations have lost not only people, but also part of their experience base. They have lost replaceable expertise, for example, knowledge of facts and figures or skills that can be brought in or perhaps even automated. Davenport and Prusak (1998) observe that after employees have left an organisation as a result of downsizing it is realised that the organisation has lost some essential knowledge, and efforts are made to buy in the equivalent of this knowledge from outside.

Downsizing and outsourcing also result in the loss of a less easily replaced knowledge, over and above the replaceable skill that has been lost; that is the experience of how work is done in the organisation. As companies have cut out middle management, they are finding out that they have lost people who knew the details of the organisation — how to deal with different people, who to approach for specific problems, who best to use for different tasks, in short, who knew how to make things happen, and who had the knowledge required to get things done. Leonard and Sensiper (1998) noticed the same: "tacit knowledge also underlies many competitive capabilities — a fact driven home to some companies in the wake of aggressive downsizing, when undervalued knowledge walked out of the door" (p. 112).

The problem is not new. Rainbird reported in 1986 on the impact of new technology in the workplace. The technology was used to monitor highs and lows in labour demand thus enabling a greater use of part-time and temporary labour. It had, however, not been recognised that people accumulate experience and knowledge that they then apply while undertaking their work. The result, according to Rainbird, was that:

> *In their haste to let people go, they lost skills which were essential to production. These skills, though not formally recognised, had been acquired through experience and were based on knowledge of the system, the product and an ability to identify faults in the functioning of production lines ... the company had to bring back these unskilled women workers who had been made redundant, many of whom had subsequently found alternative employment, to train the new employees (p. 11).*

This trend has continued up to the present as companies continue to outsource and downsize or euphemistically, "rightsize," but they continue to have the same problems. It is not so long ago that companies were proudly stating that their people were their greatest asset. Now some of those companies are getting rid of people to cut costs, but they don't realise what they are losing. In some cases they have lost whole swathes of middle management — the very people who knew how things worked and how to get things done.

This intangible aspect was evident in a description by Button and Sharrock (1994) of a group of software engineers who were developing the embedded software for a new photocopier. When using a method (for example, Structured Systems Analysis and Design Method — SSADM), it is sometimes assumed that the method can be followed and that cheaper, less experienced personnel can be used. Button and Sharrock's example shows that this is not the case: the software project had problems, not least with lack of access to the original designers and difficulties with language. The project was only a success in the end because of the experience of the team who had to make the method work. This all shows that loss of personnel could create a problem as organisations move to cheaper, less knowledge-rich workers. This loss of knowledge causes a historical problem, in that the knowledge of skilled people needs to be available for those who come later.

Globalisation is a separate issue that impacts most organisations in some way — even the smallest companies may depend on goods that are produced abroad. It affects their knowledge resource in a different way from outsourcing and downsizing. Castells (1996) observes that the development of globalisation has been rapid and has led to an informational and global economy. It is informational in that — partly due to the influence of new electronic communication media — the success of many participants in the global economy is dependent on their ability to create and process electronic information. It is global in that most of the important parts of the economy are organised on a global scale. This may be through multinationals, networks of smaller organisations, or smaller organisations that work with the larger corporations, perhaps in the form of suppliers. Even those companies that do not expand or restructure to take advantage of the global marketplace are finding that they are being subject to competition from companies that are doing exactly that (de Geus, 1997). Globalisation means that transactions, collaboration, cooperation, and the sharing of data, information and knowledge occur over vast distances. This means that organisations must cope with the difficulties posed by physical and temporal distance, and organisational and national cultural differences. Information and Communication Technologies (ICTs) have been both drivers and enablers in the internationalisation of business operations, and there have been studies to explore the issues that arise when Information Technology (IT) is applied in the international field (Deans, Karwan, Goslar, Ricks, & Toyne, 1991).

Global competition is forcing some organisations to undergo some restructuring in order to operate successfully in the new global arena. Multinational companies have been in existence for many years, but new forms, such as international, global, and transnational have been identified (Ives & Jarvenpaa, 1992; Karimi & Konsynski, 1991). Recent years have also seen many mergers and acquisitions, joint ventures, and alliances. These have led to a structural form described by Castells (1996) as a Network Enterprise. These are networks formed by corporations of all sizes working together and are based on extensive application of networked communication media. Similar organisational forms have also been discussed by Barnatt (1997), and Lincoln, Ahmadjian, and Mason (1998), who observed how networks of small specialist companies could outperform large corporations. These changes mean that information and knowledge will have to be shared between companies who might never have imagined having to work together, but it is the *sharing* of the knowledge and expertise that will make a network enterprise successful. The successful organisation will be one that is able to process information quickly and generate new knowledge. The global economy changes rapidly in terms of both culture and technology and to be successful organisations need to be able to respond quickly and be innovative — and for this they need to capitalise on the knowledge within the organisation.

## The Need to Manage the Knowledge Resource

The result of the downsizing, outsourcing, and globalisation pressures is a need to share knowledge distributed.

(a)   Over time: downsizing and outsourcing result in a need to share knowledge between people in two different time periods. It is a historical perspective in that knowledge has to be taken from people who are in the organisation at one time and be kept and passed on to people who come later.

(b)   Over space: globalisation has resulted in a need for knowledge sharing distributed over space, that is, a physical distribution between people in different locations.

This means that organisations must realise that knowledge is a valuable resource, with Nonaka (1991) describing it as the "one sure source of competitive advantage" (p. 96). The importance of knowledge can also be seen in the growing number of "knowledge workers" in commercial organisations. Knowledge workers use the knowledge they have learned in education rather than using strength and muscle as do manual workers. Drucker (1992) points out that they still use tools (for example, computers, technical instruments, etc.), but previously the worker was subordinate to the machine in that what he or she did and when he or she did it was defined by the machine; whereas in the case of the knowledge worker, the machine is unproductive without the skill and knowledge of the knowledge worker. Knowledge workers are more capable of solving a problem themselves using what they know, rather than having to stick rigidly to some externally defined procedure. Their experience is an essential part of their ability to do their jobs. Kidd (1994) explained that knowledge workers see their value in being able to understand some specific body of knowledge and from that understanding can generate new interpretations and knowledge that may benefit the organisation and the customer in some way.

> *They are highly motivated ... actively to learn can change their thinking throughout their careers. This means that if the individual doing a job changes, then the company gets a different product as a result. This is not true for other kinds of workers (p. 187).*

Organisations have also realised that, as a valuable resource, knowledge needs to be managed. Knowledge Management (KM) is a fast growing field that claims to tackle the need to share knowledge in both the temporally and physically distributed environments. As a result it has attracted much attention in both academic and commercial circles. The field of KM is interdisciplinary and the researchers and practitioners working in the field of KM represent a wide range of backgrounds. A glance through a KM journal reveals contributions from business and management specialists, psychologists, social scientists, information scientists, and computer scientists.

KM is a field that is now well established. For a long time KM was pursued through Artificial Intelligence (AI), viewing knowledge as a commodity that can be stored, transmitted, and codified. Expert systems were created to "capture" the knowledge of experts. Efforts were also made to capture knowledge in databases, manuals, books, and reports and then share them in this hard form. Emphasis was also placed on managing codified knowledge assets that were tangible in the form of patents, trademarks, and documents. It is only recently, however, that attention has been paid to other forms of knowledge that are more subtle than that currently pursued by the AI field. The newer KM strand sees knowledge as being less structured (Allee, 1997; Kidd, 1994; Manville & Foote, 1996; Skyrme 1998) and not so easily abstracted, codified, and stored for sharing. This means that in downsizing and outsourcing there is a type of knowledge lost that is not easily replaced. Examples of such knowledge might be skill, expertise, and intuition. Craftsmen making musical instruments work to fine tolerances but they "know" when a part is not up to standard, when it does not "feel right" (Cook & Seely Brown, 1999). Such knowledge cannot simply be captured and recorded for future workers. When a worker leaves the organisation, the skill and expertise also leaves. As it cannot easily be abstracted and captured, it is also not easy to share. Knowledge, which is easily captured in books, leaflets, and instructions, can be transmitted all over the world using modern technologies. The sharing of more subtle knowledge clearly poses different problems if it cannot easily be abstracted and captured. Global working leads to an increased need to share knowledge but poses further problems for the sharing of more subtle knowledge in the forms of time and distance.

In this book we will explore this less structured knowledge in more detail and see how it can be "managed" through communities called Communities of Practice (CoPs) where this type of knowledge is created, sustained, and nurtured. Despite the importance of the current trend to globalisation, these are communities that, up until recently, have been explored in co-located situations. There is, therefore, scope for exploring how CoPs function in the distributed international environment, and what particular requirements there may be for this to happen. This should provide insights into how the more subtle kinds of knowledge may be managed in such environments.

**Chapter II**

# Knowledge Management

*In this chapter, we will explore the field of KM in order to set the context for the study. We will examine the tools and techniques for the management of knowledge from a historical perspective and also explore the issues for managing knowledge in a spatially distributed environment. We will see that there is a tension between different views of knowledge and, for the purposes of this book, we will regard knowledge as "soft" and "hard" as a working definition.*

## INTRODUCTION

We have already seen in Chapter I that commercial organisations have come to recognise the value of the knowledge that is held in the organisation. As knowledge has come to be recognised as an important resource and a valuable asset, it has also been recognised that it must be managed as such. KM is a rapidly growing field that is dismissed by some as simply the most recent management trend but recognised by others as essential if organisations are to cope with pressures brought about by downsizing, outsourcing, and globalisation.

There is a wealth of definitions of KM available, most of which will have different meanings for different people. However, if something is to be managed, many people feel it must be able to be quantified, counted, organised, and measured (Glazer, 1998), and it must be able to be built, owned, controlled, and its value maximised (Allee, 1997). This view of "management" has influenced attempts to manage knowledge and led to attempts to quantify, capture, and control it as an object. More recent developments in KM have demonstrated that this approach to the management of knowledge is too restricted and that some aspects of knowledge cannot be captured. Therefore, the concept of KM has had to be broadened to include elements of sharing, learning, the generation of new knowledge, and the application of knowledge.

## MANAGING KNOWLEDGE FROM THE HISTORICAL PERSPECTIVE

In Chapter I we saw that organisations have lost personnel through downsizing and outsourcing activities. As staff have left the organisation, they have taken knowledge with them. As a result of this, initial attempts at KM consisted of trying to "capture" knowledge in order to be able to use it when people had left or at least to be able to pass it to new people who may be less skilled than their predecessors.

This approach views "knowledge as information" and as an object that can be codified. This led to attempts in the 1980s using AI to extract the knowledge of experts in order to create "expert systems." Von Krogh (1998) refers to the aim of this approach as being "to create information-processing machines that would resemble human intelligence. These machines would, like the brain, manipulate symbols and thereby solve predefined problems" (pp. 148-149).

The difficulty of this approach was demonstrated by Roschelle (1996), who explored the use of computers in learning. He was particularly interested in whether representing the mental models of experts was sufficient to help novices. As a result of his studies he came to the conclusions that:

> *Gaps between world views prevent students from interpreting displays literally, and thus limit the extent to which communication can be achieved by representing knowledge accurately. Hence, rather than merely representing mental models accurately, designers must focus on supporting communicative practices (p. 15).*

The expert systems failed to live up to expectations and only a few of the expert systems developed in the 1980s were still in use in the early 1990s

(Davenport &Prusak, 1998). Part of the reason for this may well be the exaggerated predictions made for such systems, which perhaps led to unrealistic expectations. The expert systems attempted to capture knowledge as explicit decision rules. Most of the systems did not meet expectations because decision rules have a limited scope and are not able to cater to rapidly changing environments (Davenport & Klahr, 1998), and because knowledge is not like this.

Berg (1997) describes the difficulties in developing and implementing two medical expert systems and observes that the systems did not work as intended. That is, in order to function at all, the practice in the environment had to be changed, and the systems failed to fulfill the original expectations of the developers in terms of power and scope and also the original aim of single-moment intervention. The systems had to become localised — both in scope and in space. They were localised in scope in that the original hopes for the system had to be drastically scaled down, and they were localised in space in that they did not transplant to other environments, both in terms of a more universal application and in terms of the same application in a different environment.

Despite the failure of expert systems to live up to expectations, the view of knowledge as an object that can be captured continues to dominate the KM field, with some researchers still viewing the capture of knowledge as the main challenge (Alavi & Leidner, 1997). Work continues in AI under the heading of Knowledge Engineering and using ontologies (Buckingham Shum, 1998; Vasconcelos, 1999), and Case-Based Reasoning[1] (CBR) (Davenport & Klahr, 1998).

Later attempts at KM continued to view knowledge as an object, but the emphasis shifted from trying to encode knowledge into expert systems to the creation of systems for capturing it and storing it for subsequent sharing. This is still a view that is prevalent in many definitions. This approach continues to focus on the capture-codify-store cycle and attempts to separate knowledge from people. This approach views knowledge as something which can be abstracted and which is embodied in documents (for example, books, reports, presentations) and which can be stored using databases, knowledge bases[2] and data warehousing[3].

There are, however, successful examples of this approach to KM. In attempting to manage knowledge in line with the view of management as quantification and control, many companies looked for tangible examples of what they termed their "intellectual assets," such as patents, copyrights, trademarks, and documents. Allee (1997) and Cohen (1998) both cite the example of Dow Chemical. Dow Chemical concentrated on screening patents to ascertain which should be exploited, licensed, or abandoned. This area was previously under-explored and exploiting it has resulted in $40 million savings over ten years and $125 million in licensing income. Other examples are of companies creating organisational directories or "Yellow Pages" of staff members with specific expertise. Others speak of the organisational knowledge in manuals, databases, document repositories, and filing cabinets. This is the most common use of technology in KM — to create a repository of structured or explicit knowledge (Davenport & Prusak, 1998), but this has more in common with Information Resource Management (IRM). Indeed, IRM is a necessary *part* of KM, but, in some cases, what is presented as being KM is simply IRM with a new label. This is reflected in the offerings of Knowledge Management Systems (KMS). Many of these are marketed as being total solutions for KM needs, but in fact many are simply the vendor's information retrieval system that has been given a new name to capitalise on the KM market.

Unfortunately the total KMS does not exist. As KM is not a single simple process but a range of processes, the needs of KM are too broad for any one system to be able to cater to them all. More important, however, is the recognition that IT is not a solution but an enabler and a support.

Despite this recognition, there is still a bias in the trade literature to approaches that view knowledge as an object. As a result, many organisations still equate knowledge with information and regard it as an object that exists on its own and can therefore be captured, stored, and transmitted. This leads to a technology driven approach to KM, as discussed by Fahey and Prusak (1998):

> *This orientation is in turn reflected in and reinforced by the pervasive information technology approach to the management of data and information: capture, store, retrieve, and transmit. Although organizations obviously need to manage their data and information using these technology-centered models, knowledge is a substantially different thing and thus needs different models (p. 267).*

From all this we can see that in the management of knowledge from a historical perspective one specific view of knowledge has been prevalent, that is, as a commodity that can be represented, stored, and manipulated. As a result, two primary routes have been followed:

1.   To capture the knowledge structure or mental model of an expert and encode it into an expert system. This was an approach that did not live up to expectations.
2.   To capture, store, and disseminate knowledge, for example, in books, databases, and reports. This has led to a need to cope with information overload and has more in common with IRM than KM; however, it does demonstrate that IRM is an essential part of KM.

# GLOBALISATION — THE NEED TO MANAGE KNOWLEDGE DISTRIBUTED OVER SPACE

Unlike outsourcing and downsizing, which have resulted in attempts to share knowledge across time by capturing and codifying it and then storing it for later use by other people, globalisation is a pressure that requires knowledge to be shared across space. This raises different issues and problems.

A major difference is that the two communication partners, generally speaking, have access to each other. There is a time element in that they may be in different time zones and communicating asynchronously, but the time perspective is on a different scale and they do have the opportunity to communicate.

Globalisation has not only increased the need to communicate in a physically distributed environment, but it has also extended the scale of this to distribute the environment across international borders. This causes issues of time differences, as mentioned above, and also physical distance, problems of language, and of culture.

In addition to the globalisation of technology, economy and communication, Castells (1996) also observes the impact globalisation has on identity and social change. He demonstrates this by defining two main areas: the Net and the Self. For Castells, the Net is the interaction of technological innovation and social relations. The Self, on the other hand, is how society is defined by the way social groups define their identity. Castells also notes that the Net and the Self are inseparable, for social and technical changes are interrelated. Society cannot be understood without its technological tools. The result of the most recently developed technological tools is what Castells calls the "space of flows." That is, the integrated global network that is made of three parts: the technology (the infrastructure), the places (that is, the hubs and nodes of the network with local cultural and social conditions), and the people. The space of flows has brought about a culture of what Castells terms "real virtuality." Here time is timeless and space is placeless. The result of this is that global economic effects are felt in local communities. People are working in the space of flows but are living in the physical world. Castells terms the result of this clash a "condition of structural schizophrenia" and suggests that people are losing their sense of self and are having to look for their identity in new forms. Thus organisations operating in the global environment have the advantages of access to a vast pool of staff and expertise and modern communication media that render barriers of time and space practically irrelevant but which also raise different cultural and social barriers. This raises the question as to how companies might best manage their knowledge in such an environment.

It could be said, particularly by exponents of the KM approaches outlined earlier in this chapter, that these issues are not major hurdles and that knowledge can still be captured, stored, and then shared by electronic transmission. This may well be true according to the view of knowledge as a capturable commodity; however, language and cultural issues could nevertheless create barriers to the successful sharing of the knowledge. Of more importance, alongside the barriers created by globalisation, there has been a recent realisation that there is some knowledge that cannot be captured. If the knowledge cannot be captured, codified, or stored, this means that sharing it, both over time and space, is even more difficult and presents KM with different issues and challenges for the management of such knowledge. It is only recently that the need to manage knowledge that cannot be captured and codified has been recognised.

## WHAT IS MISSING?

Until recently what was missing was an acknowledgment that not all knowledge can be captured, codified, and stored. This has now been recognised and has started to receive attention. Interestingly, it has also been acknowledged within the community that could be seen to be most firmly entrenched in the capture-codify approach (Buckingham Shum, 1998), where a recognition has been made of the importance of socially constructed knowledge:

*There appeared to be a strong sense at a recent symposium on AI's role in KM ... that formal representation of knowledge*

*seems to have a limited role to play in organizational knowledge
management, with the emphasis shifting to supporting the
social, coordinated processes through which knowledge is
constructed (p. 74).*

This recognition that not all knowledge can be treated as an object has
raised other difficulties. In the first place, if there is knowledge that cannot be
objectified, this has implications for the management of knowledge. The view
of KM as quantifying, measuring, and controlling is no longer sufficient and the
definition of KM needs to be broadened. This has led to a further difficulty.
There is now a wide variety of KM definitions to the point where there is no real
consensus as to what KM *is*. This was demonstrated by Alavi and Leidner
(1997), who investigated KM views among Chief Information Officers (CIOs),
Information Systems (IS) Managers, and functional area executives, and found
it to be the case even among business practitioners. In fact, they found three
strands:

- An information-based view that is often the dominant view, that is, of
  knowledge being codifiable, then being captured, stored, and transmitted.
- A technology-based view that sees KM in terms of IT solutions.
- A culture-based view that is based on a different view of knowledge.

*Table 1: Perspectives on the Meaning of Knowledge Management (Adapted
from Alavi & Leidner, 1997, p. 13)*

| Information-based | Technology-based | Culture-based |
|---|---|---|
| Actionable Information<br>Categorizing of Data<br>Corporate Yellow Pages<br>Filtered Information<br>Free Text and Concepts<br>People Information Archive<br>Readily Accessible Information | Data Mining<br>Data Warehouses<br>Executive Information Systems<br>Expert Systems<br>Intelligent Agents<br>Intranet<br>Multimedia<br>Search Engines<br>Smart Systems | Collective Learning<br>Continuous Learning<br>Intellectual Property Cultivation<br>Learning Organisation |

Alavi and Leidner's (1997) survey reveals the tension between the views.
The information-based view is the traditional view of KM, treating knowledge
as an object. The technology-based view is a continuation of this but also
reflects the view of those people who consider that KM consists of simply

implementing technology in order to manipulate the abstracted knowledge. The shift to recognising the importance of knowledge that cannot be captured is reflected in the third view that places more importance on "learning." This still only reflects the beginning of a shift in views; the long list of examples in the information- and technology-based views (Table 1) demonstrates the long-established work that has been done in this field. The four examples given for the culture-based view show that, while people finally recognise the importance of this area, there is still some way to go to understand fully what is needed to manage this type of knowledge.

Karl Sveiby (n.d.) explains the difference in more detail. He identifies two distinct approaches to KM, which correspond with the information-based and culture-based views encountered by Alavi and Leidner (1997):

- Track 1: This track views knowledge as information. To researchers and practitioners in this field, it is an object that can be captured and handled in an information system. People in this field will have a background in computer science or information science and will be involved in AI and information management systems. Sveiby states that this is a new and fast growing track, based on developments in IT.
- Track 2: Sveiby feels that this is an old track that is not growing very fast. People in this field regard knowledge as processes, constantly changing skills, and expertise, and have their backgrounds in philosophy, psychology, sociology, and management. This track corresponds more closely with the culture-based approach.

Sveiby also categorises KM on two levels:
- the individual level where the focus in research and practice is on the individual; and
- the organisational level where the focus is on the organisation.

This view is summarised in Table 2.

*Table 2: Sveiby's Knowledge Management Perspectives*

| | Knowledge Management | |
|---|---|---|
| **Track/Level** | **Knowledge = Object** | **Knowledge = Process** |
| **Organisation Level** | "Re-engineers" | "Organisation Theorists" |
| **Individual Level** | "AI Specialists" | "Psychologists" |

The positive aspect of this view is that it recognises the different strands, but the situation has since changed. The information track was the fastest growing as a result of developments in IT; however, although the knowledge-as-process track subscribes to an older view of knowledge, it is only recently that its importance to the organisation has been recognised. Sveiby's identification of the strands is helpful but still does not explain the different challenges that this poses to KM — this type of knowledge is so tied to people that when they leave an organisation, the knowledge leaves with them, despite the best efforts of knowledge engineers with their rules and formulas.

This poses the question that if this knowledge cannot be captured and codified, what does "management" mean? There is, therefore, a need for a more all-encompassing approach to defining KM, moving from quantification, measurement, and control to involve a generative aspect (for example, learning and knowledge creation), sharing and application, retention, trying to organise it, and ensuring it is available where and when it is needed. The American Productivity and Quality Center (APQC) with the consulting company Arthur Andersen (now known as Accenture) has jointly developed a KM framework that shows the importance of managing *all* knowledge resources, and not just concentrating on the capture/codify/store cycle.

This diagram represents all the elements that APQC and Arthur Andersen believe require consideration when managing knowledge. It acknowledges the views of knowledge as object and process. It views KM as dynamic

*Figure 1: Knowledge Management Framework (From Finerty, 1997; O'Dell & Jackson Grayson, 1998)*

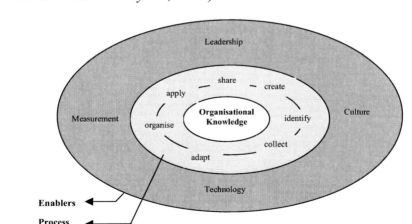

processes, and therefore shows two "orbits," one that shows the organisational enablers of technology, culture, leadership, and measurement. The second, inner orbit shows KM processes. Identify, collect, and organise refer more to the "knowledge as object," or "knowledge as information" aspect and relate to the capture-codify-store approach that has thus far been dominant. Create, apply, and adapt are KM processes that are applied when knowledge is viewed as a process. Sharing knowledge is necessary for all knowledge. How the knowledge is shared differs according to the type of knowledge.

A positive aspect of the diagram is the recognition of enablers, including technology. This is in contrast to some of Alavi and Leidner's (1997) respondents who regarded the implementation of IT as being KM itself. Figure 1 suggests that IT is simply an enabler, not a solution, and that more than IT is essential. It shows that culture is important — for example, if an organisation has not or cannot create a sharing culture, then KM initiatives will not be successful. In order to create such a culture, effective leadership is important. Measurement as an enabler is perhaps the weakest point of the diagram. Many people have the view that if something is to be managed, it must be able to be measured. Applying measurement criteria to KM initiatives may convince some skeptics of their use; however, quantification is not easy with a subject such as knowledge and as such could perhaps only be applied to tangibles such as training courses, books, databases, and database transactions — all of which are instances of "traditional" KM. Measurement would be difficult to apply to the management of this other type of knowledge.

The wider definition of KM helps — it shows the need for more than quantification and control by demonstrating the need for the generation of new knowledge, for sharing, for distributing, and for retention — but it still does not explain how this might be done for knowledge that cannot be captured and stored. This poses further questions for the KM community — what knowledge can be stored and what is the knowledge that cannot be captured?

These questions have led to a confused picture of knowledge within the KM community as researchers and practitioners have sought to define the knowledge that can be captured and that which cannot.

## KM Views of Knowledge

In exploring more subtle types of knowledge the prevalent view in KM has been that such knowledge is "tacit" (Nonaka, 1991; Polanyi, 1967) and that codifiable knowledge is explicit.

The interest in tacit knowledge in KM has come about because of an Eastern influence in the field of KM. Cohen (1998) points to Nonaka and Konno (1998) as an example of the differing approaches between East and West.

Table 3 shows how the Western view of KM reflects the dominant view of knowledge as being an object that can be captured and codified. The Japanese or Eastern view places more of an emphasis on tacit knowledge.

*Table 3:  West-East KM Contrasts (Adapted from Cohen, 1998, p. 24)*

| West | East |
|---|---|
| Focus on Explicit Knowledge | Focus on Tacit Knowledge |
| Re-Use | Creation |
| Knowledge Projects | Knowledge Cultures |
| Knowledge Markets | Knowledge Communities |
| Management and Measurement | Nurturing and Love |
| Near-Term Gains | Long-Term Advantage |

Explicit knowledge is knowledge that is easily expressed, captured, codified, stored, and reused. It is easily transmitted as data and is therefore found in databases, books, manuals, reports, and messages. Tacit knowledge, however, according to Nonaka (1991) is something very personal and difficult to articulate (and therefore difficult to communicate to other people). Nonaka also explains that it is rooted in action and consists "partly of skills — the kind of informal, hard-to-pin-down skills captured in the term 'know-how'" (p. 98).

He described how tacit knowledge is shared in a "spiral" of knowledge (Figure 2).

*Figure 2: Nonaka's Spiral of Knowledge*

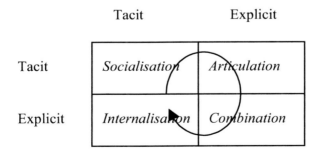

He explained this with the example of a developer who was part of a team trying to design a bread-making machine. As the team had problems, one of the developers had the idea of apprenticing herself to a master baker. She trained with the master baker, observing the special way he stretched the dough. She returned to her team, and after a long period of trial-and-error, the team came up with the successful specifications for the design of the machine. Nonaka described the developer's period of "apprenticeship" with the baker as the time when she was being "socialised" into the craft; that is, there was tacit knowledge transfer. Returning to her team, he says she was able to "articulate" or externalise the knowledge she had acquired, moving it from her tacit knowledge to explicit knowledge in order to communicate it. The following stage in the spiral is where tacit knowledge of one field is combined with tacit knowledge of another field, as in the example of the externalised tacit bread-making knowledge being combined with the knowledge of the development field. Finally, the new knowledge is internalised and becomes tacit knowledge. Nonaka emphasises that the sharing of tacit knowledge is exchanged through joint activities and requires physical proximity, and that externalisation needs tacit knowledge to be translated into forms that can be understood by others. However, an important aspect of tacit knowledge is that it is, by definition, extremely difficult to articulate. In fact, there are different opinions about whether tacit knowledge is articulable at all. Some commentators are of the opinion that tacit knowledge can, in fact, be captured (Huang, 1997); some feel it is merely "difficult" to articulate (Teece, 1998); others feel it cannot be codified without being invalidated (Buckingham Shum, 1998); whereas others feel it simply cannot be captured or codified at all (Chao, 1997; Leonard & Sensiper, 1998; Star, 1995). For example, Goguen (1997) gives the following examples of tacit knowledge being inarticulable:

> *People may know how to do something, without being able to articulate how they do it. In the social sciences, this is called the say-do problem. Some examples are riding bicycles, tying shoe laces, speaking languages, negotiating contracts, reconciling personal differences, evaluating employees, and using a word processor (p. 33).*

In fact, Nonaka's (1991) examples are *impossible* to articulate — a master craftsman with rich experience who cannot articulate the principles behind what he knows or does; the master baker who can teach someone the principles only by taking them through a period of apprenticeship. In Nonaka's spiral of knowledge, tacit knowledge is transferred by the interpersonal interaction of the apprenticeship element. The tacit knowledge is not articulated expressly; rather, the learner develops the tacit knowledge in a situated environment under the guidance of a mentor by becoming immersed in the practice itself. The weakness of the spiral comes in the tacit-explicit stage. If tacit knowledge is inarticulable, this stage simply cannot work.

Nonaka's (1991) suggestion for overcoming this problem is the use of metaphors, which is similar to the use of stories. Orr (1990), in his study of photocopier repair engineers, described how an engineer encountering a problem not covered by the procedures found in the manual would consult with a supervisor or colleague. They would discuss the problem, try new approaches based on experiences of similar problems, and usually manage to solve the problem. The story of the problem and its solution would gradually circulate among the community of copier repairers and would become part of the stock of knowledge. They referred to this as the telling of "war stories." Goldstein (1993) encountered something similar when observing supermarket managers using computer-based data. He noticed they would examine the data, look for unexpected results, and try to make sense of them. They would then share this with peers by telling "stories." This still leaves a problem—the metaphor and the story are being "articulated," as in explicit knowledge. This raises the questions of what knowledge is being shared in the story, how it is being received by the learner, and what form does the knowledge take in the story?

Perhaps because Nonaka's (1991) tacit-explicit distinction does not answer the questions, other KM researchers and practitioners have made other distinctions. Rulke, Zaheer, and Anderson (1998) focused on the knowledge of an organisation that they termed transactive knowledge, which was made up of the organisation's self-knowledge (knowing what you know) and resource knowledge (knowing who knows what).

Conklin (1996) uses the terms "formal" and "informal" knowledge to distinguish between the types of knowledge of interest to KM practitioners. He describes formal knowledge as that found in books, manuals, and documents, and which can be shared by training courses. He observes that it is easily and routinely captured in organisations. Informal knowledge, on the other hand, is the knowledge that is applied in the process of creating formal knowledge. As examples, he gives ideas, assumptions, decisions, and stories. It is process-oriented and is difficult to capture. Part of this is symptomatic of another distinction that is made by the KM community; that is the distinction between knowledge as information and knowledge as process. In this view, knowledge is regarded by some as being a superior kind of information and by some as being the process of knowing.

Kogut and Zander (1992) differentiate between information and know-how, and Seely Brown and Duguid (1998) make a similar distinction with "know-what" and "know-how." They explain that "know-what" is explicit knowledge and easily shared, whereas the "core-competency" aspect of organisational knowledge needs more. It needs the "know-how" in order to put "know-what" into practice. However, even in this distinction there is an inconsistency in that know-how can have an "explicit" component, for example, procedures can be seen as a codified form of "know-how" that guides people in how to perform a task.

All of these distinctions are viewed in the form of opposites, but none of them have proved to be truly satisfactory in that they still seem to be limited, and in some there are distinct inconsistencies. Leonard and Sensiper (1998) try to tackle this by moving from a dichotomy to a continuum. They define tacit knowledge as "semiconscious and unconscious knowledge held in people's heads and bodies" and place it at one end of the spectrum. They define explicit knowledge as "codified, structured, and accessible to people other than the individuals originating it" and place it at the other end, with most knowledge somewhere in between.

Even this view, however, despite terming it a continuum, still places some types of knowledge at the ends of the spectrum and views them as opposites.

This move to exploring the management of less structured knowledge is explained by von Krogh (1998) as a shift in perspectives. He describes the more recent emphasis as being from a "constructionist" perspective, as opposed to the cognitivist perspective. He explains that the constructionist perspective regards knowledge as an act of construction or creation, with tacit knowledge being highly personal and difficult to express. As examples, von Krogh offers "physical skills, such as putting the movements together in a high-precision luxury watch, as well as perception skills, such as interpreting a complex seismic readout of an oil reservoir" (p. 134).

Von Krogh's (1998) constructionist view is based to a large degree on earlier work he did comparing the representational or cognitivist view of knowledge with a particular type of constructionist view — autopoiesis. Autopoiesis is a view of knowledge that is based on observations of cell reproduction in neurobiology. According to von Krogh, Roos, and Slocum (1996), it does not view the world as a state that can be represented:

*Rather, that cognition is a creative act of bringing forth a world. Knowledge is a component of the autopoietic (self-productive) process; it is history dependent, context sensitive, and ... at the individual level, knowledge is not abstract but rather is embodied in the individual (p. 163).*

A key aspect of autopoiesis is that it is self-referential; i.e., it includes potential future knowledge as well as past knowledge. People use established knowledge to determine what they see and to make distinctions in what they see. They also use what they already know to select what they are looking for in the environment. In other words, we use what we already know to decide what to look for in our surroundings (von Krogh, Roos, & Slocum, 1996). Changing those surroundings is undertaken by making different and finer distinctions and new interpretations (Vicari, von Krogh, Roos, & Mahnke, 1996), thereby evolving to higher states of knowledge.

The differences between the traditional and autopoietic perspectives are summarised in Table 4.

*Table 4: Autopoietic vs. Traditional View of Knowledge (Adapted from Vicari et al., 1996)*

| Autopoietic view | Traditional view |
|---|---|
| Knowledge is creational and based on distinction making in observation | Knowledge is representation of a pre-given reality |
| Knowledge is history dependent and context sensitive | Knowledge is universal and objective |
| Knowledge is not directly transferable | Knowledge is transferable |

Underlying the arguments of von Krogh, Roos and Slocum (1996) regarding the use of autopoiesis theory is the idea that knowledge is socially constructed. This is perhaps the central debate between the views of knowledge in the field of KM, that is, knowledge as data and knowledge as reasoning and culture. In anthropological, socio-psychological, and sociological work, knowledge tends to be regarded as a social product, whereas cognitive psychology has tended to emphasise representational and perceptual knowledge (Aadne, von Krogh, & Roos, 1996; von Krogh & Roos, 1995).

Traditional cognitivism assumes human cognition is a form of information processing and views the world as "pre-given" with the aim of creating the most accurate representations of the world. It regards knowledge as being representations of the world held in the minds of individuals in the form of knowledge structures, or schema constructs (Walsh, 1995). In this form, it regards the individual as an information processor. Von Krogh and Roos (1996) observe that representationism has formed the basis of much strategic management literature and has contributed to the view of knowledge as information.

There is, however, a different view in cognitive psychology that recognises the importance of the social context and culture. Bruner (1990) argues that we should move away from the notion of the individual merely as a processor of information and move the emphasis to meaning and how this is negotiated in a community, as individuals cannot exist independent of culture. He observes that symbols and codes (for example, the digits we use, mnemonics) that humans use to create meaning exist in and are developed in culture and communities. Wenger (1998), too, stresses that "information stored in explicit ways" is only a small part of the picture and that knowing is primarily something that comes about by active participation in communities. Hutchins (1995), in developing his theory of Distributed Cognition, also noted that looking for knowledge structures inside the individual fails to recognise that human cognition always takes place in a complicated social cultural environment and must therefore be affected by it. He emphasises that we must see cognition as part of a cultural process.

Although von Krogh (1998) describes the shift in perspectives as being from a cognitivist/representational approach to a constructionist view, the opposite views described earlier generally seem to still be rooted in the cognitivist/representational approach. This might explain why the management of the unstructured knowledge is proving such a challenge — although it is so difficult (perhaps impossible) to articulate, capture, codify, and store, the same approach is being taken. Attempts to manage such knowledge seem to focus on making tacit knowledge explicit and converting less structured knowledge to a form whereby it can be captured. There is clearly a need for a different view of knowledge in order to overcome this challenge of managing knowledge that cannot be captured, codified, and stored.

## Viewing Knowledge Differently

Cook and Seely Brown (1999) have also come to the conclusion that a new view of knowledge is required; that is, they emphasise the need for a move from possession to practice. As a result, they emphasise that tacit and explicit knowledge are distinct types of knowledge and it is impossible to move from one to the other; that is, tacit knowledge *cannot* be made explicit. This is unlike the general KM approach that is to try to make tacit knowledge explicit in order that it may be more easily used and managed.

Cook and Seely Brown (1999) retain the notions of tacit and explicit but note that each does work that the other cannot. To illustrate this point, they use the example of riding a bicycle. In order to ride a bicycle, one must have (tacit) knowledge of how to remain upright. They emphasise that this is not the activity of riding, but knowledge used in riding. The rider still has the tacit knowledge even when (s)he is not riding. It is the tacit knowledge that enables the rider to remain upright, and this is something that explicit knowledge cannot do. Instructions could be given regarding how to ride a bicycle. This would be explicit knowledge that could be given to a novice, but it would not be able to do all the work that would enable someone to know how to ride. The tacit knowledge can only be gained by actually riding the cycle. Although each form of knowledge does work that the other cannot do, each can be an aid in acquiring the other; for example, the explicit knowledge may help a beginner get started while (s)he acquires tacit knowledge. It is important to note, however, that there is no conversion — one can be used to *generate* the other.

Cook and Seely Brown (1999) also add in another dimension — that of "knowing." In their bicycle example, they note that tacit and explicit knowledge are not sufficient to develop the ability to ride a bicycle. The act of riding itself is also necessary. They call that which is possessed "knowledge," emphasising that it is *used* in action but is not itself action. Knowing, on the other hand, is described as being *part* of action. They refer to it as doing "the epistemic work that is done as part of action or practice" (p. 387). Knowledge and knowing are not opposites — they are complementary to each other. Cook and Seely Brown refer to this as being "mutually enabling."

> *Knowledge is a tool of knowing, ... knowing is an aspect of our interaction with the social and physical world, and that the interplay of knowledge and knowing can generate new knowledge and new ways of knowing (p. 381).*

These authors consider that the interaction between knowing and knowledge is generative — it leads to new knowledge being created. Using this approach they view Nonaka's (1991) example of the bread machine from a different angle. In Nonaka's account, the designer obtained the tacit knowledge from the master baker and then articulated it (made it explicit) for her colleagues in the design team. Cook and Seely Brown (1999) reject the idea that the tacit knowledge was made explicit. Rather, they consider that in addition to the knowledge (tacit and explicit) of all of the members of the group, there was also knowing — the way the group members interacted with each other, the dough, and the machine parts, that finally led to the creation of new knowledge.

Cook and Seely Brown's (1999) work is interesting and useful for the move to find a different view of knowledge from that used by most KM practitioners and researchers. The extra aspect of "knowing" that has been added to the picture is helpful in that it reinforces the view that the tacit-explicit pairing is not sufficient to explain the knowledge that cannot be captured and shows that an epistemology of practice is also necessary. However, knowledge is also still regarded as something that is possessed, and the "practice" part is something extra. What is needed is a view of knowledge that incorporates the practice, the socially constructed, the elusive knowledge. Perhaps in the first place a more general distinction is needed as a working hypothesis. For the purposes of this book, the terms "soft knowledge" and "hard knowledge" will be used. As a starting point, hard knowledge will be used to describe that knowledge that can easily be captured, codified, and stored. Soft knowledge will be used for the elusive knowledge that is posing a challenge to KM. However, soft knowledge in particular needs more examination, for it has already been mentioned that the predominant view of this type of knowledge still has its roots in representationism. However, von Krogh (1998) has shown that there is a shift to constructionism.

We have seen in this chapter that there *is* a shift to looking at soft knowledge, but that the attempts to define it have resulted in a variety of opposites, all of which are hard or soft. The management of hard knowledge is well established, but the management of soft knowledge is posing a challenge to KM. In Chapter III, therefore, we will explore in more detail the notion of soft knowledge in order to refine the concept and to attempt to understand the relative roles of representationism and constructionism.

**Chapter III**

# What is Soft Knowledge?

*In order to further inform the notion of soft knowledge, in this chapter we will explore three areas of literature with different views of how work is supported by knowledge: Distributed Cognition, Common Ground, and Communities of Practice. The different views show, to a greater or lesser degree, that the capture-codify-store approach is probably the wrong metaphor. The exploration of these views also indicates that the simple soft-hard distinction is not as simple as it appears.*

## INTRODUCTION

So far we have seen that organisations have lost knowledge through the pressures of downsizing and outsourcing and are having to share knowledge as a result of globalisation; that is, they are having to collaborate with other organisations, often in other locations, or they are having to operate in other locations themselves with the result that their staff have to operate in a distributed environment. We have also seen that KM has not been totally successful in helping organisations manage their knowledge, with the result that there is a shift in views of knowledge from knowledge as an object that can be captured to recognising that there is some knowledge that cannot be captured. KM tends to view these as opposites, but we have also noted a shift in perspectives — away from representationism and more to constructionism. We have used the terms "hard" and "soft" knowledge to try to simplify the different views of knowledge. We can regard the management of hard knowledge as being the result of a representationist view. This is well established. It is soft knowledge that poses the challenge to KM, and therefore, in this chapter, we will explore and refine the notion of soft knowledge in order to ascertain whether it really does map to a constructionist view. We will undertake this exploration by exploring three different views of how work is supported by knowledge:

- Distributed Cognition;
- Common Ground; and
- Communities of Practice.

# DISTRIBUTED COGNITION

The capture/codify/store approach suggests that knowledge relevant to work can be externalised, made explicit, and embedded in representations that are unproblematically storable by others. A good example of such knowledge is an encyclopaedia. Recent work in the field of Distributed Cognition (DC) has analyzed work practice from the perspective of the way information is represented and propagated around a network of people and technology and shows the important way in which physical artefacts come to embody knowledge relevant to the work practice.

Distributed Cognition is a theoretical framework which has been developed by Hutchins, (1990, 1995a, 1995b) and colleagues. Its aim is to explain cognitive activities as being embedded in the work settings where they occur. Rather than seeing the individual as the unit of analysis it takes "a culturally constituted functional group" (Hutchins & Klausen, 1991), because, generally, most cognitive work is not done in an individual's head but is spread out between people and across artefacts and time (Halverson, 1994). The importance placed on enculturation indicates that this may be a view that can help refine the notion of soft knowledge.

Hutchins (1995a) points out that DC is to be found in all collaborative work and therefore is of use to the field of Computer-Supported Co-operative

Work (CSCW), which has paid much attention to shared artefacts. As a methodological framework with the intention of aiding design, DC has been found to be suitable for application in areas where work activities are complex and socially distributed and use a variety of artefacts. It has been applied to a range of areas including marine navigation (Hutchins, 1990, 1995a), airplane cockpits (Hutchins & Klausen, 1991; Hutchins, 1995b), air traffic control (Halverson, 1994; Fields, Wright, Marti, & Palmonari, 1998), and aircraft failure management systems (Hicks, Wright, & Pocock, 1998), end-user programming (Nardi, 1993), the flow of work in a German Ministry (Mambrey & Robinson, 1997), work in a hospital radiology department (Symon, Long, & Ellis, 1996), and ambulance control (Martin, Bowers, & Wastell, 1997).

The DC view of knowledge being embedded in artefacts and representations that are propagated across different media and states is interesting, but it needs further exploration to ascertain whether it is predominantly hard or soft.

## What is the Distributed Cognition View of Knowledge?

With the DC view of cognition, representations are viewed differently from "traditional" views of cognition (Zhang &Norman, 1994). They are not regarded as schemas and knowledge structures — more emphasis is given to external representations of both information and knowledge, that is, how information is processed across both the internal mind and the external environment. This is perhaps best explained by going to a key point of DC: how a problem might be represented to make its solution easier. If a problem is presented in one way, it may well be difficult to solve, but if presented in another way, the solution becomes immediately apparent. It is clear that not every problem can be easily re-represented to a state where its solution is obvious, and different individuals will see the solution more or less quickly depending on their knowledge and experience.

Hutchins (1990, 1995a) applied this idea when he undertook an ethnographical study of a navigation team on a US warship. He observed traditional computational problems, such as plot fixing, and saw the artefacts, such as navigational tools, that were being used to assist with the navigation. The tools, for example, an alidade[4], a nautical slide rule, logs (the depth recorder's book and the bearing logbook), and a chart were designed to make the task much easier — they had represented the problem in a different way. Also of interest is the way these representations are propagated across different media and states (Hutchins & Klausen, 1991; Rogers & Ellis, 1994).

The fix cycle provides a good example of this. It determines the current position of the ship and predicts its future position. According to Hutchins (1995a), "The fix cycle is accomplished by the *propagation of representational state* across a series of *representational media*" (p. 117).

Landmarks are selected from the chart by an officer. These landmarks are then assigned to the bearing takers (one starboard and one port) by the bearing recorder. The bearing takers sight the landmarks and measure their direction from the ship using an alidade. When given the instruction to mark the bearing, the time is recorded in the time column of the bearing log, a fathometer operator reads the depth of the water from the display, speaks the depth into the phone circuit, and records the time and the depth in his own book. After the depth is given, the command "mark" is given by the bearing recorder, and the bearing takers can speak their bearings. The Quartermaster Chief records the bearings in the correct column in the bearing record log. The plotter reads the bearing as it is being written in the log and using an one-armed protractor draws lines on the chart to match the lines of sight between the ship and the landmarks.

In his example, Hutchins (1995a) is not breaking down the individual task of each member of the team; rather he is focusing on the way knowledge is being transmitted between the team members and how information is being propagated across different artefacts. The representation of the ship's position moves from the alidade, to the spoken word, to the bearing book in the domain of written numbers, to the plotting tool, and finally to the chart that is the domain where the information is now more easily interpreted. Rogers and Ellis (1994) describe it as:

- Remembering the name and description of the landmark: mental coordination of representational states.
- Coordinating name and description of landmark with external sighting using alidade: technologically mediated coordination of representational states.
- Bearer reports readings over phone circuit to bearing recorder: socially distributed and technologically mediated coordination of representational states.
- Bearing recorder records bearings in logbook: technologically mediated coordination of representational states.
- Information passed to plotter either verbally: socially distributed coordination of representational states.
- Information passed to plotter by plotter reading from logbook: mental coordination of external and internal representation states.

- Fix plotted on chart using instruments: technologically mediated coordination of representational states.

The use of the artefacts is central to DC because of the representations that they carry and the idea that they can contain embedded knowledge. The tools mentioned above were not only re-representations of a problem — they also represented the knowledge of previous generations of mariners via whom the artefact had come into being. For example, the chart represents the collection of more observations than any individual could make and therefore embodies generations of observation, experience, and measurement. The knowledge is *embedded* in the artefact — the knowledge and practice are crystallised in physical structures:

> *Physical artefacts became repositories of knowledge, and they were constructed in durable media so that a single artefact might come to represent more than any individual could know (Hutchins, 1995a).*

This shows how knowledge relevant to work practice can be captured, codified, and stored in artefacts in ways that are more subtle than the explicit propositional forms of encyclopaedias and expert systems.

Hutchins (1990, 1995a) also observed that artefacts do not have to be physical. In some cases, procedures act as artefacts. Standard Operating Procedures are standard practice and are commonplace in navigation. Hutchins (1995a) describes the procedure as a mediating artefact, that is, mediating the relationship between the performer and the task. He emphasises that it is not to be seen as something that stands between the two but as one of the structural elements that are being brought into coordination.

The emphasis on information artefacts and propagation of the representations suggests that as far as Hutchins goes in his books (1990, 1995a), his model of DC is representational and not constructionist. He believes in and argues for the distribution of information but he does not emphasise any differences in the types of information or knowledge. In Hutchins' model of DC, there is no distinction made between physical representation and representation in the head. There is some consideration and acknowledgment of cultural issues, but the view appears to be that cultural knowledge can somehow be embedded in the material artefact, and again the emphasis is on the importance of representational artefacts.

Even with the emphasis on representational artefacts, Hutchins (1990,1995a) downplays the importance of other forms of knowledge that are required by the users of such artefacts. For example, Goguen (1997) argues that all representations have both wet and dry components; Robinson (1997) in his study of models and procedures argues that the knowledge to use such things is different; Berg (1997) has shown how expert systems have failed to capture the social, organisational knowledge required to make sense of the output of expert systems; and Orr (1997) points to the importance of the more subtle aspects of knowledge required to work with explicit representation. An example of this is the case of a street map and a telephone book — if positions are simply shown as addresses it may well be difficult to get an idea of distance between them. This shows that other knowledge is needed to *use* the artefact and is not in the artefact itself. This is supported by another aspect that is emphasised by Martin et al. (1997): many artefacts (as opposed to communication technologies) afford possibilities and occasions for social interaction in the workplace. They expand on this with different knowledge being found in the interaction between people and between the users and the artefact, not in the artefact itself.

The DC emphasis on representational artefacts and their propagation shows us that, although cultural aspects are acknowledged, the approach is primarily representational. It is clear that some other kind of knowledge is needed to *use* the artefacts, the representations. A key issue is also how soft knowledge can be managed in a distributed environment. The DC examples do not deal with virtual or distributed teams, therefore, further exploration is needed.

An area where soft knowledge may be more apparent, therefore, is where the artefacts (the representations) are used in different communities. We have already seen that different knowledge is needed to use the artefacts, and this will probably be exacerbated when the artefact is being used in different communities or social worlds as would be found in a distributed environment. As the artefacts move between communities, we might expect that difficulties would arise with the translation of the softer aspects of knowledge, that is, the artefact would have totally different meanings in the two communities.

## Boundary Objects

Boundary objects address the problem of common representations in different social worlds that border one another, for example, across different disciplines. They also provide a further opportunity to consider the softer aspects of knowledge as they are highlighted by the interaction in different social worlds. Star and Griesemer (1989) use boundary objects as an analytical concept and describe them as objects that are found in different intersecting social worlds and that satisfy the informational requirements of each. They are strong enough to retain a common identity but are nevertheless flexible enough to adapt to local needs. Star (1989), and Star and Griesemer (1989) based their notion of boundary objects on artefacts that do not change but are able to convey information over a distance. The boundary objects are therefore robust enough to travel between communities and also have local interpretations. Although they have a structure that is recognisable in different worlds, they can have different meanings within those worlds.

Star (1989) and Star and Griesemer (1989) identified four types of boundary object:

*Repositories*

They describe repositories as being "ordered piles of objects that are indexed in a standardized fashion" (Star, 1989, p. 48). They give the examples of libraries or museums that can be accessed by the different social communities for their own purposes. Repositories show that, although based on immutable *mobiles*, a boundary object does not have to be mobile to be a boundary object.

*Ideal Type or Platonic Object*

Star (1989) gives the example of an atlas as being an ideal type. It does not accurately describe the details of any particular site or thing. It may be vague because it is abstracted from several domains. It is precisely for this reason that it is adaptable to a local site. It is a means of communicating symbolically with all parties.

*Terrain with Coincident Boundaries*

This is described as "common objects which have the same boundaries but different internal contents" (Star, 1989, p. 49). As an example they give maps for different groups of people working at a museum. Maps for collectors and conservationists emphasise features such as trails and campsites. The professional biologists, on the other hand, have maps (showing the same state boundaries) that emphasise shaded areas representing ecological concepts.

*Forms and Labels*

These are boundary objects deliberately designed for communicating across dispersed workgroups, for example, a standardised form. They are the boundary objects most closely based on the immutable mobile — they contain unchanging information that can be transported across long distance. They have the advantage that they delete local uncertainties. They may become part of a repository.

Boundary objects are part of the representationist approach and therefore are predominantly "hard." Seely Brown and Duguid (1998), however, observe the different local interpretations. They describe boundary objects as being objects that are of interest to different communities that are involved in some way. These objects are used differently, or at least, regarded differently by the different communities. Through the boundary object, a community can gain some understanding about what is common and what is different about another community.

The different local interpretations, or interpretive flexibility, of boundary objects throw a different light on the shared artefacts of Distributed Cognition. It shows that the knowledge embedded in an artefact is not simply re-extracted, but that a degree of knowledge is necessary to be able to use the artefact; that is, some knowledge is not embedded in the artefact, other knowledge is applied to make use of the artefact. This other knowledge is perhaps the "soft" knowledge that cannot be represented.

It would appear, however, that the DC and boundary object view is primarily representationist with the main emphasis on hard knowledge and that DC is falling into the same trap as KM. This means that we need to look elsewhere in order to further inform the conceptualisation of the softer aspects of knowledge.

Cole (1996) felt the interaction between an artefact and the different social worlds, an under-emphasised aspect of DC, to be of great importance in the way it helped shape the artefact. The interpretive flexibility of boundary objects also points to differences in the different communities touched by a boundary object, despite the DC emphasis on hard knowledge, that aim to let the artefact move smoothly between them. This suggests that the context of the different social worlds may be able to further inform the concept of soft knowledge. One of the main issues that defines a social world is the language used by the members. The following section will therefore move to explore the notion of

Common Ground in language that Clark (1996) uses to demonstrate how interpretations are created in the context of a community.

# COMMON GROUND

Clark (1996) uses the notion of Common Ground and proposes it as being essential to communication. He describes Common Ground as "the sum of [two people's] mutual, common, or joint knowledge, beliefs, and suppositions" (p. 93). The example he gives is picking up a conch shell on a beach — he is aware that he is looking at the conch shell. He is then joined by his young son who also looks at the conch shell, and it becomes part of his son's awareness of his general situation, and therefore part of their Common Ground. The situation is the *shared basis* for their Common Ground. As they both look at the shell, they each have evidence that there is a conch shell between them, but they do not have evidence of the age of the shell. Clark calls this quality of evidence: excellent evidence that there is a conch shell, but poor evidence of its age; therefore, it is highly likely that the conch shell is part of their Common Ground but unlikely that its age is. He observes that people, in interaction with others, are constantly and unknowingly evaluating shared bases for Common Ground for their quality. The participants do not know they are doing this, they are applying their soft knowledge.

He takes the idea of Common Ground further and applies this to membership of cultural communities. For example, when meeting somebody new and getting to know him or her, one might find out that the other is a classical music enthusiast. If they are both enthusiasts they will find that they have a common stock of knowledge and language. There are different levels of cultural communities. Clark (1996) offers the example of a New Zealand ophthalmologist — this person would be a member of the communities of English speakers, of New Zealanders, and of ophthalmologists. What one would infer would depend on one's membership of these communities. One would expect that the person would tacitly know the use of English with its grammar and vocabulary. One would also assume that (s)he would know basic New Zealand geography and history, but one would only have a small part of that knowledge in common with the person. Likewise, one would expect the ophthalmologist to have detailed knowledge of eyes and their diseases. A non-ophthalmologist would only know the *types* of information the ophthalmologist would know. The ophthalmologist would know most of the particulars. Community members share a system of beliefs, practices, skills, know-how, and conventions and also have terms that have no meaning to an outsider. The ophthalmologists are an example of an occupational cultural community. Clark also gives examples of people with shared hobbies, religions, education, nationality, and employment.

A cultural community is more than a collection of people — they must have Common Ground. There are outsiders and insiders. Common Ground, according to Clark (1996), provides a means of differentiating — it shows what each knows about the community:

*Inside information of a community is particular information that members of the community mutually assume is possessed by members of the community.*

*Outside information of a community is types of information that outsiders assume is inside information for that community (p. 101).*

Common Ground is something that insiders of a community take for granted within each other — it includes "facts, beliefs, and assumptions about objects, norms of behaviour, conventions, procedures, skills, and even ineffable experiences" (Clark, 1996, p. 112), and it provides a means of defining a community.

In addition to common, shared knowledge, expertise, procedures, and beliefs, Common Ground can also take the form of a common language and a shared background. For example, the common language can take the form of language (national community), dialect (regional community), jargon, technical terminology, and shoptalk (occupational community). As an example of the shared background, Clark (1996) offers the example of a downhill skier — members of this community all know the experiences shared by each other, for example, the feeling of wind in the face, the different snow textures beneath the skis, and how to respond to the different surfaces. These are experiences that non-members cannot understand until they have themselves experienced them. Clark notes that more than facts (as in an encyclopaedia) are necessary, as facts cannot record or represent personal experience. He points out that community members do not just have shared knowledge but *know-how*, as in a community of accomplished pianists who take it for granted that each can play certain scales, play in certain modes, produce certain keyboard effects, and know what is and is not possible with regard to the piano.

Clark's (1996) focus was primarily on language, and it draws attention to soft knowledge in that he points out that the Common Ground is necessary in the interpretation of language — a phrase might have one meaning in one community and a different meaning in another community. The meaning depends on one's membership in the community. This provides a step forward in the exploration of soft knowledge, but a larger unit of analysis is needed to explore this in organisations. We need, therefore, to explore communities in the organisational context. In particular, we will focus on a particular type of organisational community that provides an environment for learning: the Community of Practice (Lave & Wenger, 1991).

# COMMUNITIES OF PRACTICE
## What is a Community of Practice?

Jean Lave (Lave, 1991; Lave & Wenger 1991) is credited with first introducing the term of Communities of Practice (CoP) (Wenger, 1998). Lave and Wenger (1991) described a CoP as:

> ... *a set of relations among persons, activity, and world, over time and in relation with other tangential and overlapping communities of practice (p. 98).*

They illustrated it with five examples of apprenticeship, emphasising that their notion of apprenticeship is not restricted to the historical idea of apprenticeship in a trade. Rather, they view it as a form of *socialisation* into a community, where the newcomer gradually becomes a legitimate member of the CoP by learning the practice, the language, and the conventions of the community by having access to and interacting with established members. The key point here is the emphasis on the social as opposed to information and knowledge. The learning a newcomer undertakes is situated in and cannot be separated from the practice of the community. In explaining this, Lave and Wenger emphasise the context of the community for learning and knowledge, using the example that even if a general rule is known, it does not necessarily mean that it can be applied in relevant specific circumstances; that is, the "power of abstraction" is situated in the culture of the community.

Their "apprenticeship" examples are from different traditions and cultures and take different forms — formal arrangements, informal arrangements, and a community where membership was purely voluntary — but in all of them what is common is the importance of the access that newcomers have to old-timers who are long standing members of the community and from whom newcomers will learn. Their five examples were Yucatec midwives, Vai and Gola tailors, quartermasters, butchers, and non-drinking alcoholics. For the tailors, there was a formal arrangement between the apprentice and a single master; the quartermasters were part of a formal arrangement; the apprenticeship of the butchers followed the historical notion of apprenticeship more closely, but it was also the one that did not work as it should because of the lack of access to the old-timers. The apprentices were taught specific tasks, that is, the hard aspects of their domain knowledge, but in being denied access to interaction with old timers, they were not being given the opportunity to develop the softer aspects of their knowledge in the context of the community. The Yucatan midwives had an informal arrangement — in many cases the newcomer was the daughter of an existing midwife who would accompany her mother. The non-drinking alcoholics also had a purely voluntary "apprenticeship." The process is from alcoholic to non-drinking alcoholic. An "apprentice" will attend meetings several times a week. There will be other people at the meetings, who are at different stages in the process and who, together, make up the community. In general meetings, the "old-timers" tell stories of their lives as alcoholics. These stories can have taken years to reach the stage of polish at which they are presented. In discussion meetings, the focus tends to be on one smaller part that will eventually be part of the whole of the life story. There are also 12 steps through which the newcomer must go. These steps basically represent the process from peripheral to full participation in the community. For the absolute newcomer, the first participation, apart from attending the meeting, may be as simple as a declaration of intent to abstain from drinking in the next twenty-four hours, in the form of picking up a white chip at the end of a meeting. From there, the newcomer will develop his/her story and pass through the "12 Steps," which culminates in being recognised as an old-timer and trying to persuade someone else to become a member of the community.

All of Lave and Wenger's (1991) examples show this difference between newcomer and old-timer and the process of moving from one way of being to another. The members achieve this shift in state by learning the practice of the community. They do this by participating in the practice of the community, gradually moving from peripheral to full participation. This process is what Lave and Wenger term Legitimate Peripheral Participation (LPP).

*Legitimate Peripheral Participation*

For Lave and Wenger (1991), LPP is the defining characteristic of apprenticeship as a form of learning. Newcomers learn the practice of the community by being situated in the practice and by having access to established members. LPP is part of the process by which a newcomer becomes an established member of a CoP.

In CoPs, newcomers learn from old-timers by being allowed to participate in certain tasks relating to the practice of the community and gradually move from peripheral to full participation in the community. For example, the daughter of the Yucatec midwife may start simply by knowing what the life of a midwife involves, such as having to go out at all hours, the kinds of herbs that need to be collected, etc. The midwife may then start taking her daughter with her on visits. The daughter will hear stories of cases. She may then proceed to running errands and taking messages. Eventually, she may assist at a birth or give a massage to an expectant mother. As time goes on, if she has decided to pursue this line of work, she will gradually take over more and more of the workload.

Lave and Wenger (1991) saw a Community of Practice as "an intrinsic condition for the existence of knowledge" (p. 98). They saw the learning that took place in such communities not as narrow situated learning where instances of practice are simply replicated but "learning as Legitimate Peripheral Participation" (p. 34). LPP is not merely learning situated in practice but learning as an integral part of practice: learning as "generative social practice in the lived-in world" (p. 35).

LPP is complex and composite in character. Lave and Wenger (1991) state that each of its three aspects — legitimation, peripherality, and participation — is indispensable in defining the others and can not be considered in isolation. Legitimation and participation define the characteristic ways of belonging to a community, while peripherality and participation are concerned with location and identity in the social world. Although Lave and Wenger stress the composite character of LPP, it is useful as an analytical convenience to consider the three components and their relationships separately.

Legitimation is the dimension of CoPs that is concerned with power and authority relations in the group. In Lave and Wenger's examples, legitimation does not necessarily have to be formal. For example, for quartermasters, tailors, and butchers, there is a degree of formal legitimacy that comes from hierarchy and rank, but for the midwives and alcoholics, legitimacy is more informal. For example, the alcoholics gain legitimacy, as the stories they tell of their experiences become more mature and closer to those of an old-timer. The legitimation bestowed by a story was also noted by Orr (1997), who described the stories as artefacts for sharing experience.

> *Once war stories have been told, the stories are artefacts to circulate and preserve. Through them experience becomes reproducible and reusable ... They preserve and circulate hard won information and are used to make claims of membership or seniority within the community ... They also amuse, instruct and celebrate the tellers' identity as technicians. Such tellings are also demonstrations of one's competence as a technician and therefore one's membership in the community (p. 26).*

Peripherality is neither a physical concept as in core and periphery nor a simple measure of the amount of knowledge that has been acquired. Lave and Wenger (1991) use the terms peripheral and full participation to denote the degree of engagement with and participation in the community, but note that peripherality "must be connected to issues of legitimacy of the social organisation and control over resources if it is to gain its full analytical potential" (p. 37).

For Lave and Wenger (1991), it is participation that provides the key to understanding CoPs. CoPs do not necessarily imply co-presence, a well-defined or identifiable group, or socially visible boundaries. However, CoPs do imply participation in an activity about which all participants have a common understanding of what it is and what it means for their lives and community. The community and the degree of participation in it are in some sense inseparable from the practice.

*Expanding the Model*

Lave and Wenger (1991) emphasised that CoPs were not restricted to an apprenticeship model, and other researchers have attempted to extend the concept in order to apply CoPs in a KM setting, that is, by applying the concept to commercial organisations and regarding them as a new organisational form. Some researchers have even used the term to refer to the wider community of a specific group of practitioners. For example, Hutchins and Klausen (1991) refer to the Community of Practice of pilots and their shared knowledge. Classifying such a large community as a CoP gives us two tiers of CoPs—the wider community (for example, of pilots) and more compact CoPs (for example, a team of pilots who work for a particular airline and who are based at a particular airport). Clark (1996) provides a basis for both types of CoP with the notion of Common Ground described earlier. When using language within a community, the Common Ground forms part of the basis of the communication and can manifest itself in conventions within the community. Common Ground will also include terms and jargon — a language shared by members of a particular community.

Seely Brown and Duguid (1996) have noticed similar aspects when exploring the role of CoPs in learning. Their examples of learning how to become a physicist or a football player do not only entail learning formulae and plays. The newcomer must "learn how to act as one, talk as one, be recognised as one — it's not the explicit statements, but the implicit practices that count" (p. 13).

The people who fail to learn the language and practices of the community, that is, those who fail to become a member, are those who simply learn the outside information (that is, the harder aspects) and thus give themselves away as outsiders. Indeed, it is often only knowing the explicit statements that betray an outsider. This does, however, show the importance of the Common Ground, in the form of developing the softer aspects of knowledge in the context of the community.

Common Ground alone, however, is only one constituent of a CoP — in extending the concept, different characteristics have been identified and many definitions have been suggested. Manville and Foote (1996) place their version of CoPs firmly in the organisational context and emphasise the informality that may be found in CoPs. The CoP does not have to be an official grouping. Membership may be totally voluntary. They also allude to the tackling of common problems and refer to the knowledge that can be created within the group through the tackling of those problems. Conceição, Gibson, and Shariq (1997) also restricted their version of a CoP to an organisational context, referring to the knowledge that is to be found in a CoP and observing that CoPs can be cross-functional, in that they are not restricted to specific business functions. They cross the borders between the different parts of the organisation.

Seely Brown and Duguid (1991, 1998) took the notion of CoPs and applied them to a study of technical photocopy technical repairers undertaken by Orr (1990). They describe the copier repairers as a CoP and relate how narration, in the form of war stories (as described in Chapter II), was used to help solve problems and create new knowledge. The story might be told at a later stage and become part of the community's stock of knowledge. Lave and

Wenger (1991) explain the importance of stories by relating them to knowledge being situated in the context of a community.

> ... any "power of abstraction" is thoroughly situated, in the lives of persons and in the culture that makes it possible. On the other hand, the world carries its own structure so that specificity always implies generality ... That is why stories can be so powerful in conveying ideas, often more so than an articulation of the idea itself. What is called general knowledge is not privileged with respect to other "kinds" of knowledge. It too can be gained only in specific circumstances. And it too must be brought into play in specific circumstances. The generality of any form of knowledge always lies in the power to renegotiate the meaning of the past and the future in constructing the meaning of present circumstances (p. 34).

In Orr's (1990) example, the story is heard being re-told in the lunchroom and Seely Brown and Solomon Gray relate how technical repairers gather round the coffee pot to swap stories. They point out that whereas many people might regard this as "dead" time, the repairers were in fact carrying out valuable work — as field service is a social activity, they were swapping and producing insights as to how better to repair the machines. Davenport and Prusak (1998) widen this to ad hoc conversation in general, showing that informal ad hoc communication is an essential part of interaction within a community, during which valuable work gets done. They observe that when people are having a conversation at the water cooler, the coffee machine, or in the company cafeteria knowledge transfer is often taking place. Unfortunately, some managers often regard this as wasted time, but in general most of the conversations will be about work — current projects, solving problems, asking advice, etc.

The extension of the concept of a CoP has led to some inappropriate usage of the term. For example, Lindstaedt (1996) referred to them as project teams and interest groups, and Sandusky (1997) equated them to business functional units. It is wrong to define CoPs in these terms, for project teams, interest groups, and business function units are formally constituted groups. CoPs per se are not formally created. It may be the case that a formally constituted group, such as a project team, develops into a CoP by virtue of the relationships between its members, but this only shows that such a group *can* develop into a CoP, *not* that all such groups are CoPs.

*Putting Together a Covering Definition*

In order to draw the CoP characteristics together it is perhaps best to regard the term Community of Practice as an umbrella term, covering a range of groups, some of which might have more of some characteristics than others.

*Figure 1: Community of Practice Characteristics*

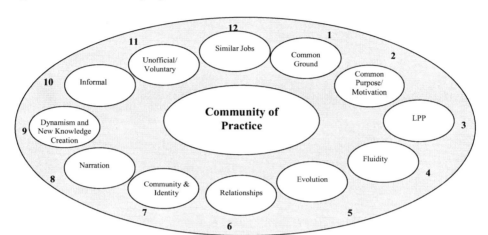

Figure 1 shows that there are a number of characteristics that would appear to be present in most CoPs to a greater or lesser degree:

**Common Ground:** Clark (1996) classified and defined cultural communities by the use of Common Ground — the knowledge, beliefs, and suppositions shared by members of the community. As described in Chapter III, this provides us with two tiers of CoP — at a higher level, for example, a community of dentists who share a common language, background, and experiences, and at a lower level, there is the smaller CoP. In the case of the dentists, it may be a group of dentists who work in a particular practice and who have evolved into a CoP. They may have newcomers, practice-specific jargon, and nicknames. They may have developed strong working relationships and have a common goal for the practice towards which they are working. They will also have practice-specific Common Ground, for example, relating to particular incidents or tricky operations within the practice.

The members of the CoP have some sort of shared or background knowledge. This is generally, but not necessarily, related to the common interest of the group. Nardi and Miller (1991) term this the "domain knowledge." Of more interest here is the soft knowledge that forms part of the Common Ground.

**Common Purpose/Motivation:** The members of the group will feel that they have a common purpose, which will give the group an internal impetus. The motivation of the members of a CoP is also a key element of what makes it a CoP. There is an *internal* motivation that provides the group with its impetus. Even when the group is formally constituted, part of what makes the group a CoP will be the internal motivation that drives the group rather than any external pressures. The CoP members are self-motivated in what they do within the CoP.

**Legitimate Peripheral Participation:** (Lave, 1991; Lave & Wenger 1991) As described earlier, LPP is the process by which a newcomer to the group gradually becomes an established member of the CoP. In Lave and Wenger's (1991) examples, this was based on a form of apprenticeship. Even in CoPs where a newcomer already has a degree of domain knowledge, there will be group- and organisation-specific aspects that the newcomer has to learn as (s)he works him/herself into the group. This might be, for example, the particular practices of the group and organisation, "the way things are done here," or relevant people to contact.

**Fluidity/Regeneration:** The fluidity of the CoP refers to the arrival of newcomers and the eventual departure of old-timers. Newcomers arrive, learn the language, domain knowledge, and practices of the group, go through the process of LPP, and themselves become acknowledged old-timers. This is how the CoP regenerates itself and ensures its stock of knowledge is not lost.

**Evolution:** A CoP will go through some sort of evolution. It may be simply that the CoP owes its very existence to evolution in that it developed through a group of people having a common interest. On the other hand, the group may originally have been formally created but has developed or evolved into a CoP as a result of the relationships, inner momentum, and feeling of community that have developed into an identity of its own over time.

**Relationships:** The relationships are a key part of what makes a CoP. It is possible for a team to become a CoP as informal relationships begin to develop and the source of legitimation changes in emphasis. The relationships that develop are central to developing the sense of trust and identity that defines the community.

**Community/Identity:** The internal motivation and the development of relationships contribute to a feeling of community and identity. The members feel they belong to the community. They may even go as far as giving the group a name.

**Narration:** Narration takes the form of story telling and is seen by some commentators as a key means by which CoP members share knowledge (Goldstein, 1993; Orr, 1990; Sachs, 1995). This was shown as a central part of the transition from newcomer to old-timer in Lave and Wenger's (1991) community of non-drinking alcoholics. Orr (1997) also showed that the qualities of the stories bestowed members of his copier repair engineers with a form of legitimation and confirmed their status in and membership of the community.

**Dynamism/Creation of New Knowledge:** The dynamism aspect relates to the social distribution of the knowledge in the group. Over a period of time, as the group's work progresses, the members will learn different things at different paces. There will be members of the group who have specialised knowledge in certain aspects, that is, they are "gurus" (Star, 1995). Other members will be able to consult them for help, but as time passes, the social distribution of the knowledge will shift – it is dynamic, not static. This dynamic process can also create new knowledge as demonstrated by Orr's (1990, 1997) photocopier technicians. In swapping stories and bouncing ideas off each other, the two technicians finally arrived at a solution that was then added to the community's stock of knowledge.

**Informal:** It is often the case in a CoP that there is no hierarchy and the group has no specific deliverable. The group is run on informal lines. This has close links with the legitimation aspect (in LPP). In such an informal group, the legitimation is bestowed by the informal relationships and not by an externally imposed rank. In the case of an officially created group that has evolved into a CoP, the official hierarchy of the original group will still be present and functioning, and such a group may still have deliverables.

This factor may then be less essential than some of the other aspects. It is particularly interesting, however, when the informal legitimation and externally imposed rankings clash, as in the Chief Petty Officers of Hutchins (1995a) having to "break in" the new officers.

**Unofficial:** In many cases a CoP is not formally created by an organisation. The example of the technicians in Orr (1990) is a good example – the company was unaware of the technicians' ways of working and collaborating. It can also often be found that membership in a CoP is voluntary, possibly because the CoP is unofficial. This does not, however, preclude voluntary membership of an official group or team.

**Similar Jobs:** This characteristic is where a CoP is situated in an organisational context and refers to the identification of CoPs. In many cases a CoP may form around a particular job, the job is the practice — as in the example of photocopier repairers provided by Orr (1990), or, on a wider level, the ophthalmologists suggested by Clark (1996). The fact that CoPs may form around similar roles or jobs in an organisation provides a starting point when looking for potential CoPs, particularly in a distributed environment where they might not be so obvious. There will be individuals doing similar jobs and closer contact would be beneficial to them.

In a Community of Practice it is important to emphasise the social aspects, which feature heavily. Several of the characteristics described above point to the importance of the social features. A CoP cannot be created, merely facilitated, for without the internal motivation and the relationships that the members develop, a group will fail to evolve into a CoP. This is demonstrated particularly well by the Legitimation aspect where the legitimation of a member in the community comes not from some formal and externally imposed hierarchy but by his/her gaining the acceptance of the other members.

The relationships developed between the members are also important, for the socially constructed softer aspects of knowledge are to be found there. This raises the question of what impact this will have on the knowledge loss problems posed by outsourcing and downsizing. CoPs cope with the loss of members by a process of regeneration — as old-timers leave they are replaced by newcomers moving to full participation. However, if the whole community were to be lost in a program of staff reduction, knowledge would be lost which could not be captured and stored for the use of the organisation.

*Managing CoPs*

The extension of the concept (as in Figure 1) has also led to some consultancies trying to formalise CoPs to the extent where consultants are told to go and create CoPs. CoPs per se cannot be created, or "managed" in the traditional sense of closely controlled, because they depend to such a great extent on the social issues. Perhaps a better approach is one of facilitation, enabling, and coaching. For example, it is not possible to say to a group of people that it is now a CoP and that it should go away and work as one. A group can be supported with facilities that facilitate interaction, and it may be that as relationships in the group develop, the group develops into a CoP. By the same token, a CoP per se cannot be managed — however, there will be the case where a formally managed group develops into a CoP. In that case, it is the formal group that is being managed; it just happens that that group is a CoP. The management was put in place for the original group, whether it was a CoP or not. Wheatley (1992), in trying to move away from rigid structures, emphasises the importance of relationships, interactions, and of linking people but acknowledges that precise outcomes cannot be pre-determined.

O'Dell and Jackson Grayson (1998b) see this from an ICT point of view and report on how Chevron has tried to nurture and support CoPs when they have appeared. Support and facilitation does not, however, have to be technological. Stewart (1996) recognised the value of IT but also of simpler support. He explained that managers can help CoPs in a number of ways. In the first place, simply recognising CoPs and their importance is a step forward. Once CoPs have been found, they can be supported initially by letting them build an intranet, or use a conference room, or by funding a get-together.

*How do the Ideas of CoPs Inform Soft Knowledge?*

LPP allows the development of both hard and soft knowledge. Hard knowledge can be articulated and may be exemplified by tasks that can be demonstrated. Soft knowledge is that which the newcomer cannot learn simply by demonstration or instruction; for example, in a craft situation the newcomer will learn to develop a "feel" for the material to be able to tell when the artefact being worked on "feels" right. (S)he can learn this through LPP, through working on tasks with the old-timers. Soft knowledge also goes further than this — it includes learning the language and unspoken conventions of the community. These softer aspects are learned through being socialised into the community through interaction with the existing members. The stories provide a good example, as well as demonstrating legitimation in a CoP. The utterance of the story itself is an articulation of the teller's hard knowledge. The quality of the story will depend on the soft knowledge that has been developed through interaction with the other members of the community. The members' soft knowledge is also necessary for understanding the story. An outsider or newcomer who has not yet developed the soft knowledge would not gain the same understanding as an old-timer who may also be in a position to make new inferences and interpretations from the story.

Part of the soft knowledge developed in a CoP, however, is still knowledge from a representationist/cognitivist view. This goes against the simple distinction expressed earlier that hard knowledge equates with the cognitivist/ representationist and soft knowledge equates with the constructionist viewpoint. What this shows is that it is problematic to seek soft knowledge on its own. Knowledge is not made up of opposites. Regarding knowledge in these terms appears to be a false dichotomy. On the contrary, rather than regarding knowledge as opposites, it should perhaps be regarded as consisting of complementary facets. It needs to be regarded as a duality. Therefore, in order to move forward we will not regard knowledge as opposites but as a *duality* with hard and soft aspects; that is, all knowledge is to some degree hard *and* soft, simply the balance varies (Figure 2). The softer aspects of knowledge are those that cannot be captured, the harder aspects are those that can be articulated, captured, and stored.

*Figure 2: Soft-Hard Knowledge Duality*

This has a number of benefits; for example, it uses the "knowing" idea of Cook and Seely Brown (1999) as a different view of knowledge that cannot be captured, but it shows this in a simpler form. "Knowing" is one of the softer aspects of knowledge. The duality is not exclusive; it caters to those types of knowledge described earlier — those "types" of knowledge that cannot be so easily captured are some of the softer aspects. It can apply to those types of knowledge that are difficult to express or capture even if they are being viewed from a representational perspective, but it can also cover knowledge viewed from the constructionist perspective as softer aspects. Most importantly, it shows us that both perspectives are needed and must be taken into account for managing knowledge.

Viewing knowledge as a duality could explain some of the failures of KM initiatives. When the harder aspects are abstracted in isolation, the representation is incomplete — this is analogous to copying one side of a banknote and regarding it as a complete banknote, however, the softer aspects of knowledge must be taken into account as well. Hargadon (1998) gives the example of a server holding past projects, but developers do not look there for solutions. As the developers put it, "It's all in people's heads," that is, such solutions only represent the harder aspects of the knowledge. For a complete picture, the softer aspects are also necessary. Even the knowledge "in people's heads" is not sufficient; there is also the interactive aspect of Cook and Seely Brown's (1999) "knowing" that must be taken into account. This is one of the key softer aspects. As they explain it:

> We act within a social and physical world, and since knowing is an aspect of action, it is about interaction with that world. When we act we either give shape to the physical world or both. Thus "knowing" does not focus on what we possess in our heads; it focuses on our interactions with the things of the social and physical world (p. 388).

Including the management of these softer aspects of knowledge in KM poses different challenges. Certainly there should be a shift from capturing and leveraging knowledge to supporting learning and the sharing of softer knowledge. The harder aspects of knowledge are managed by capturing them, storing them, and then disseminating them, for example in training sessions, books, or reports. The management of the softer aspects, however poses different problems — how can they be managed if they cannot be captured and there is no possibility for face-to-face interaction; that is, if individuals want to share such knowledge across time and space? Technology does have a role to play, but the emphasis needs to shift from trying to package knowledge as an object to using technology in a different context to try to share experience. This is a view supported by Davenport and Prusak (1998), who emphasise the communications aspect of ICT, with their potential to link people: "the more rich and tacit knowledge is, the more technology should be used to enable people to share that knowledge directly. *It's not a good idea to try and contain or represent the knowledge itself using technology*" (emphasis added) (p. 96).

Recognising this, Junnarkar and Brown (1997) point to the potential of technology such as tele- and video-conferencing. The technology currently receiving the most attention for supporting the sharing of softer knowledge is the intranet[5], but at the moment even intranets seem to mainly be used for the sharing of the abstracted hard aspects of knowledge in the form of reports and documents.

Clearly IT itself is not enough and some emphasise the need for physical contact (Leonard & Sensiper, 1998). However, even with physical contact, there are still difficulties involved in the sharing of softer knowledge, for example, the importance of speaking the same language, not only the same national language but the same professional background language as well. Drucker (1992) gives the example of the American civil servant who would be at ease discussing bureaucratic issues with a Chinese counterpart, but who would be lost if he had to sit in a marketing meeting of a major retail organisation.

Developing the notion of the soft/hard duality indicates an area needing further exploration: the development and management of the soft aspects of knowledge needs joint activities and physical proximity for interaction; however, the increase in globalisation is resulting in an increased need to share knowledge in a physically distributed environment. This therefore raises the question as to how the softer aspects of knowledge can be managed in the physically distributed global environment.

To some the answer to this problem would be simple — the softer aspects of knowledge could be made hard, making its management a trivial matter. For example, are the war stories of the photocopier repairers (Orr, 1990) not soft knowledge made hard? This view falls into the same trap as traditional KM and attempts to view the softer aspects of knowledge from a representationist perspective. It also fails to recognise the essential feature of the duality, namely, that all knowledge is soft *and* hard. It is only the balance that differs and that only some aspects of knowledge can be hard. The war stories are only one aspect of the knowledge — without the softer aspects, they are of limited value. If they were taken outside the community, that is, removed from their context, people hearing them would obtain only very limited benefit. The softer aspects of knowledge are required to maximise the value of the stories; for example, the community members have worked closely with each other, have learned the language of the community and have interacted together. Interacting with each other and telling the stories enables different interpretations to be made and new knowledge to be created. Viewing knowledge as a duality helps to explain some other discrepancies in KM: the expert systems described in Chapter II failed because they concentrated solely on the harder aspects of knowledge. Ignoring the softer aspects meant the representation was incomplete, and the system could not be transplanted to a different environment.    Another inconsistency was indicated in Chapter II: Seely Brown and Duguid (1998) differentiated between know-how and know-what. It was pointed out, however, that know-how can have an explicit component in the form of procedures that help people perform a task. Viewing this through the soft/hard lens explains the apparent contradiction. A procedure is a codified form of some of the harder aspects. Someone who had been doing a procedure for some time, that is, doing the activity, working the practice, would reach the point where (s)he would not need to rely on the procedure, could circumvent it if a work-around was needed, and would possibly be able to improve the procedure.

Some successes were also described in Chapter II, namely Dow Chemical's screening of the patents. However, using the soft/hard lens shows that it is not simply the fact that Dow has the patents (that is, the harder aspects of knowledge) but what it did with them that brought the success.

Viewing knowledge as a soft-hard duality poses the question of how this could be managed. We have noted that CoPs are groups where the softer aspects of knowledge are created, nurtured, and sustained. Recent work done in the area of CoPs provides an interesting avenue for exploration.

### Recent Work in Communities of Practice

In 1998, Wenger brought the theory of CoPs up-to-date. He revisited the earlier (Lave & Wenger, 1991) work in the light of moving CoPs into a business environment. He based his study in a commercial organisational environment (in a claims processing department). He divided the book into two parts. In the first part, he concentrated on providing a series of characterisations of the concept of Communities of Practice. The essential part of this is practice. In the second part, he examined the concept of identity. This is the development of the members of the community as they join the community and participate in its practice.

**Practice:** Wenger considers "practice" to be much more than the everyday practice of a community. He prefers to explore practice as meaning; in particular, *"practice is about meaning as an experience of everyday life"* (p. 52). He states that it is this meaning as an experience that interests him and that it is located in a process that he calls the "negotiation of meaning." This negotiation of meaning involves the interaction of two processes that form a duality: participation and reification. This duality is central to bringing the concept of CoPs up-to date. Participation is one of the elements of LPP (Lave & Wenger, 1991), but while Wenger does not ignore legitimacy and peripherality, it is participation that he extracts as being key, showing it to be one of the constituent processes of his negotiation of meaning.

For Wenger (1998), participation is more than engaging in some activities with certain other people. Learning is *social* participation; that is, it is a fuller process whereby people are active participants in the practice of a community through which they can develop identities in relation to that community. Wenger's description of participation is an excellent example of how CoP members could develop softer aspects of their knowledge. For him, participation describes:

> *the social experience of living in the world in terms of membership in social communities and active involvement in social enterprises ... Participation ... is not tantamount to collaboration. It can involve all kinds of relations, conflictual as well as harmonious, intimate as well as political, competitive as well as cooperative (pp. 55-56).*

A key aspect of participation for Wenger (1998) is mutuality — there must be reciprocal recognition. This does not necessarily imply respect and equality. He gives the examples of parents and children, and workers and direct supervisors. The relations between these people are mutual because the participants "shape each other's experiences of meaning" (p. 56). It is through the mutual interaction that CoP members gradually learn more and more about being a member of the community and thus develop the softer aspects of knowledge that cannot be directly articulated.

As knowledge has both softer and harder aspects, so participation and reification are also inextricably linked. Having concentrated on the participation aspect of LPP, Wenger (1998) emphasised that it remains undefined without the other constituent process that makes up the negotiation of meaning: *reification*. This is taken to mean giving concrete form to something that is abstract. He uses the concept of reification to refer to the process where experience is given a "form," somehow made concrete. He uses the term to cover a whole range of processes that include "making, designing, representing, naming, encoding and describing, as well as perceiving, interpreting, using, reusing, decoding and recasting" (p. 59).

He explains that any CoP will produce artefacts, tools, stories, procedures, and terms that reify something of its practice. Like the shared artefacts in DC, the artefacts reified here have knowledge embedded in them; however, the duality shows that it is the harder aspects that have been reified.

Wenger (1998) emphasises that these two constituent processes are separable analytically but are a *duality*. One cannot replace the other. Participation is undefined without reification and vice versa. They are not a dichotomy; they are a complementary pair in that they differ in how they affect the negotiation of meaning. In participation, mutuality is essential as members of a community recognise themselves in each other. In reification, however, our meanings are *projected* on to the world and attain an independent existence.

*Figure 3: The Duality of Participation and Reification (Wenger, 1998, p. 63)*

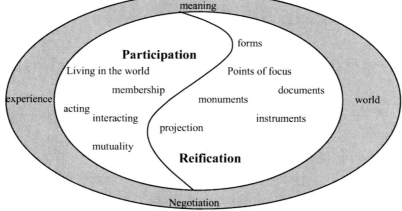

Another key point in the Participation-Reification duality is the proportion of each of the constituent processes. They need to be in a correct proportion so that one will balance the shortcomings of the other. The correct balance is necessary to achieve coordinated practice through Common Ground. Wenger (1998) points out:

> *If participation prevails — if most of what matters is left unreified — then there may not be enough material to anchor the specificities of coordination and to uncover diverging assumptions. This is why lawyers want everything in writing. If reification prevails — if everything is reified, but with little opportunity for shared experience and interactive negotiation — then there may not be enough overlap in participation to recover a coordinated, relevant, or generative meaning. This helps explain why putting everything in writing does not seem to solve all our problems (p. 65).*

The participation/reification duality maps very closely to the hard knowledge/soft knowledge duality proposed earlier, particularly with regard to the proportions. Knowledge was said to be a soft/hard duality in that all knowledge is hard *and* soft — it is simply the proportions that may differ. This is also true of participation and reification. If knowledge is predominantly soft, then the participation proportion of the duality will be higher. Conversely, the harder the knowledge the greater the reification proportion. This provides an indication as to why the capture/codify/store approach fails to provide a whole KM solution. The capture/codify/store is reifying the harder aspects of knowledge and not accounting for the softer aspects, that is, the participation part of the duality.

Wenger (1998) also takes the reified artefact beyond the boundary of the CoP, because CoPs do not exist in isolation, and in many cases a lot of the work has to be done in coordination with other communities and groups. As the artefact bridges the boundary between communities, it functions as a "boundary object" (Star, 1989; Star & Griesemer, 1989). Boundary objects can be artefacts (for example, a document) around which CoPs can organise their interconnections.

The role of the artefact as connecting different communities provides interesting possibilities. Wenger (1998) refers to this role of the artefact as a "reificative connection" and explains that, as such, artefacts can help us overcome the time and space limits of participation. As examples, he observes that we cannot be everywhere, but we can read newspapers. Similarly he points out that we cannot live in the past, but we have monuments left by people from long ago.

However, he does also point out the limitations of the artefact alone. There are the possibilities of different interpretations, as reification must accommodate different viewpoints. Therefore, it is preferable to have people and artefacts travel together to take advantage of the complementarity of reification and participation — it has already been pointed out that an artefact by itself has a meaning projected on to it. As it functions as a boundary object, the receiving community will make its own interpretations. Having people and artefacts travel together redresses the proportions between reification and participation and enables a more fruitful negotiation of meaning.

In addition to practice as meaning supported by reification and participation, Wenger (1998) also explores practice as the property of a community, pointing out that it has three dimensions: mutual engagement, joint enterprise, and shared repertoire.

*Figure 4: Dimensions of Practice as the Property of a Community (Wenger, 1998, p. 73)*

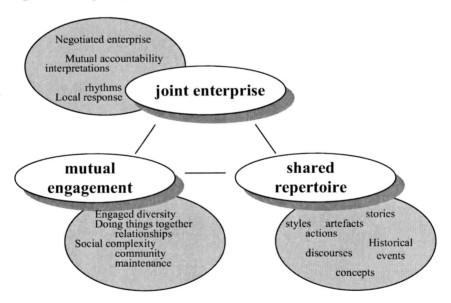

**Mutual Engagement:** Mutuality is a key aspect of engagement. Wenger (1998) explains that practice exists because people engage in actions, and they have to negotiate the meanings of these actions with each other. Therefore, he states that practice is not to be found in books or tools (although it may involve many kinds of artefacts). Practice is to be found in a community "and the relations of mutual engagement by which they can do whatever they do" (p. 73).

**Joint Enterprise:** Joint enterprise is key to keeping a community together. Wenger (1998) explains that it is not simply a stated goal; rather, relations of mutual accountability are created between and among the members of the community and this becomes part of the practice. The joint enterprise is also defined by the members of the community as they are in the process of pursuing it.

**Shared Repertoire:** Over time a CoP will create resources for negotiating meaning as the participants pursue the joint enterprise. These resources can include procedures, routines, tools, stories, concepts, and artefacts that the community has produced and that have now become a part of the practice.

These areas provide further support to the soft/hard duality. The harder aspects are clearly visible in the shared repertoire, and the softer aspects of knowledge are necessary for the success of the joint enterprise and mutual engagement.

*Identity*

Participation and reification also play a part in the second part of Wenger's (1998) book where he examines the concept of identity. This is the development of the members of the community as they join the community and participate in its practice. Identity and practice are closely linked. Wenger observes that to develop a practice needs the members of the community to engage with each other and acknowledge each other as members of the community; that is, it involves the members each negotiating ways of being a person in the context of the CoP.

Identity is partly defined in terms of the relations that develop in a community. Engaging in the practice of a community develops relations that constitute a form of legitimation — it defines a member's place in the community. It defines, among other things, who has specific expertise, who is central, who is peripheral. For Wenger (1998), identity is defined socially in practice because it is a result of participation in communities. However, participation and reification are a duality and a balance of both is needed: "An identity, then, is a layering of events of participation and reification by which our experience and its social interpretation inform each other" (p. 151).

People learn how to work, they learn how to engage with each other, and as they do so they can play a part in the relations that define the community. They also learn how to interpret and use the community's repertoire of practice. This includes a community's artefacts, actions, and language and makes use of the community's history in the form of references and memories. Identity then, like legitimation, is a form of competence that is constantly being renegotiated over time.

Having brought CoPs up-to-date Wenger (1998) provides a list of possible characteristics that he feels define a CoP. Many of them overlap the characteristics identified in Figure 1[6] but some points add to the concept, for example:

- When members offer a description of who "belongs," there is substantial overlap in the descriptions.
- Introductory preambles are non-existent. It is as if conversations and interactions are simply continuing an ongoing process.
- The members know what each other knows, what they are able to do, and how they can make a contribution.

Wenger (1998) is of the same view that it is not possible to create a single, tight definition, but rather it is preferable to use the term CoP as an umbrella term. Making a definition too broad would devalue the concept, yet having too narrow a definition would reduce its usefulness.

> *It is not necessary, for instance, to develop a simple metric that would yield a clear-cut answer for each of the social configurations ... by specifying exact ranges of size, duration, proximity, amount of interaction or types of activities (p. 122).*

There is however a limitation in the descriptions of CoPs, even when brought up-to-date by Wenger (1998) — that Communities of Practice are essentially a co-located phenomenon. It is only recently that much work has been done in the development of virtual CoPs. We have seen in Chapter II that the internationalisation of business is impacting an ever-increasing number of organisations and causing more and more work to be undertaken in a distributed, often international, environment. Lave and Wenger (1991) pointed out in passing that CoPs do not necessarily have to be co-located; that is, the term community does not automatically imply co-presence. However, all of the examples were co-located. Wenger (1998) goes slightly further. He states that geographical proximity alone is not sufficient to develop a practice, but that it can be advantageous to have physical proximity. Wenger tackles the issue of locality of practice and within this context he introduces the notion of a *constellation* of communities of practice able to move out of physical co-location. Initially, he gives the examples of large communities such as speakers of a language, a city, or a social movement, and some smaller ones such as a factory, an office, or a school. He acknowledges the movement to a global environment and states that these configurations are better viewed as constellations of interconnected CoPs.

Work that has been done in the field of virtual CoPs has concentrated on on-line communities that regard themselves as CoPs. In this book, we are more concerned with organisational CoPs that have to function in a distributed international environment where knowledge (both soft and hard) needs to be shared across physical and temporal distance. It is not clear what effect such an environment will have on Wenger's reification/participation duality. This is an important question and we will explore it further in Chapter IV.

## INFORMING THE OTHER VIEWS REGARDING SOFT KNOWLEDGE

Earlier we came to the conclusion that the Distributed Cognition and boundary object approaches are primarily representationist. We also saw that in CoPs and with Common Ground dealing with soft knowledge on its own is problematic. This resulted in the suggestion to regard knowledge as a duality. Wenger's (1998) work in CoPs with his emphasis on the participation/reification duality provides us with a meta-framework to help clarify the Distributed Cognition and boundary object, Common Ground, and CoP approaches, adding further weight to the duality view.

### Distributed Cognition

There is an apparent contradiction in Distributed Cognition. Hutchins and Klausen (1991) in applying DC to an airline cockpit refer to the pilots as members of a CoP, although in this case they are referring to the wider CoP of pilots in general. Hutchins (1995a) also emphasises the cultural aspect of the artefacts:

*Although some of the representations are internal, they are still cultural in the sense that they are the residua of a process enacted by a Community of Practice rather than idiosyncratic inventions of their individual users (p. 130).*

There are numerous other examples of the groups where DC has been applied that could very well be CoPs, for example, the medics examined by Cicourel (1990) and the radiology groups of Rogers and Ellis (1994) and Symon et al. (1996). The best example, however, is provided by Hutchins (1990, 1995a) with his description of the quartermasters, and indeed we find that the quartermasters themselves are described as a CoP by Lave and Wenger (1991).

Although, Hutchins and Klausen (1991) emphasise the cultural aspect and refer to a CoP, we have already noted that Hutchins' Distributed Cognition approach is primarily representationist.

It is perhaps not surprising that the groups described in some of the DC literature bear such a strong resemblance to CoPs because of the emphasis it places on some CoP characteristics. Hutchins (1995a) emphasises the fluid self-perpetuative nature of the community and the social distribution of the knowledge. There are experts or gurus regarding specific aspects, but as time passes, there is a sharing of knowledge through interaction. The social distribution of knowledge gradually changes — it is the "dynamic" part of the CoP. The social distribution of the knowledge also indicates that there is some overlap. Members do know some of the same things. Hutchins (1995a) emphasises the importance of this overlapping knowledge distribution in cooperative work as it makes the system robust and able to cope with difficulties. He shows this with the example of the navigation team by criticising those analysts who see knowledge distributed between cooperative participants in a mutually exclusive manner. In the navigation team, there is some clear overlap between the knowledge of the plotter, the bearing taker, and the bearing timer-recorder, leading to a robust system. Hutchins (1990) also shows that the artefacts support this distribution of knowledge among the members of the navigation team to make it robust should an individual component fail.

Hutchins' (1990, 1995a) representationist approach is perhaps best seen in the artefacts. Wenger (1998) also uses shared artefacts in the reification part of his duality. Wenger's use of shared artefacts in the form of boundary objects and the use of shared artefacts in DC should not be seen as dichotomous but rather as complementary. DC concentrates on externalised representations of knowledge and absolute meaning, whereas boundary objects have an interpretive flexibility. This shows that domain and soft knowledge are necessary in order to benefit from the knowledge embedded in the artefact, be it a document, a tool, or a story. An outsider will understand little, a newcomer with some domain knowledge would be able to understand the story at face value perhaps and what it means, but the old-timer will be able to see new possibilities and make different interpretations.

Robinson's (1997) description of procedures as artefacts has great importance for CoPs. Procedures embody the knowledge of previous practitioners; they provide a form of accountability and cover if something goes wrong. Just as important, they are a "way-in" for newcomers to the community. A newcomer will follow the procedure. Gradually, as the newcomer becomes proficient, (s)he will not have to think as explicitly about the steps to be taken. As (s)he becomes an old-timer, (s)he may develop the soft knowledge to omit some steps or even to conceive of improvements to the procedure.

Wenger's (1998) reification/participation approach helps us to understand the apparent contradiction of Distributed Cognition being a representationist approach but referring to CoPs. The difference lies in the emphasis. As we saw earlier, the use of artefacts in DC concentrates on the harder aspects of knowledge. Wenger's duality shows us that what is lacking in DC is a consideration of the participation. His emphasis on the duality is also a reflection of Cole (1996), who emphasised the dual nature of the artefact itself, thus moving away from the hard representational aspect. Cole's view of artefacts is that they are dual in nature. They are both ideal (conceptual) and material. Their material form is made up of the physical characteristics, but they are also *ideal*, that is, conceptual. This means that the material form is a result of changes that have been brought about by use. The changes might also have been brought about by participation in interactions with other artefacts, with actions and with human social worlds between which they mediate. This is supported by Cook and Seely Brown (1999) who, as explained earlier, emphasised the importance of interaction. Cole's view would suggest that cultural aspects are not embedded in the artefact in the "hard" sense, as suggested by DC, but are to be found in the "ideal" form of the artefact.

DC also provides us with a complementary view to LPP. Whereas LPP is concerned with the social structure of the community and how newcomers learn, DC is concerned with the process of how work gets done, thus providing us with a functional view of the community to complement the social view.

## Boundary Objects

Wenger (1998) used Star's (1989) ideas of boundary objects to further describe the role of the artefacts in his CoPs. In Wenger's case, the artefacts as boundary objects crossed boundaries between different CoPs. He explains that the connections that boundary objects create between CoPs are reificative. By this he does not mean that they do not involve participation, but, being artefacts, they use forms of reification and thereby are able to bridge different forms of participation. They enable coordination between different communities without creating a direct link, or, as Wenger calls it, a bridge.

He also explains how a boundary object reflects the relations between the communities. He gives the example of a memo created for wide distribution. A memo appears as a self-contained artefact and one would assume that the memo tells its own story. However, Wenger (1998) observes that the memo gives rise to different meanings, and these are a function of the relations between the practices involved:

> *When a person reads the memo, what is really going on involves not merely a relation between the person and the memo but also a relation between communities of practice: those where the memo originated and those to which the person belongs (p. 108).*

He points out that this means the problem of communication is one of both reification and participation, and therefore designing artefacts also means designing boundary objects. Designing a boundary object (which is reification in the form of an artefact) means designing for participation, thus moving the emphasis from the harder aspects to the softer.

## Common Ground

When we were exploring the notion of soft knowledge earlier in this chapter we observed that there are some of the softer aspects of knowledge to be found in Common Ground. Wenger's (1998) emphasis on the duality adds weight to the view of knowledge as a soft/hard duality and enables us to see that there are both soft and hard aspects in Common Ground. The softer aspects are in the knowledge that the members of a community have built up and with which they can understand each other. The harder aspects of knowledge are in the utterance itself. The softer aspects allow the members to understand the correct meaning. The conch shell in the example given earlier shows that an artefact can provide a shared basis for Common Ground and the Common Ground can determine the interpretation of an artefact within a community.

## MAKING SOFT KNOWLEDGE HARD

We have already noted that, although KM practitioners and researchers recognise that there is knowledge that is difficult to articulate and capture, most are still approaching the problem from a representationist point of view and are trying to proceed by exploring ways of representing the unrepresentable, by trying to make soft knowledge hard so that it can be represented. Wenger's (1998) duality gives a clearer view of why this is perhaps the wrong route to follow.

A key aspect of the three different views is the importance to a greater (Distributed Cognition) or lesser (Common Ground) degree of objects. The information that the artefacts contain is not the same as the knowledge required to use them, which may be socially constructed—this is the softer component, or the participation component of knowledge. This provides some indications that sharing the softer part of knowledge is not as simple as making it hard.

Distributed Cognition would imply that the softer aspects of knowledge could be made hard by embedding them in artefacts, for example, procedures, physical artefacts, and stories. However, the predominantly representational approach of Distributed Cognition is shown by CoPs to be lacking. The CoP approach shows that the participation aspect is overlooked in Distributed Cognition. The participation and socially constructed component does not become apparent until the artefact becomes a boundary object and crosses the boundary to another community. Boundary objects show that if the knowledge was simply softer knowledge made hard, then it could be easily extracted. This is not the case, as boundary objects demonstrate that a degree of knowledge is needed to be able to use the artefact — there is a degree of interpretive flexibility. A newcomer to the community could possibly understand the artefact at face level, a member with more experience would understand more of the artefact, but an old-timer with a greater store of softer knowledge would perhaps be able to make new inferences from it and so develop new knowledge. This is especially true of artefacts in the form of procedures that serve as a framework and support for newcomers who follow the procedures, whereas old-timers develop the experience and skill to be able to "break" the procedure where necessary to work more effectively or efficiently. In becoming a boundary object and crossing to another community, the artefact is also being moved out of the context of the community in which it was created. Context plays important roles. It is closely linked with identity, for example, if a member of a community does not know who has created an artefact (s)he might not have confidence in it. Goguen (1997) also shows that some aspects of meaning are also context dependent. As an example he offers:

> "Do you want a cup of coffee?"
> "Coffee keeps me awake."

The question can be understood at a literal level; however, the answer could be affirmative or negative. It is not clear without the context. In making softer knowledge hard, the literal parts could be captured but the context-dependent components would be lost. This shows that the utterance is what is hard and the understanding of the meaning is the softer aspect. Clark (1996) expands the notion of context into Common Ground. In losing the context of the community in which an artefact is created, there would only be the Common Ground of the wider community available, for example, the community of English speakers. According to Clark (1996), this is also to be seen in personal experiences that cannot be represented as such and are recorded in a mental "personal diary" and provide a context and a Common Ground. This shows that softer aspects of knowledge are to be found in Common Ground and also indicates that in trying to make the softer aspects of knowledge hard, the context (and, with it, Common Ground) would be lost.

As softer knowledge cannot simply be made hard, this has implications for KM and the use of IT for managing knowledge.

Some attempts have been made to manage soft knowledge by recording "war stories" of the people involved in the work of the organisation. The importance of war stories and chance conversations at the water cooler have been recognised as being so important that a Hewlett-Packard (HP) division developed a system using Lotus Notes in order for the company trainers to be able to enter any insights, tips, tricks, observations or insights (Davenport & Prusak, 1998). This was regarded as a form of knowledge repository and was initially very successful. Of late, however, it appears not be used to the same extent. This indicates perhaps that its initial impact may have had some novelty value and that more is needed to maintain its use. This points to the importance of the "people" aspect when trying to share softer knowledge.

It also raises the question as to what form the knowledge takes in a "war story" — has the softer knowledge simply been made hard? If this were the case, it would be a simple matter of reversing the process and retrieving the softer aspects. This is clearly not the case. During the transition, there is always a degree of abstraction. In order to get something back out, more softer knowledge is needed. Someone who had concentrated on the harder aspects of knowledge (for example, a newcomer) would understand the story at face level, the more experienced practitioner would get more out of it, but different people would not get out what was put in. People would have different interpretations (Kidd, 1994), and some might be able to make new inferences and create new knowledge. For this they need to develop the softer part of their knowledge, as in the potential future knowledge of autopoiesis.

DC has shown us how artefacts can have knowledge embedded in them. The same question as to whether they are softer knowledge made hard also applies to the artefacts. The answer is also the same — the process cannot simply be reversed to retrieve the softer knowledge. Something else is necessary. It is, in this case, interesting to note that the artefact is of little use outside the context of the community in which it is created, for example, the navigational aids described by Hutchins (1990, 1995a) could not easily be used by someone who was not in the community of people with navigation skills. As expressed by Interrogate the Internet[7] (1996), "knowledge taken out of context is really just noise." This is also true of the expert systems described by Berg (1997) in Chapter II. They were even less successful when tried in a different environment; that is, they were of little use outside the context of the community in which they were developed, a fact also noticed earlier by Cicourel (1990). This shows how such systems concentrated on the harder aspects of knowledge that could be captured and codified, but failed to take into account the softer aspects. The systems were therefore incomplete.

Hutchins (1995a) points out that although artefacts have the knowledge of other people embedded in them and represent a problem in a different way in order to make its solution easier, they do not change our cognitive abilities — rather, they present the situation to the user in a way that requires a different ability. He suggests that this is, in a way, rather like the attempts made at creating expert systems in the 1980s. But these artefacts work, unlike the expert systems that were disappointing in their results. They are more like tools that the user can use. It is a different view of codifying knowledge. It has not been codified in the way of AI. Davenport and Prusak (1998) explain it:

> *Some knowledge that is quite complex and initially tacit can be externalized and embedded in a company's products or services. The knowers use their expertise to develop a process or product that contains at least some of what they know (p. 83).*

The fact that the artefact is of little or no use outside of the community in which it has been created means that — although knowledge is embedded in the artefact — newcomers to the community still need to learn how to use it. This knowledge is often learned from people who are already members of the community.

The importance of the social context, the learning of softer knowledge from existing members of a community, and the lack of success of trying to see IT as a solution all indicate the importance of the human aspect to the sharing of softer knowledge and suggests something more is needed. In fact, if human factors are not taken into consideration during a KM project, can we really call it KM? Fahey and Prusak (1998) consider not catering to human interaction to be one of their 11 deadliest sins of KM. They explain that IT is an enabler and its strengths lie in the transmission and distribution of data and information. However, they point out that dialogue between people has a "rich interactivity" that enables communication and learning.

> *Knowledge is primarily a function and consequence of the meeting and interaction of minds. Human intervention remains the only source of knowledge generation (p. 273).*

In catering to the sharing of the softer side of knowledge, we should therefore ensure that there is sufficient time devoted to personal contact. Relationships need to develop for the meaningful sharing and transfer of softer knowledge to take place. Therefore, rather than simply attempting to implement technological solutions, a key part of the management of the softer aspects of knowledge is facilitating communication and interaction — connection not collection. Sachs (1995) reports on studies that suggest that the webs of relationships that workers develop in communities are more important than seeing the workers as cogs in a wheel. How important this is in the organisational context is illustrated in Table 1. The table shows that Sachs' "explicit"

*Table 1: Views of Work as Both Tacit and Explicit (Adapted from Sachs, 1995)*

| Explicit Organisational View | Tacit Organisational View |
|---|---|
| Training | Learning |
| Tasks | Know-How |
| Position in hierarchy | Informal political systems, network of contacts |
| Procedures and techniques | Conceptual understanding |
| Work flow | Work practices |
| Methods and procedures | Rules of thumb, judgement |
| Teams | Communities |

view demonstrates the usual emphasis on the harder aspects. She recommends her "tacit" view where the softer aspects receive more emphasis.

These challenges are perhaps well met by the management of the softer aspect of knowledge by using Wenger's (1998) approach encompassing the three views (Distributed Cognition/Common Ground/CoPs) that we used to refine the notion of soft knowledge. His reification/participation duality provides a way forward for KM, as it takes into account the need to maintain the balance between the harder and the softer aspects of knowledge. However, we need to look more closely at a solution for managing the softer aspects of knowledge in a distributed environment.

As the softer aspects are found in relationships, are constructed in a social context, and are difficult or impossible to articulate, they pose particular difficulties to KM, namely, how can they be managed, and how can they be managed in the global environment? The dominant capture-codify-store approach is not suitable for sharing soft knowledge, for it is not a simple matter of making the softer aspects hard. In his work on CoPs, Wenger (1998) showed that the reification of knowledge/practice cannot be divorced from participation, for the meaning of artefacts does not reside in the artefact alone — knowledge as practice is distinct from knowledge as representation. CoPs are groups where the softer aspects of knowledge are created, nurtured, and sustained. They can help with the temporal distribution of knowledge caused by the loss of staff (unless the whole CoP is lost) in that, with LPP, newcomers are constantly learning from old-timers, and the CoP is constantly undergoing a re-generation. As organisations are having to operate in an increasingly distributed environment, the question is raised as to how the management of the softer aspects of knowledge might be achieved through sustaining CoPs virtually. This leads to the question, How does a CoP function in a physically distributed environment? This will be the focus of the CoP that we visit in Section Two of this book. However, before we meet the CoP, it will be useful to see what issues are involved in working in Virtual Environments (VEs) and with Virtual Teams.

**Chapter IV**

# Going Virtual

*Before meeting our CoP we take the opportunity to explore issues which may affect a CoP which needs to function in a distributed international environment.*

## THE ISSUES IN GOING VIRTUAL

As most organisational CoPs tend to be co-located. It is a useful exercise to appraise ourselves of the issues involved in Virtual Environments (VEs) and Virtual Teams. This will give us some idea of the issues that a CoP may face when it has to operate in a distributed environment.

### Virtual Working

In order to gain the necessary flexibility for operating in the global environment, firms are increasingly turning to teams and communities (Castells, 1996; Lipnack & Stamps, 1997; Finerty, 1997). Much of the research into virtual communities and knowledge sharing has been undertaken in the field of sociology (for example, Fernback, 1997, and Jones, 1998) and has focused on the communities that develop on the Internet (Argyle & Shields, 1996;

Breslow, 1997; Chen & Gaines, 1998; Danet, Ruedenberg, & Rosenbaum-Tamari, 1998) and Internet-based media such as Multi-User Dungeons[8] (MUDs) and Object-Oriented MUDS (MOOS) (Bromberg, 1996; Conkar & Kimble, 1997; Seely Brown & Duguid, 1996), and Usenet and discussion groups. Exploring the communities that have come into being on the Internet has led to debate whether a virtual community is a community at all (Bromberg, 1996; Porter, 1997; Wilbur, 1997), comparisons of virtual and physical communities (Mitra, 1997; Zickmund, 1997), and the general study of communities that have grown up in a VE (McLaughlin, Osborne, & Ellison, 1997; Watson, 1997).

Castells (1996) describes virtual communities as "a self-defined electronic network of interactive communication organised around a shared interest or purpose, although sometimes communication becomes the goal in itself" (p. 362). This was also shown in Conkar and Kimble (1997). In that case the community that had formed around a MUD was referred to as a Community of Practice, and the medium *is* the practice; that is, the MUD is not only the medium by which the community communicates, but the purpose of the community is interaction within the MUD. The MUD is the principal reason for the existence of the community. Newcomers have to learn the language of the community, how to use the MUD, and the etiquette of the community.

However, discussion of the Internet as a medium for sharing knowledge across time and distance has led several researchers to observe that what is found on the Internet is primarily information, as opposed to knowledge. They argue that the knowledge resides in the human agents using the medium (Interrogate the Internet, 1996; Thu Nguyen & Alexander, 1996), that information can be retrieved from the documents, but discourse is needed for knowledge sharing (Chen & Gaines, 1998). Seely Brown and Duguid (1996) come the closest when they describe a MOO that was set up at the University of Pennsylvania for graduates of Medieval Latin. It was more than a simple chat line; it was a virtual complex with quadrangle, classrooms, a common room where Latin was spoken, and a virtual Coke machine where people could gather and chat. This grew to include scholars from other locations.

The importance of teams and communities to organisations that are having to cope with the pressures of internationalisation has led to a variety of terms being coined and groups being studied; for example, "self-directed work teams" (Evans & Sims, Jr., 1997), "network communities" (Carroll, Langton, & Rosson, 1996), "'self-managing work groups" (Williams, 1994) and "Virtual Teams" (Barnatt, 1997; Lipnack & Stamps, 1997). These are all types of group that have recently been identified in the modern organisation. Virtual

Teams are not to be equated with CoPs but they can help acquaint us with the issues, because they play a role in directly tackling the practical problems posed by distributed international working, that is, problems such as time, place, culture, and language differences.

*Virtual Teams*

Virtual Teams are teams that, according to Lipnack and Stamps (1997) are teams like any other but that routinely cross boundaries. These boundaries may be national and cultural if the work is spread across different countries, or they may be organisational and cultural, for example, if collaboration is being spread across different organisations in the case of an inter-organisational collaboration or as a result of a merger or acquisition. In doing so they have to cope with the major difficulties of different cultures, different languages, temporal distance, and physical distance.

The problems of overcoming different cultures and languages have been recognised by many (for example, Barnatt, 1997, and Li & Williams, 1999), with culture having received the most attention (for example, Dyrkton, 1996, Chao, 1997, and Pearce, 1997). Cultural differences can involve moral standards (Shade, 1996), or social, learning and organisational differences (Sumner, Domingue, & Zdrahal, 1998). In fact, it can be the organisational cultural factors that can cause the most problems — both between partnership organisations as in Castells' (1996) Network Enterprise or within different areas of the same organisation, perhaps as a result of a merger.

The problem of communicating across different time zones means that there are times when it is not possible to contact a colleague, for example, by telephone. However, the greatest difficulty is that posed by physical distance. As distance increases, social awareness is reduced and the potential for collaboration decreases. As observed by Lipnack and Stamps (1997), "The probability of people communicating or collaborating more than once a week drops off dramatically if they are more than the width of a basketball apart" (p. 8).

To overcome the problems of time and distance, great possibilities are offered by 'new" media, or computer-mediated communications (CMCs) such as e-mail, voice mail, tele- and video-conferencing, group discussion, and mailing lists, the Internet, including Internet Relay Chat (IRC), and MUDs and MOOs, which are developing into VEs using virtual reality (VR) technologies.

These "new" media with their possibilities have been one of the drivers to the internationalisation of business. As Voiskounsky (1998) puts it, CMCs

*Figure 1: Collocated to Virtual Distance (From Lipnack & Stamps, 1997, p. 9)*

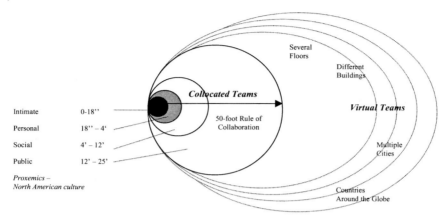

assume no time zones and their use in large distributed organisations has attracted interest (Hinds & Kiesler, 1995). They manage this because some of them are asynchronous — it is no longer necessary for a communication partner to be at his/her terminal at the same time. Communication no longer has to take place in real time as on the telephone — an e-mail can be sent that will be waiting for the communication partner when (s)he arrives at his/her desk. Despite the advantages they bring, however, they do have some drawbacks. E-mail (and mailing lists), as the oldest of the CMCs, has received the most attention (for example, Robinson, 1991, and Rudy, 1996), much of it focusing on its negative aspects such as e-mail overload (Dawley & Anthony, 1998; Mackay, Malone, Crowston, Rao, Rosenblitt, & Card, 1989) and the lack of "richness" (Ngwenyama & Lee, 1997) in the medium that can lead to loss of bodily cues and misunderstandings (Rivera, Cooke, & Bauhs, 1996; Witmer & Katzman, 1998).

It is the lack of bodily cues that has interested many and, as a result, voice mail and video conferencing have attracted attention (Fish, Kraut, Root, & Rice, 1992; Kristoffersen & Rodden, 1996; Sellen, 1992). However. these have also been felt to be lacking in richness and inferior to face-to-face communication (Fish et al., 1992; Hollan & Stornetta, 1992). This is a weakness that runs through much of the above CMC literature; that is, CMC is compared with face-to-face communication, and there seems to be a constant striving to achieve the equivalent of face-to-face communication through CMCs. Rather than comparing the new media with face-to-face communication and more "traditional" media, CMCs should be regarded as media in their own right (Hollan & Stornetta, 1992; Rafaeli & Sudweeks, 1998). We should compare like with like (Shields, 1996), and concentrate on using the correct medium for the correct task in the correct context (Rice, 1987). Indeed, what are now regarded as relatively old technologies, such as the telephone and television, were once revolutionary new technologies and had their critics (Shade, 1996; Jones, 1997).

The importance of work in a distributed environment has also attracted researchers in the Computer-Supported Cooperative Work (CSCW) field (for example, van House, Butler, & Schiff, 1998; Poltrock & Engelbeck, 1997), who have looked at using IT to support distributed communities and groups. Some of these are looking to web-based systems for knowledge exchange (Buckingham Shum, 1998), while others are looking to further develop video-based systems (Adler & Henderson, 1994; Tang & Rua, 1994), for example, to increase awareness and assist ad hoc communication.

> *Key concepts are social browsing, proximity and unplanned interaction ... this has become the equivalent of supporting the ability to meet informally  (Kristofferson & Rodden, 1996, p. 17).*

However, despite the technologies that are being researched and applied to distributed international working, it is clear that they will not succeed unless certain cultural factors apply. Even if the most advanced technology available is put in place, it will only be successful if participants want it to be. If there is not a culture of sharing in place, then the organisation will have to take steps to actively encourage and promote it. To ensure the organisational culture encourages teamwork, it will be necessary to emphasise the team above the individual and to foster an atmosphere of collaboration rather than competition. People must be encouraged away from hoarding their knowledge to sharing it — teams are much more successful in organisations with a culture of information sharing. Such organisations are also likely to be based on trust, to be helpful, and encourage debate and consultation.

Button and Sharrock's (1994) example of software engineers developing embedded software for a photocopier gave a good example of this need for information sharing and teamwork. The software engineers had access to the original Japanese development team. There was a language problem in that the managers the team had originally met spoke English, but the engineers to whom they really needed to speak, did not. The original design documents were also found to be in Japanese. Therefore, when they encountered problems, they could not simply use the phone or e-mail, as queries and replies had to go through a translation process. There was also a cultural problem in that even when the team finally received replies, the replies were incomplete, and it was felt that the Japanese part of the company was deliberately resisting the dissemination of its expertise.

In addition to the importance of the cultural factors and the possibilities offered by the "new"' media, there still seems to be a necessity for a face-to-face element in "virtual" teams and communities (Barnatt, 1997; Li & Williams, 1999; Lipnack & Stamps, 1997). In fact, Castells (1996) even reports on a community that grew up electronically but whose residents have now reached the point where they meet face-to-face to further develop the community. The community, SFNet, is based in the San Francisco Bay area. As most of the community regulars live in the Bay area, some of them hold regular parties in order to get to know each other better. Powell (1998) talks about the continued importance of co-location despite the range of new technologies that would technically enable people to collaborate from anywhere in the world. This shows that more than technology is needed, and Powell reports that many people still feel that face-to-face interaction is the only way for tacit knowledge transfer. This need for face-to-face interaction is demonstrated even in the field of "virtual" teams. Lipnack and Stamps' (1997) emphasise the importance of face-to-face interaction to solidify the teams with the result being a mixture of face-to-face meetings and electronic communication to reduce the degree of travel rather than replacing it. This reinforces the earlier point that IT is simply a support or an enabler, not a solution, and suggests that the human element remains essential.

### Communities of Practice and Virtual Teams

The previous section highlighted some interesting points that can be useful in CoPs and virtual teams but the groups described above are not CoPs. For the purposes of this book, it is specifically CoPs that are of interest and, therefore, it is necessary to be able to differentiate between a CoP and a team.

Wenger (1998) is very clear that the term Community of Practice is not synonymous with group, team, or network, but it is certainly possible for a formally constituted team to develop into a CoP. CoPs tend to be informal, but it may be the case that a team is put together with a brief and with deliverables. However, as time goes by, that team may develop closer working relationships, go beyond their original brief in unofficial ways, and evolve into a CoP.

The difference between a CoP and a formal team or project group lies in the relationships that are developed between the members. One way of looking at this is to consider the aspect of legitimacy. The form of legitimation that is present can be used to differentiate between a team and a CoP. In a team, the legitimation is derived from the formal hierarchy (for example, externally imposed structure and membership). In CoPs, legitimation is more informal and comes about by members earning their status in the community, for example by the newcomer being accepted and gradually working his/her way to full participation.

It is possible for a team to become a CoP as informal relationships begin to develop and the source of legitimation changes in emphasis. Hutchins (1990, 1995a) provides an account of how a formally structured team may also function as a CoP in his study of a navigation team on an American warship. There is a formal structure to the team provided by military rankings. However, when the team gets a new officer, the informal CoP provides the forum for the learning that takes place. It is one of the Petty Officers, lower in rank but with more experience, who has to supervise the newcomer and "break in" the new officer.

Having ascertained the difference between a team and a CoP, we can now move on to see what specific issues there could be, and what there could be to learn for a CoP that is operating in a physically distributed international environment.

## A Virtual CoP?

As operations in the distributed international arena are becoming ever more important, it is becoming ever more pressing to support the sharing of the softer side of knowledge when workers are not co-located. In fact, Holtshouse (1998) considers this one of the most pressing issues for KM:

> The issue ... is how to provide the effect of ... knowledge exchange without workers necessarily interacting face-to-face and being co-located (p. 278).

This has also been considered by others in their desire for a "virtual coffee pot" (Berman, 1990):

> The meetings by the coffee machine are usually central ... We want to be able to have meetings by the coffee machine, but to

*be able to do so 80 miles apart via the video and audio links on
the workstation (p. 14).*

From an established KM viewpoint, the solution would be to make
knowledge harder, capture it, and share it, but we have already seen that this
approach does not work and that CoPs are where the softer aspects of
knowledge are sustained and nurtured. This poses the question of how to make
a CoP distributed, even international.

Some aspects of a CoP should translate from the co-located to the virtual
world relatively easily, for example, finding a shared interest. Co-location is not
necessary for some aspects of Common Ground: if the members are doing
similar jobs, then there will already be a shared domain language, knowledge,
and background.  However, if Common Ground is based on a shared
perception of an artefact, event, or action, this may be affected by distribution.
Clark (1996) refers to this as "perceptual copresence." Co-location is also not
necessary for fluidity — working in a distributed environment could even
increase the degree to which newcomers arrive and old-timers leave.

We have seen that narration and the telling of stories are used for
knowledge sharing.  At first glance, it should be easy to transfer stories to a
distributed operation by simply recording the stories and making them available
to members, similar to the Hewlett-Packard Trainers' Trading Post. However,
even the use of narration is not simply a matter of making softer aspects of
knowledge hard.

Distribution may also cause a problem in the following areas:

**Relationships:** Relationships are a key aspect of a CoP.  They determine the
motivation and the legitimation of the members, which in turn determine
the identity and the trust and confidence of the members. The question
arises as to how effectively relationships can be developed and sustained
in the distributed environment. The relationships will also affect the feeling
of community and identity that develops in a CoP.

**Common Purpose/Motivation:** Although people doing similar jobs might
share an interest, the development of a common purpose is more closely
tied with the motivation of the members. Can the motivation be maintained
when the members are not co-located?

**Informal and Unofficial:** Often CoPs are informal and unofficial. They evolve
from a group of people with a shared interest.  It may be that it is difficult

for a CoP to come about because the prospective members do not know of each other's existence, and if they do start to evolve into a CoP, there is the question of how it can be facilitated or enabled.

**Legitimate Peripheral Participation (LPP):** Other issues might concern the question of how Lave and Wenger's (1991) concept of LPP would translate to a distributed environment. The learning undertaken with LPP is situated, as is some of the knowledge created during problem solving. Whether the CoP moves easily to working in distributed mode might depend on the reason for the situatedness. If the members need to be co-located because they share resources such as a document, then the CoP should translate to the distributed environment relatively easily. If, however, the learning is situated because the face-to-face element is essential for seeing and learning how the job is done, then the distribution will have more impact.

The concept of peripherality may also be affected. In Lave and Wenger's (1991) CoPs, the periphery is a social periphery. However, in a distributed environment, there will also be a physical and a temporal periphery that will have certain connotations for the notion of participation.

The transition to a virtual environment also raises the question of whether it will be more difficult to gain legitimacy in such a community, but perhaps the most difficult area will be the facilitation of participation. Wenger (1998) observed that participation is more than simply collaboration and engagement in practice. It is experiencing living in the social world of the community and involves the relationships between the members. It is central to the evolution of the community and to the creation of relationships that help develop the sense of trust and identity that defines the community.

*Specific Issues for the Case Studies*

Perhaps the greatest possibilities for helping a CoP function in the distributed environment are offered by shared artefacts as described in Wenger's (1998) duality of participation and reification. We have already seen how Wenger alluded to the possibilities offered by the reificative connections. This raises a number of questions that need to be explored:

- Are the softer aspects of knowledge shared through artefacts?
- What form might the artefact take?

- How does the CoP function in the distributed environment? Is it a matter of linking CoPs or is the CoP spread over national boundaries? What movement is there either between the linked CoPs or over the national boundaries? Is this movement of people, artefacts as boundary objects, or both?
- What is the role of the boundary object/artefact?
- What are the implications for legitimation, peripherality, and participation?
- If participation is the most difficult part of LPP to obtain in a distributed environment, does that mean that there will be correspondingly more reification, and if so, what consequences does this have for the balance between the two?
- Does the apprenticeship form of LPP play a role?

Other, more general, questions that are raised are:

- What sort of structure would a distributed CoP have?
- Are distributed CoPs totally virtual?
- How do they interact and communicate?
- How is the CoP maintained?
- What media are used? Why are particular media selected?
- Common Ground — how is perceptual copresence established in a virtual environment?
- Social processes (trust and relationships) are important in a CoP. How are these affected in the distributed environment?

# SECTION II:

# LIVING WITH THE COMMUNITY

# Chapter V

# Living with the CoP — Stage One

*This chapter describes Stage One of the case study, which is designed to obtain an inside view of how a distributed CoP works, how the softer aspects of knowledge are shared, and how participation is achieved. To start with we are introduced to the members of the community, and then we spend some time with them. Before we move to Stage Two, we take the opportunity to examine some issues that arise from this first stage.*

## INTRODUCTION TO THE COMMUNITY

The community that provided the focus for the research in the case study is in the IT support for the research arm of a major international organisation. It exists in three locations — Japan, the UK, and California. It consists of the IT support group in a UK location, a larger IT support group in a Californian location, and an IT support member in Japan. They had seen a need for structural change at an early stage and for over two years have been working to try to provide a global infrastructure for the organisation's research arm, to try to undertake joint development work, and to try to deploy distributed resources more effectively.

*Figure 1: Structure of Case Study CoP*

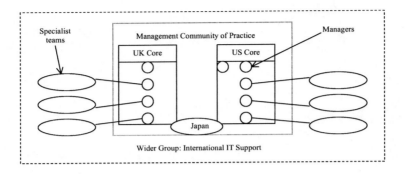

The UK core consists of an overall manager, Wayne, and three other managers: Dave, who is responsible for the Infrastructure Team; Stan, who is responsible for the Informatics Team, and Mike, who leads the PC Support Team. The first stage of the main case study concentrates on the UK core, but the members frequently and regularly interact with Chakaka, the support person in Japan, with the US core, and with people from a number of project groups.  Figure 2 shows the relationship between the people who are present in the study.

*Figure 2: The People Involved in Case Study*

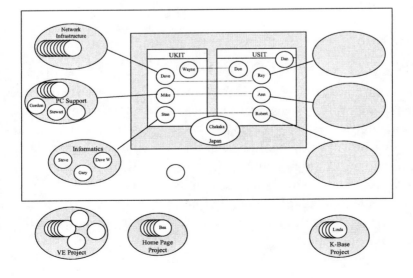

The situation is very similar in the American location. There are specialist teams headed by an individual manager. The teams correspond broadly to the teams in the UK core. The main difference, however, is that the American teams are much larger. The Japanese location is much smaller overall and is served by one member: Chakaka. Although there is an obvious hierarchy within the US group, as evidenced by the presence of an overall manager (Dan), the group considers itself to be a Community of Practice and the members justify this by defining a CoP with the following characteristics:

- Has a common set of interests *motivated* to do a common set of something.
- Is concerned with motivation.
- Is self-generating.
- Is self-selecting.
- Is not necessarily co-located.
- "Has a common set of interests *motivated* to a pattern of work, not directed to it."

This is consistent with the CoP characteristics outlined in Chapter III but is interesting for the importance it attributes to the internal motivation. Also interesting is the fact that they do not feel co-location is necessary for a CoP to function.

Other CoP features were also in evidence; for example, there was a sense of a common purpose, and the group had a strong feeling of identity, even to the point of giving itself a name. The group had its own terminology — as well as the technical domain language, there were also group-specific acronyms and nicknames. Although the group is an official group, it is a group that has evolved from a need and that is driven by the members themselves.

The group originally evolved from getting together to act as a bidding organisation that sought to make innovative bids to make new investments in the IT structure. At the end of that process, the members of the group found that they had got to know each other quite well and had developed good relationships. They had developed into regarding themselves as a worldwide IT organisation, changed the group's name and have since continued to move forward and evolve, with relationships constantly developing. They consider the management team of the IT organisation (WWITMan) to be the CoP, as that is where the strongest relationships have developed and where the closest collaboration takes place. However, relationships are constantly developing in the wider group (WWIT), and joint projects and cooperation are becoming more and more the norm — it may therefore be possible that other CoPs will come into being in WWIT in the future.

# A WEEK IN THE LIFE OF A DISTRIBUTED INTERNATIONAL COP

The vignettes describe the work of the group as it was observed during the period of the contextual interviews. The main events are summarised in Figure 3.

*Figure 3: The Main Events of Case Study Stage One*

| | Case Study Stage 1 Timeline |
|---|---|
| Monday | ➡ Semi-structured interview with Wayne in order to obtain the background to the CoP and set the study in context<br>➡ Late afternoon: Mike, Stan and DaveW have electronic meeting with 2 colleagues (Don and Linda) in Palo Alto about the development of the Knowledge Base |
| Tuesday | ➡ Stan has a team meeting with his vertical team (Gary, Steve and DaveW ). They discuss the UKIT Planning Document<br>➡ After the meeting Stan works on the Planning Document<br>➡ Stan, Dave, Mike and Wayne meet to discuss and work on the Planning Document<br>➡ Mike goes to an e-meeting with the overall head of WWIT (Dan)<br>➡ Stan works to solve a problem being encountered by one of the sub-groups of which he is a member<br>➡ Stan goes home and spends more time working on the planning document |
| Wednesday | ➡ Stan, Dave, Mike and Wayne meet to continue yesterday's discussion centred round the planning document<br>➡ Wayne and Dave meet with one of the research groups with a view to piloting some of the research<br>➡ Stan joins them for the demonstration of the research<br>➡ Wayne and Stan meet with Bea from the Communications Department. They are meeting about the internal home page project (one of the sub-groups of which Stan is a member)<br>➡ Wayne makes phone calls and sorts out some e-mails tasks<br>➡ At home Stan continues to work on the Planning Document |
| Thursday | ➡ Wayne, Mike, Stan and Dave have their regular weekly meeting, continuing to discuss the Planning Document in preparation for this evening's e-meeting<br>➡ Dave uses documents received from his team members to feed into the Planning Document and to help him plan the Y2K action<br>➡ In the evening Dave, Mike, Stan and Wayne have an e-meeting with their peers in Palo Alto, using the Planning Document to drive the meeting |

# Welcome to the World of WWIT

*Monday, 16.00 — E-Meeting*

The time is late afternoon UK time and the beginning of the working day in California. Mike, DaveW and Stan are struggling to set up MS NetMeeting for an electronic meeting with their colleagues in California. The purpose of the meeting is for the UK group to leverage the experience of the Californian group. The Californian group has already implemented a system to act as a computer-support "knowledge base" that can be used by technicians and end users. The members of the UK team want to develop something along similar lines but do not want to "reinvent the wheel" and prefer to build on the experience of their colleagues, if possible. They have identified an opportunity for collaboration and have arranged this meeting with a colleague, Don. Don is the manager of the Applications Team in the US and is Stan's opposite number. Also to be present at the meeting is the person responsible for the administration of the knowledge base, Linda. This meeting is a result of Mike having explored the American knowledge base. He has also spoken on the phone with a colleague in the American group, and he has discussed the knowledge base informally with Stan. This formally arranged meeting is only one of the means by which they communicate — there are also numerous informal conversations taking place over the Atlantic via phone and e-mail in the normal course of events.

Debating the possible causes of the problem between each other they still fail to see the image of the lap top screen on the big white screen in the office. They are having a problem getting the system to work satisfactorily. They debate the possible causes of the problem between each other but still fail to see the image of the lap top screen on the big white screen in the office. They use the polycom (phone unit with keyboard, speaker and three microphones — Figure 4) to dial Don in America. He is due to be present at this electronic

*Figure 4: Polycom*

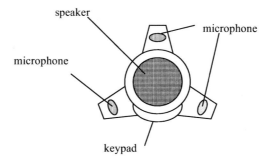

meeting, but they can only reach his voice mail. Mike leaves a voice mail saying, "We're here, waiting for the meeting."

As Mike and Stan discuss the possibility of the drivers being the cause of the problem DaveW goes to bring his personal computer (PC) to use instead of the laptop. He returns and sets up his PC and manages to get the screen image on the big screen. Mike relates the tale of a colleague who bolted a handle to his PC and used it as a "portable." DaveW tries ringing the American group again, but still fails to get a response. The group tends to try to use the electronic media to save video and travelling costs. NetMeeting is a free application, and the small cameras (although not yet widely used) are very cheap. Connection costs are also much lower than those of the full video-conferencing suite that is also available. The advantage of NetMeeting is that applications can be shared across the network, making, for example, documents visible to all parties. It is not an intuitive piece of software, but Mike observes that they have seen an improvement in the use of NetMeeting over the three months they have been using it as they have grown accustomed to it. It has also had the advantage of making meeting records visible as they are recorded.

The connection is finally made and the meeting gets underway. On the screen is an image from the PC in America — a demonstration of the Knowledge Base, the camera image of the two people attending the meeting in America, and a camera image of the people attending the meeting in the UK.

*Figure 5: White Screen View*

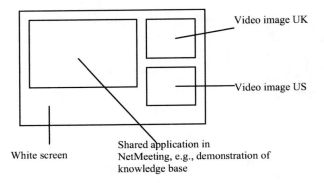

Linda and Don put the Knowledge Base interface up on the screen and remotely demonstrate it to the UK people. After a while, the UK people ask questions and start to make suggestions as to how the system could be improved or adapted for company-wide use. DaveW suggests the use of a geographic location field. This raises a host of other issues and problems. The group discusses the issues and bounce ideas off each other, eventually working up a possible solution. Don recaps the proposed solution and makes notes of it in the "chat" section of NetMeeting. This will form the minutes of the meeting. He checks that the UK people can see the chat board and then he types it in. Mike says, "No, that's not right" and corrects him. Don still doesn't fully understand, so Mike goes over the proposed solution again until the note is entered in the chat section to everyone's satisfaction.

The Knowledge Base is brought back on to the screen and the discussion moves into technical issues and finds another problem. Further discussion reveals a possible solution at the American end. This is something that Stan needs to look into and they agree that the American end will help him with this. They return to the Knowledge Base demonstration on the screen and agree that it would be preferable for the UK members to build on it rather than develop a totally fresh one. The discussion now moves into the practicalities of doing so, with issues of speed and replication causing concern. They identify the issues and some possible solutions and note them on the chat board for further investigation. Don flags up an issue regarding further development of the Knowledge Base with links and cross-indexing to other web pages, for which he would like advice. The Knowledge Base disappears from the screen and a web page appears. Stan offers a solution. It is accepted that the solution would work, but there is one area within Stan's solution for which they would need further information. They do not have the answer but know a local expert at their site in California. They make a note of this on the chat board.

Suddenly the sound disappears — Mike has pressed the wrong button. Laughing, he types his apologies onto the chat board and re-establishes the sound connection. After a short period of joking and laughter with the American pair, the discussion returns to the next steps to be taken. The discussion returns to the earlier problem of identifying location with another possible solution being suggested. This is noted as an action item. Don asks if they can go back to the Knowledge Base one more time as he wants to demonstrate another aspect. Don is demonstrating, but he is unsure of exactly what he is doing and is guided by Linda who is sitting next to him. Part way through, the demonstration makes Mike think of something else, and he asks Don to move onto the department home page in the US and then to the UK's departmental home page. He points out the inconsistencies and suggests they standardise the two. This is also noted as an action item. They decide that Linda (in California) will work with DaveW (in the UK) on this issue. They decide that there will be another e-meeting in three weeks, but that informal phone and e-mail communication will continue in the meantime as necessary. They end the meeting, and the three UK members discuss the meeting among themselves as they put away the equipment, and declare themselves happy with the outcome.

*Tuesday Afternoon — Vertical Team Meeting and WWITMan UK*

The following afternoon Stan has a meeting with his Informatics Team, comprised of himself, DaveW (the Webmaster who was also present at last night's meeting), Gary (the applications developer), and Steve (the Notes developer). Stan explains the purpose of the meeting as being to discuss how the three vertical teams can better learn from each other and what they need and expect from each other. Gary points out that an alternative model would be to have one large team rather than three separate ones. In this model there would be individual specialists or wizards and people would have better opportunity to learn from one another as they would not be operating so much in separate environments. At the very least, Gary emphasises the need for cross-team collaboration.

Stan hands each member of the team Draft 1.0 of WWITMan's planning document. This had already been worked on by the UK management team at an off-site meeting five days earlier, and Stan wants to use it to communicate with his team and to get its input. In the first place, he wants to use this draft document to discuss some project priorities. Scanning through the document, wry comments are made about the number of new projects and the number of times Informatics people are mentioned. They continue to discuss the document, leading into a discussion of who they would need for some projects. Talking about the skills of a particular individual in UKIT leads to a general discussion of PC support and the type of detailed domain knowledge that is now necessary. The conversation moves round to work with the Infrastructure Team and cross-team collaboration on backups, and on who to consult for specific problems — they need to know which expert to consult. Gary notes that there is a desperate need for an overall understanding and level of knowledge that crosses the teams, so Stan suggests that Informatics offer a series of seminars on the projects and applications that they deliver. Gary suggests that there should also be an accompanying web page. The discussion of the document continues. The discussion brings up various issues that are followed through and talked about. The team gets so involved that it fails to notice the time and are only made aware of it when other people arrive to use the meeting room for another meeting.

Stan has half an hour before another meeting so he returns to his cubicle and updates his PalmTop computer from his PC so that all his MS Exchange files are synchronised. His next job is to work on the planning document. He has got lists of objectives from the other members of the UK management team and he wants to merge them all to a common form to feed into the planning document. He scans the documents and spends 20 minutes doing the Optical Character Recognition (OCR) corrections. Dave arrives and informs Stan that Wayne and Mike have not arrived yet for the next meeting. Dave and Stan discuss briefly what Stan is doing with Dave's objectives list, what Dave agrees with and what he would prefer handled differently. Their conversation then moves onto the forthcoming e-meeting with their American peers and how the planning document will help them. Dave suggests using the same headings as in a similar document produced by the American group. They compare the two documents and use them to see how they can adapt theirs so that there is some consistency. After this informal interruption, Dave and Stan go to the meeting with Wayne and Mike. The planning document is driving this meeting, and Stan hands out the updated version on which he has been working. Wayne wants to discuss the latest version that Stan has prepared and move from that to how they can present it to their American colleagues in the e-meeting. They take the document as the starting point and discuss how to prioritise. From there the discussion moves to what the drivers are for the projects, and then to whether the emphasis should be on development or consolidation, and from there to the Year 2000 problem that is a major element of the planning document. The planning document again becomes the focus of the discussion and this cycle continues — issues arise and are discussed, problems get flagged up from the discussions about the document. They talk about the problems and arrive at solutions or plans of action, always bringing their attention back to the document, the focal point of the meeting. Mike gets paged — he is due at an e-meeting with the overall manager of WWITMan (Dan). He leaves and Dave, Wayne, and Stan remain chatting informally for a few minutes and then adjourn, intending to continue the meeting the following morning. Stan returns to his cubicle and makes a phone call. As he finishes his phone call one of his team arrives to inform Stan of a problem — he cannot get onto the Exchange server. Stan makes a phone call to a colleague in California and leaves a voice- mail message. He also sends an e-mail message. These are both in connection with another project that Stan is working on with American and UK colleagues. They are developing a bibliographic reference database, and in advance of a meeting scheduled for tomorrow the UK people should have been able to access the directory on the American server, but they are not able to do so.

They can see the directory, but the system is denying them access. Stan has been trying to get the problem sorted out, but has not yet managed to do so. With only 15 minutes to go before leaving for home, Stan synchronises his laptop with his PC. Another team member arrives to ask if there is a problem with the Exchange server. Stan says there is and packs up to go home where he spends more time melding the remaining objectives documents into the single planning document.

*Wednesday Morning — More WWITMan UK*

The day starts with a continuation of yesterday's meeting. Wayne summarises what was said in order that they do not go over it again, finishing up with the final point that was discussed yesterday — resourcing. This had actually been pencilled in for today's meeting, but discussion of the document had already flagged it up yesterday, so the subject has already been broached. There is some debate about what Mike had said, with Dave interpreting it slightly different from the others. They continue to talk around the resourcing issue, making a number of suggestions, with Mike referring to what happened when a similar problem arose a couple of years ago. The resource discussion leads in to a discussion about learning from each other, which at the moment is a matter of asking a "guru" when there is a problem. There is some recognition that Mike's team could do with more training on certain aspects, but it comes back to a resource problem. Mike offers his preferred solution but acknowledges the problems that it would cause. Another solution is offered but is a non-starter because of finance problems. The discussion follows other suggestions but keeps coming back to the non-starter. Mike gets paged so they take a break. Stan goes and gets a cup of tea and Dave and Wayne continue the discussion informally, moving on to a chat about an international football match. They resume the meeting, continuing the resourcing topic for quite some time, revisiting previously suggested solutions, and encountering new issues, in particular the idea that they should be putting different people together to learn from each other and generally raising skill sets. They finally decide to move the resourcing issue on to the planning document in order to treat it as a longer term issue and take a much needed break. Stan and Dave leave the room so Mike takes the opportunity to discuss with Wayne a letter that he has received highlighting a problem. An informal chat enables Mike to suggest a solution. Wayne agrees, and the problem is solved.

After the break, the planning document is again brought to the fore. Stan explains that he has done some more melding and got the raw data in, but he explains the structure that he is aiming for, which will make it easier to use in the meeting with the American group. They continue the discussion about priorities and the Year 2000 problem and then work their way down the document looking for immovables and imposed deadlines, making notes on their individual copies of the document. As they work their way through the document, it fires up discussion about different issues, technical problems, and issues of timing. The purpose of the document at this stage is to be able to use it in the forthcoming e-meeting with the American colleagues so that they can show what they have done in trying to identify areas for collaboration. At the end of the morning they break for lunch. Stan will continue to work on the document, taking into account what has been discussed in the meeting and will change the structure of the document.

*Wednesday Afternoon — Some Cross-Team Collaboration*

After lunch, Wayne has a meeting with Dave and three members of one of the research groups. They have been working on an area of 3-D audio and VEs. One of the CoP members in the US has seen something of the research and would like to incorporate it as a product. The meeting itself, however, is a direct result of Wayne bumping into one of the researchers in a corridor and having a chat. The presenters describe the product that is a visual space with avatars[9] and 3-D sound. After the presentation and some discussion, Wayne collects Stan and goes with Dave and the researchers for a demonstration. After the demonstration, Wayne and Stan meet with Bea about the internal web design project, which is being run with colleagues from America so is working as a distributed team. Wayne is concerned that there are too many people involved to be able to make good progress. There is an e-meeting scheduled with the people in the States for the following Monday, and Wayne would like the strategy worked out in advance. Stan has e-mailed Lucy (the team leader in America) to inform her that he, Wayne, and Bea would be meeting today. Bea expresses concern that she was not aware of this, and Stan apologises that she may not have been copied in on all the e-mails. Lucy had expressed a desire for all the people listed to be at the e-meeting. The concern for Wayne, Stan, and Bea is that there are too many people for one meeting and that no progress will be made. Their preference is to break it up. Bea expresses annoyance that Lucy had found out that they were wanting a smaller meeting *before* today's discussion. They continue to talk around the problem of numbers, but are basically in agreement that they feel the proposed e-meeting is too large and will not achieve anything. Discussion turns to the format of the proposed internal web pages. The aim is to have multiple web pages that have a consistent look and feel. They discuss the style and the technology. The basic format of the home page has been designed, and they still feel that adding more people to the group will slow the project down. The talk moves to what it is they will be trying to produce, and Wayne expresses a concern about the design. He feels that Lucy, as an information scientist, will not produce a suitable design, as evidenced by the fact that when he visits the home page at the American site he cannot find the USIT page. Stan suggests that a preferable meeting format would be to have a maximum of five people for the design and *then* bring in other, technical people. The time is up and Bea has to leave so the meeting finishes. Wayne returns to his cubicle and checks his e-mail. E-mail is one of the four main media he uses — e-mail, telephone/voicemail, video conferencing and NetMeeting. He also has formal meetings with his team and with other people, but most of the communication with people on site is ad hoc and informal. For distant communication, his preferred medium is the telephone but this brings problems of time distance — it is most likely that his communication partner will not be there, and he will have to use the voice mail. He likes e-mail when he has the time to put together an accurate message, but he doesn't really bother with video conferencing as it takes a lot of setting up and doesn't add much extra over the phone. He would prefer to use NetMeeting in conjunction with the telephone — he feels it adds an extra level of communication. The phone rings and Wayne answers. It is a personal call. Having completed the call he checks his voice mail and finds three messages. One is from the person who has just called. He dials the number of the second person, who answers the phone with "Hi, Wayne" as the phones have caller display. There is a financial problem left from the last time the American colleagues visited. Wayne says his department will absorb the cost and solves the problem. Wayne makes his second call, which is to an external consultant and concerns some problems the company is having with building contractors. They discuss the problems, and the consultant agrees to keep pressure on the contractors. After the problems have been discussed, there is some informal chat during which the consultant gives Wayne a piece of useful information — off the record — regarding another consultant who has moved to another company. Wayne now has to arrange a meeting with two other people. One of them is not available, so he chooses one of two suggested options and pencils it in for them, voice mails them both, and suggests that they only respond if there is a problem. He has one final task to do before he leaves. He has to call the overall head of WWIT, Dan, in the States to discuss the forthcoming e-meeting. He has had to wait until now to make the call as it is now 08.30 in America. Unfortunately, Dan is in meetings all day, and Wayne only gets to speak with the secretary. As

Wayne cannot get to speak with Dan, he leaves the secretary with a list of agenda items, and she agrees to e-mail the list to all the participants. Wayne rings off and goes through his e-mails deciding which he can delete from the system. Mike arrives with a quick question that Wayne can answer. They then chat a little and Wayne passes on the information he received from the external consultant. This raises a problem with training, and they discuss this a little. Mike leaves. Wayne finishes managing his e-mails. He sees one that has just arrived that he feels he ought to forward to Stan. One of the members of Stan's Informatics Team, Gary, has been working on a resource booking system with which they are highly delighted. The aim is to be able to use it between the UK and America, for example, if Wayne was going to California, he could book the room and resources he needed there from his desk in the UK. The new e-mail has come from someone in another part of the company indicating that a corporate solution for room-booking systems has been selected! The time is now 17.40 and Wayne leaves for home.

*Thursday Morning — More Meetings*

08.45. Wayne arrives for the regular weekly meeting scheduled for nine o'clock. Mike also arrives at 08.45, and the two have a spontaneous informal chat about something that they feel should not be discussed in open forum. A couple of minutes later Stan arrives and they move the discussion on to the technical details of a hotline database. Mike is paged and leaves to go and solve a problem. Dave has not yet arrived so Wayne rings his desk and leaves a message on the voice mail. Wayne tells Stan about an interesting technical paper he read the previous evening, and then they chat about the VE meeting they had yesterday with the research project group. There has been a lot of interest and there is scope for testing it between America and the UK within WWIT. Mike sends a message that he has been held up with solving the problem but will return as soon as he can. Wayne and Stan chat about the planning document. Stan carried on working at home last night and has the document as up-to-date as possible for this evening's e-meeting, and he has managed to keep it fairly consistent with a previous American document. Wayne is pleased with the result and feels that it is starting to take shape, making a suggestion about the addition of a further column so it could be used as a communication tool. Stan has also added an extra section that meets with Wayne's approval. He feels that it is already better than what they did the previous year. While discussing what Stan has done, the issue of NT and UNIX print drivers arises and the discussion moves onto a technical footing. At a quarter past nine, Dave arrives — as there have been so many meetings this week, he had not realised which day it was. Stan and Wayne chat informally about the web page project meeting they had yesterday and the tension between some of the participants. After the meeting, Stan called the American team leader just to keep her informed. He preferred to call because he felt he could better smooth the situation when she could hear his voice, plus there were things he did not want recorded on paper.

At 20 past nine, the meeting finally gets under way. Wayne recaps on the document and what came out of it. Before they get too far into discussing the document, Stan raises a problem — Steve in his team will be away on holiday, so they might have problems with the Lotus Notes system. How can they support it while Steve is away? They come to the conclusion that between them, although they will not be doing any development, they will be able to work out how to support it, and if they are stuck they can call on their American colleagues for advice. As a matter of course, Steve generally keeps the American people informed. Therefore, the UK people can keep an eye on the system, and the American people can keep a distant eye on it as well. However, they will get Steve to brief them in more detail about the system before he goes on holiday.

The discussion moves on to the planning document. Wayne now feels that it will make a good communication tool, but will not *yet* be adequate as an internal project tool. Mike points out that the document has now lost detail of priority and who will do what. Stan replies that it has not been lost — there are sections for that, but he has just not had time to populate that area of the document. Dave asks what the significance of the asterisks is. Stan replies that they are simply mistakes in the OCR reading and he still has to correct them. They take on the most pressing issue from the document, that is, the Year 2000 (Y2K) problem preparations. They had started discussing this yesterday and now carry on discussing the preparations in detail, moving onto strategy. Dave outlines the plans he has made for tackling the problem. One of his ideas is to create a dummy infrastructure for testing. They could also collaborate with their American colleagues on this. The discussion moves onto planning and timing. Referring to the planning document, Wayne suggests a solution as to how they might tackle the planning and timing issues. They continue their discussion, bringing it back to the document, and trying a different approach with the document. They finally decide to keep the Year 2000 problem as the single immovable issue and plan everything else around it. They move on to comparing their planning document with the earlier document from America. The meeting ends, and Stan goes to adjust again the structure of the document, which will be used in the evening's e-meeting, but they will emphasise that it is in a first draft stage.

Dave returns to his cubicle. He wants to do some further work on the documents he initially passed over to Stan for inclusion in the planning document (a) because some parts have not translated very well, and (b) because there is more work to do on planning the tackling of Y2K. He e-mails his opposite number, in the States, Ray, to see if they need to discuss anything in advance of the e-meeting. Normally he would have done this earlier, but he is aware that Ray has been away for a while. Dave has worked with Ray on several joint projects, and they have been encouraging members of their vertical teams to work together on projects and problem solutions. He checks his e-mail and deletes "the rubbish." This is habit, and he does it periodically during the day. He reads the ones of interest. One is a request for help from someone on Mike's team. The message has come to Dave because the person who would normally handle it is away. Dave deals with the request by going to find who would be the most suitable person on his team to take care of it. He leaves the problem with that person and replies to the e-mail to say what he has done and who will be sorting the problem out. He is expecting Stan to e-mail him the most up-to-date version of the planning document, but it hasn't arrived yet. While waiting for the document to arrive, he fills his time by preparing for a meeting for tomorrow, when he will be meeting people from another IT department within the organisation. They meet periodically to keep up-to-date with what each other is doing. He then continues with some work on the planned schedule for checking the millennium compliance of the various servers. He prints the document. While getting the print, he happens to see Stan and asks why he hasn't mailed him the planning document. Stan has sent it; it just hasn't arrived. Further discussion reveals that there are other documents from Stan that were sent but which Dave has not received. Dave has previously suspected this, but this is the first time he has had confirmation. There is clearly a problem. Dave sends a test e-mail to Stan who will send a reply. While waiting for the e-mail, Dave takes the print-out he had just collected across to one of his team and asks for comments. He leaves the print-out with his colleague and returns, just as Stan arrives. Stan thinks he has figured out the problem — they need to put a "forward" in Dave's Exchange configuration (or change Stan's address book entry). The problem is solved. Dave has received the updated planning document, and he can get on with it. He wants to add more detail to it. He also has input from his team members that he wants to include — some of this is on paper, and some is in e-mail format. When he did his original document on which his section of the planning document was based, he hadn't got all the input in from his team. Now he can finish it. Before he starts, he does what he calls a "sanity check," that is, he checks through the planning document to see that his input has all translated satisfactorily to the current version. He feels that there is currently too much that is UK-specific for using the document as a communication tool with the US. Stan has added the extra column that Dave wanted so he starts entering the Y2K items. In entering them he finds that some of the text has scanned incorrectly in the OCR program, meaning that some of the acronyms are absolutely meaningless. He corrects them. He breaks for lunch and then continues to work on adding detail to the planning document and seeing if he can reword some of it to make it less team-specific.

*Thursday Evening — The E-Meeting*

16.00.   The e-meeting is due to start.  Wayne is still setting up the equipment and chatting with the three people (Dan, Linda, and Jim) in California as he does so. Five minutes later Stan arrives and says "Hi" to everyone. He chats informally with the three in California as Wayne continues to set up NetMeeting. He gets the signal projected on to the large electronic white screen, but then the signal starts to break up. Stan helps set up NetMeeting. Dan asks if they are going to see us today. They won't, but the camera has been ordered. Mike arrives and sets up the smartboard. Dave arrives. Stan asks the people in Palo Alto if they have got the chatboard up. Mike helps set up the connections and checks with Palo Alto confirming that they can see what

*Figure 6: Room Layout for E-Meeting*

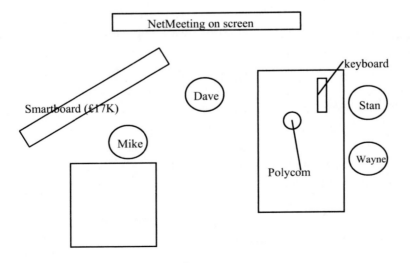

is on the smartboard.  The equipment is almost ready, Stan is working on NetMeeting, and Mike is using a remote keyboard for use with the smartboard.

There is still one small problem.  Mike says to Palo Alto, "On your smartboard, you need to switch the button to send the video to me rather than your portable." Now the smartboard displays a picture of them. It is a small picture, not bad, but not wonderful.  The UK staff see three people in the American meeting room. They wave, but express disappointment that they cannot see the attendees in the UK. Wayne repeats that Mike has ordered a camera.  Dan in Palo Alto asks who is present on the UK side, and Wayne runs through the names of those present.  The first action is to pick up from the last meeting where they had a list of actions.  As there has not been enough time to complete most of the actions, they decide to leave them and move straight on to the planning document.  There is a slight delay while they change the documents over in NetMeeting.  The people in Palo Alto take the opportunity to get a quick drink. Wayne gives a bit of background, but Dan interrupts almost immediately as he can see the scope for joint projects.  Dave starts going through the document highlighting the parts that are particularly interesting to him. Dan interrupts and asks him to put the cursor on the point he is addressing. As he goes through the items, they realise there is a problem with encryption and US export regulations.  Attention is turned to discussion of the problem, with the result that Palo Alto can solve the problem.  They continue working through the document and come to the virus section.  This triggers a debate.  They discuss the virus protection and decide to collaborate and work towards a common solution.  Mike handwrites this as an action item on the smartboard. They move on to the next item, which is messaging.  This is something where they are giving out different messages, but they recognise it as an area where they would really benefit from working together.  Mike writes this as an action item on the smartboard.  They move to the next item but something Dan says moves Palo Alto off on a tangent, and they move the discussion to the policy regarding Linux support.  Dave explains the policy of the UK group.  Dan suggests another issue where a tool has been launched by the organisation that might be able to help them.  The UK people had not heard of this so he suggests that they go and look at some presentation slides that are on the intranet.  He feels it might be an area where they could usefully collaborate.  Mike notes it as an action item.  Wayne is aware of the pressure of time and pushes the discussion on.  They move back to the planning document and Mike starts going through his section.  He reaches a section regarding a proprietary printer technology. This triggers questions from Palo Alto.  Stan has already sent a document to Dan.  He has not received it yet.  He says that he will forward it to his colleagues and they will provide feedback on it. The people in Palo Alto complain that Mike is hard to hear. He moves nearer to the polycom. He goes through the rest of his section and then Wayne starts with the audit section. As they work through, they find other areas where they can collaborate on joint action. When Wayne has finished his section Stan takes over. He reaches a technical section on 16-bit obsolescence. This sparks a discussion that leads to Palo Alto deciding to leverage from the UK team and doing joint work. Mike again notes the action items. The UK team seems to be six months ahead, and they have the opportunity to work together to provide a WWIT strategy. The next item also sparks a debate, with several people trying to get in to say something. The Palo Alto people have several concerns, but Mike points out that they are mistaken in their understanding of how the technology under discussion actually works. Stan moves down through his section of the document to multimedia publishing tools and raises a point that has been causing a problem. Through discussion of the topic they find that they have already found a solution for the problem in Palo Alto. The discussion moves into calendaring, but Dan totally misunderstands. The UK group manages, with some difficulty, to clarify the concepts. Suddenly, the UK group erupts into laughter — on the screen they have seen someone come into the room behind the Palo Alto people and walk off with a chair. One more issue is flagged up which is causing a problem for Stan's team. Dan suggests that they have a local expert who could perhaps help. They reach the end of the list, and Dan asks if they can have a copy of the planning document so they can track the revisions. Mike tries to send it through NetMeeting — he explains the settings that Palo Alto has to change, and he transfers it into one of their directories. Dan in Palo Alto says he would prefer the document to be e-mailed to everyone. They also decide to copy Chakaka (the Japanese member of the CoP) in on the e-mail. There is a problem with the printer in the American room — it has suddenly stopped. Mike had tried to send the action list that he had written on the smartboard to their printer and had forgot that the settings were for A4 paper on the smartboard and letter size on the American printer. They cancel the print job and arrange the next meeting for three weeks later, to start at 15.00 UK time and 07.00 Pacific time. In the meantime, Dan would like to examine the document more closely in order to see if the UK and American planning documents can be integrated into one document. He and Wayne agree to get together electronically before the main meeting to discuss this further. Palo Alto signs off, and Wayne, Mike, Stan, and Dave decide to book the room for an earlier time and set the equipment up in advance of the next meeting. They lost twenty minutes of the meeting today to set-up time, which represents a high proportion when they only have a two-hour window (from 16.00 to 18.00) in which they can expect to be in contact with their American peers.

# WHAT ISSUES DID WE FIND IN STAGE ONE?

The case study was intended to provide some understanding of the work of a physically distributed CoP, and how its members make it work. This aspect was demonstrated very clearly in the vignettes — they were all about making the CoP work. A major point to emerge from the vignettes was the use of documents to make the CoP work. Other vignettes showed technology and how it was used to sustain the working of the CoP, and others indicated what individuals know about other communities and other members that helps put the right people in contact for participation.

A number of themes and issues came to light that provided a comprehensive insight into the workings of the CoP and the interactions between the members.

## The CoP

As a distributed CoP, it has an interesting structure. That is, it is not *totally* distributed — it has co-located cores and has an individual on the periphery. It would appear that the co-located core of a distributed CoP is essential, for a lot of work was undertaken in the co-located core to ensure the smooth operation of the CoP across the distributed environment.

The practice of the community *is* their normal work. However, the group was not formally created, it came about through evolution.

In the first place, it is interesting to explore the CoP characteristics (as outlined in Chapter III) that were exhibited by WWITMan.

*Marginals/Brokers — Knowing the Practices of Other Communities*

Star and Griesemer (1989) referred to "marginals" as community members who are members of different communities. Wenger (1998) used the term "brokers" to describe these people. He saw their role as helping the flow of information between communities. Brokers will have a knowledge of the customs, language, and relationships in the different communities and are therefore in a position to assist with mutual comprehension. This could be important for the management of the softer aspects of knowledge; for example, in the cases of boundary objects, a marginal who is a member of more than one community can help when the artefact is being used in the context of another community.

In WWITMan the members were all members of a range of different groups. In addition to being members of WWITMan, their own vertical teams, and WWIT, they were involved in different project groups, some of which may well be CoPs themselves. There were also some CoPs, informal groups that had arisen because of common interests to which the WWITMan members belonged. Stan, in particular, was a member of several different groups; for example the "Internal Home Page Group" and a library project group. In some of these cases, the members learned things in one group that they could use for the benefit of another group. For example, during a visit to Palo Alto, Stan had met informally with a colleague in one of his project groups and found that his colleague was involved in a different group that was developing an application that Stan felt would benefit another of his groups.

Another example of brokering in the case study was to be seen in the way the planning document was used. In creating the document, the UK core used its knowledge of the relationships between how one community uses something and how another does to create the document in a format that would be most suitable for use by the two cores.

### Gurus/Wizards

Gurus and wizards in a group are those members who are regarded as "experts" in a particular domain of the practice. They will have a high degree of technical knowledge but will also have developed softer aspects of their domain knowledge, for example, a "feel" for how things work, an intuition when troubleshooting. Other members may learn from working alongside the guru; however, part of the softer aspects of a CoP member's knowledge is simply knowing who knows what and who can be approached for help with different things. When a guru leaves the organisation, it might be possible to replace him/her with a new, technically competent staff member, but the softer aspects of the new member's knowledge will be different.

Gurus/wizards were very much in evidence in the case study; however, it was not so much an exclusive CoP characteristic but more a result of the role of the group. Although the group is a CoP, it does fulfill an official role, and the WWITMan members are specialists in their field. Moving into the wider UKIT group, there were several individuals who had developed a high degree of expertise in a specific area and who were then consulted by other members of the group; for example, Steve was the Lotus Notes expert. This situation was also evident in the USIT part of WWIT. Although WWIT as a whole was not considered to be a CoP, there was an increasing amount of collaboration being undertaken and wizards in one part would assist people in the other part; for example, during one of the e-meetings a problem was encountered, and the Palo Alto people immediately suggested that they had a local expert who could solve it.

An interesting issue that was demonstrated was how the CoP would survive when a guru was missing, and how the CoP dealt with the loss of knowledge on a day-to-day basis. Steve, the Lotus Notes expert, was going on holiday, and UKIT were concerned as to how it might manage while he was not available. The conclusion reached by the UKIT staff was to (a) be briefed by Steve who would provide as much of the harder aspects as possible, so they could maintain the system to a certain degree, and (b) to liaise with USIT as it had more expertise available there. The people in USIT would assist the UKIT people as necessary, where the harder aspects of the knowledge were not sufficient. This was also demonstrated when the UKIT managers were concerned that they might be losing a particularly capable member of UKIT, Stewart. They took a number of steps to ensure that they kept him, but they also identified another member of staff who they wanted to work closely with Stewart. Thus they provided the staff member with access to Stewart so that softer aspects of his knowledge would be shared during general work.

*Problem Solving*

In a CoP if a problem arises, a key weapon in the CoPs armory is to be found among the softer aspects of the members' knowledge, that is, knowing who has the knowledge to help and being able to obtain the participation of the people with the knowledge.

Within the wider UKIT group and WWIT as a whole, there was clearly a lot of problem solving as the group is an IT-support operation. However, there were also a lot of problems to be solved in addition to these. In some cases, during discussion of the planning document, problems arose or were foreseen. The CoP was either able to solve the problem immediately through the discussion, identify an individual with the relevant experience to solve the problem, or could organise some people to tackle the problem; for example, in the main e-meeting, Stan raised a problem with multi-media publishing tools and found that the US core had encountered a similar problem and solved it. They now had the expertise that was willingly made available to Stan.

Problems were solved within the CoP — both within the two cores and by one asking for help from the other core. If an individual had a problem to solve, (s)he had a good idea of who to ask. The members of the CoP learned from each other through the problem solving. Problem solving within the cores tended to be a result of ad hoc chat, that is, opportunistic communication or informal communication, where if an individual had a problem, (s)he would call a colleague to ask for advice. There were occasional examples of problem solving via e-mail, but in fact one of the main problems (accessing a supposedly shared directory) was not finally solved until the participants were in the e-meeting and could demonstrate the problem in real time. This also showed the importance of speed of response in the interchange for some problems. Stan had tried to solve the problem of the shared directory access for several days, over e-mail and voice mail interchange. However, it was not until they were in an e-meeting, and he could say, "Here, let me *show* you...," and actually demonstrate the problem on the screen, that the problem was finally solved.

A shared background and a shared language are part of a CoP and this was useful in solving problems, as people could discuss the problem and work up a solution.

### Language

Part of the definition of a CoP is the language shared by its members. The language is an essential part of Common Ground, where some of the softer aspects of a CoP's knowledge are to be found. This was evident in the language of WWITMan, as the members used the technical domain language and acronyms of the wider community of IT professionals (for example, UNIX, NT). In addition there was localised language that would have no meaning to an outsider, (such as organisation-specific acronyms, like "PRs" for Personal Reviews, and group-specific terms such as the names of the servers.

The technical domain language could be seen as being "hard." The softer aspects, then, would be found in the ways the CoP members speak which underlines their attitudes and impressions. For example, when one says, "Is it one of *those* meetings?," this would only be understandable to another established CoP member. A CoP member might therefore be identified as a member of the CoP by the way (s)he speaks.

### Legitimate Peripheral Participation

The participation component was very much in evidence in the importance of the social issues. As Wenger (1998) had identified participation as being the key LPP component to be part of the reification/participation duality, this will be discussed separately along with the importance of the shared artefact, which represents the reification part of the duality. However, as well as being the key to participation, the social issues were also key to legitimation. The legitimation aspect was affected to some degree by the fact that there is a formal aspect to the group with a manager both in UKIT and USIT, and an overall WWITMan manager. However, the members of the CoP did not feel that a CoP is formally created. The members of WWITMan are automatically assumed to have a high degree of relevant knowledge by virtue of the positions they hold, but there was also something more than this. The members of the USIT management team had developed very strong working relationships, and this was key to the legitimation within the group. In a formal group such as a team, virtual team, or project group, the legitimation of the members comes from the formal structure of the group. In a CoP, the legitimation comes from the social relationships that develop. As people get to know each other, they have confidence in the information and knowledge they receive from their partners. This shows the social issues of a CoP to be of major importance, and therefore does not preclude a formally constituted group or team from *developing* or *evolving* into a CoP as the members develop relationships, get to know each other well, and go beyond the formal relationships. The members of the CoP felt that key to making the CoP work, particularly when faced with the difficulties caused by distributed working, was the fact that they had developed strong relationships to the point where they would "go the extra mile" for each other. This shows that the essential factor that differentiates a CoP from a team is the "human aspect," that is, the social relationships that are formed in a CoP.

In the case study, there was evidence of a physical peripherality, as there were two co-located cores with a member situated elsewhere in Japan. This member was accepted as a member of the group but did not feature so much in the meetings because of the time difference. She was kept informed of plans and progress, but she was not able to play as full a part as other members. If she wanted to take part in an electronic conference, she had to participate in the middle of the night. She was regarded as being a full member of the group, and the other members had every confidence in her ability, but the physical and temporal distance meant she was, in some ways, a peripheral member. The physical periphery also restricted her real-time access to other members of the CoP, thus reducing opportunities for learning from them.

*Learning*

Although learning is a key aspect of CoPs, the learning that took place in WWITMan was not a formally stated goal. There were many examples of learning, but where it occurred, it tended to be a by-product. It occurred both within the CoP (WWITMan) and within the wider WWIT group.

Learning could be seen where members of the CoP were keen to leverage from each other. In this case, the knowledge existed in one person who could then help the other who would learn from the exchange. However, the prime aim here was not learning but the avoidance of re-inventing the wheel, which in itself is an important part of KM. This worked as well as it did partly because of the sharing culture of the organisation, and also because of the relationships that had developed between the members. Leverage occurred often through collaboration, which was an important part of the work of WWIT. During the e-meeting that was focused on the planning document, a primary aim was to identify areas where the UKIT and USIT could collaborate and leverage from each other. This was quite common and was regarded as standard practice within the CoP, and was being extended to the wider WWIT group. There was one example where this had not worked, but this was outside of the CoP and the wider WWIT group. Stan's Informatics Team had developed a booking system for audio-visual (AV) resources. This was proving to be a very useful tool in UKIT's armory and was being linked to the room-booking system they had developed. The goal was to be able to book the necessary room and resources anywhere in the organisation. For example, if the UK core was going to visit the US core, Wayne would not have to ask his opposite number to book resources and rooms for him at the US site. From his desk, he would be able to book all the rooms and resources for the visit, in advance. Unfortunately, towards the end to the study Wayne received an e-mail saying that a booking system had been developed in the company, and it was to be adopted as standard throughout the organisation.

Learning also occurred in the collaboration. In this case it was less a case of one person learning from another. Rather, as people worked together on a project they would both learn from the process of what they were doing and gain from experience. The collaboration might be the implementation of some technology where they would gain from the experience or it might be solving a problem, in which case the people would apply their knowledge and experience to the problem and among them would work up a solution. Although the people involved in the collaboration learned and gained further experience, it was not evident that the opportunity was taken to provide feedback to other members of the group. It was more likely that any further sharing of the knowledge would be in a serendipitous manner. Knowing who might have a specific type of experience and who could then be consulted on it would be part of the group's stock of knowledge. In many cases, an important part of the CoP's stock of knowledge was simply knowing who to ask for help. This extended beyond the CoP to the wider WWIT group, as it might be necessary to consult an expert in the other country.

There were two examples in the case study of distributed situated learning using an artefact. In one case, people from Palo Alto demonstrated the Knowledge Base to three people in the UK using NetMeeting. They demonstrated its functionality and took them through how to use it. The other example was in the main e-meeting. The team in Palo Alto was having difficulties setting up the smartboard, and Mike took them through it step-by-step.

It was assumed that people within the group would already have a high degree of technical domain knowledge and therefore some sort of shared background. They would also therefore be able to speak the necessary technical language as a pre-requisite to further learning from each other. This was also necessary for legitimation — they each had to have confidence and trust in each other's abilities. Also as a result of the existing level of domain knowledge, much of what people had to learn would not necessarily be of a technical nature, but would be things of a softer nature — how to get things done, who to approach, how to function as a CoP, how things are done, etc. This social learning, however, was not encountered, that is, where members become enculturated in the ways and language of the CoP. The reason for this was simply a problem of time scale. The case study was under strict time limitations and was not long enough to be able to see such learning.

The learning within the group tends to be informal and ad hoc. This is part of the culture of the organisation and reflects much of the communication within the group. A lot of what the group does is serendipitous. However, the group is aware of the importance of learning and is moving towards more explicit support. This is taking place in the wider group (UKIT and WWIT) as opposed to within WWITMan. For example, the members of WWITMan are now trying to consciously get UKIT people to learn from others — they foresaw a problem occurring in the future and put one person (Charles) together with someone (Stewart) who was fully experienced in the field with the aim that Charles would learn from Stewart. WWITMan were also trying to spread this practice to WWIT as they made it an objective to encourage collaboration between members of their teams and members of the corresponding teams in Palo Alto. This was simply a means of trying to support, facilitate, and enable the sharing of knowledge so that if one key person left there would be somebody who was able, to some degree at least, to take over for him or her. The harder aspects of the knowledge could have been written down in procedures, but the CoP preferred to put people together or encourage people to get together so that the softer aspects of knowledge can also be developed.

Being aware of the need for learning, WWITMan could see that there was scope for more learning within the group. In particular, they felt they were not good at learning from the past. In this respect they were probably being too harsh on themselves, as there were several examples of where they had done exactly this. One example was when members of WWITMan were discussing a resourcing issue. This was causing them some problems until the discussion led them into territory that was a similar situation to one they had faced some years previously. Dave remembered this and remembered how they had tackled the situation then. This insight moved them on faster towards a solution this time round. The problem with this is that it is the softer side of knowledge, remembered through experience and triggered by context, and if there had not been someone there who remembered the previous time, then the knowledge would have been lost, and they would have had to go through the whole problem-solving process again. Another example of learning from the past was the construction of the planning document. The CoP members applied their knowledge to the content of the document and learned from participating in the process. Already by the second iteration of the document they felt they had done a better job than the previous year. It was not the document itself that was important, but the process of creating it. The document was not the end product, but became an ongoing, "living" document. Although it was the process from which the CoP learned, at least there was *something* concrete that came out of it that would serve as a reference— the planning document itself that embodied part of the knowledge of the CoP.

*Formal Attempts to Share Knowledge*

Knowledge was shared in a variety of ways in the case study. The harder aspects of knowledge — those easily articulable — were shared consciously and deliberately, primarily by instructional means. Documents were circulated, seminars were held, information was exchanged in meetings, and information was placed on the intranet. Two systems were also in development that would aid in the sharing of knowledge: UKIT was developing an asset database, and USIT had developed a knowledge base (K-Base) that UKIT was going to use. These two systems are different and have different purposes but end up doing something similar. The K-Base is to be placed on the intranet and provide a facility that both technicians and end-users can consult with problems. The level of knowledge that a person has will determine the extent to which (s)he can use the system. For example, some entries will be understandable to all, whereas other entries will need a high degree of domain knowledge if the information is to be taken and applied. The asset database simply records facts. It records details of items such as PCs, printers, and similar assets. Mike wanted to develop the system to also provide a history of each item, that is, as anybody did some work on an item, such as replacing a hard drive or a motherboard, then (s)he should record it in the asset database, thereby creating a full history of the item. This means that should a different technician have to work on the item at a later date, (s)he could see what had already been done. It could even be the case that there might be an ongoing intermittent fault, and a technician working on the system might see from the history that a particular mix of components was present that could be causing the problem. Therefore, the asset database could provide a focus for the softer side of a technician's knowledge — different technicians might make different inferences from what was available. Although both systems record hard facts and one was called a Knowledge Base, the softer aspects of the users' knowledge were important. This was recognised by the CoP members, as they could see that different people would get different levels of information. The softer aspects of their knowledge would determine what they could get out of the system. It was also recognised that the K-Base system would be crossing boundaries and be used by people from outside the wider IT group; therefore, the developers were using their expertise to ensure that users from outside the community would also be able to benefit.

The softer aspects of knowledge tended to be shared by interaction in collaboration, either in problem solving where solutions were developed or in collaboration on a project. However, rather than *sharing* softer knowledge, it seemed to be more the case that situations arose or were created that needed the joint application of softer knowledge — as in the case of problem solving or collaboration.

## Distribution/Globalisation

As WWITMan is an internationally distributed CoP, it is not surprising that issues of globalisation and distribution came to the fore. There were the usual problems of time, distance, and culture, but there were also some incidents that showed other problems that can arise when operating in such an environment.

The problems of distribution can be very simple (and therefore easily solved); for example, in an e-meeting Mike (in the UK) attempted to send the chat history (that is, the meeting minutes or action list) to the printer in the American room so that the people there could have a copy. The Americans were quite surprised when their printer suddenly started and then suddenly stopped. The problem was that Mike's page setup was A4 size, and he had forgot that the American printer would require letter-size media.

WWITMan often runs phone conferences or e-meetings. These are generally very good, but there are often problems if more than two or three sites are involved. This can be because of issues of turn taking, but more generally (except where cameras are being used) issues of identity — the participants find it hard to determine who is speaking. This is even worse for the Japanese member who is quite at ease with American accents but struggles with the British accents.

Perhaps the greatest problem experienced by WWITMan was part of the time zone problem. The UK core members have only a short time window when they can communicate with their partners in Palo Alto, and there is no time of day at all when Palo Alto, the UK, and Japan are all at work at the same time. Opportunistic communication is an important part of the culture of the organisation, and the CoP members find it difficult catching their communication partners at the desk. Developing relationships needs regular and frequent interaction. This decreases as one party moves out of proximity and would be helped by being able to engage more easily in ad hoc communication with other partners. This could well be helped by a system that allowed awareness of when the partner is available.

Distribution does not only bring problems, of course. WWITMan (and WWIT) feel they have benefited from access to a wider pool of expertise. The UKIT people do not feel that the USIT knows *more* than them, but that they know different things. It is becoming more common that if they have a problem they turn to someone in the parallel core. This was demonstrated in the e-meeting during discussion of the planning document when an issue was raised. USIT had a local expert who could tackle the problem.

## Communication/Collaboration

The Flow Model consolidation of the analysis (see Appendix 1) indicated that collaboration is a major part of the work of WWITMan. It also suggests that most of the collaboration is technical. This is not surprising when one considers the work of the group. The importance of the collaboration is also not unexpected when one realises that it is part of the organisational culture and that WWITMan is consciously trying to extend the spirit of cooperation and collaboration down through its teams, to the extent that members of its vertical teams are encouraged to collaborate on projects with their opposite numbers in Palo Alto. In particular, Dave has written it into the objectives of his individual team members, thus, to some degree, formalising the informal practice.

The collaboration takes different forms. In some cases there are joint projects where people work on something new (and thereby probably create new knowledge). On other occasions the collaboration might be with a view to solving a problem that has occurred, and there are occasions where people get together (or are placed together) with the express aim of one leveraging from the other.

For collaboration to take place, it is clear that communication will play an important role, especially when it must take place over a distance. Both WWITMan and the wider WWIT group are all at home with a wide range of e-media.

*Media*

The members of the group use a range of different media for their communication purposes. They use standard telephone, fax, and e-mail, but are also at ease with voice mail, full video-conferencing, phone conferencing, MS NetMeeting, and e-meetings using a mix of phone conferencing, desktop video conferencing, MS NetMeeting, and a shared smartboard.

All the media have pros and cons, and each member of the CoP had preferred media for different tasks. The telephone was liked because it was immediate and members liked to hear their partner's voice; however, in many cases the phone was inappropriate because the communication partner was not at his or her desk and the caller had to revert to voice mail. E-mail was similar to voice mail in that it overcame the problem of the time zone, but some people felt the response from their partners was not as fast if an e-mail had been sent as opposed to a voice mail. Some people perceived a voice mail to be more urgent. This was perhaps a result of the fact that many people saw e-mail, too, as an oral and therefore informal medium, not observing conventions that would normally be the case with a written medium. Video conferencing was not generally regarded very favorably. It was not felt that full-blown video-conferencing offered enough extra advantage over a phone conversation to warrant the additional expense incurred. Desktop video conferencing, in conjunction with MS NetMeeting, was starting to be used, and although the members felt the technology was not yet immediate enough, they felt that having an image (albeit a relatively poor one) provided an advantage in the form of context. It provides a social context and gives them something to observe. Because the technology was so cheap, its use was felt justifiable. They only used it in group meetings, however, expressing the view that to use it on a one-to-one basis would be using it as a toy and not a tool. Part of the problem of NetMeeting was the fact that it had a high set-up cost; that is, the technology is not intuitive, and it had taken some time for the members to be sufficiently au fait with the setting up and running of the technology for it not to get in the way of the communication. For the main e-meeting in the case study, it had taken almost half an hour to set up the communication technology. When other people use the technology, WWIT runs the meeting for them so that the participants can concentrate on the meeting and do not have to worry about the media.

It was clear that the medium used was selected for the task. In fact, media selection was regarded as being very important when working cross culturally, as a comment by Stan illustrates: "If you've got it on the wrong medium, especially if it's a different culture (that doesn't understand English humor), you can get it wrong."

In some cases the selection was unconscious, that is, the choice was based on what the user was used to or preferred. For example, Dave is used to e-mail. It is ingrained in the culture and as yet he would prefer to e-mail material ahead of the meeting rather than use NetMeeting. However, there were also occasions where the medium was deliberately selected for the task at hand. For example, Stan chose to wait and use the phone to speak with Linda because he needed to discuss a situation where there was scope for conflict; he wanted Linda to be able to hear his voice so that there would be no misunderstandings and conflict could be avoided. Another example was to be seen in the main e-meeting. Mike was going to send the plan directly through NetMeeting, but Dan in Palo Alto wanted it e-mailed so it would be easier to reach more people. The CoP members expressed the view that they would try to select the appropriate medium for the task and if it did not work, would then select another medium. It was interesting to note that the same medium was not selected for the same task each time – it also depended on context. One case study respondent said, "A key point is the rate at which you receive feedback. Deciding how important the feedback is, or if it's sensitive and needs feedback isn't often conscious. It's habit, experience. Context can change it."

There were some interesting aspects that came to light regarding the selection of a medium. Speed of response was felt to be the key, especially in problem solving. The users wanted rapid interaction. This was felt to be much more important than richness, such as in the form of video. The addition of a shared artefact was also generally felt to be more important than the video image. If the meeting's purpose is discussion, they feel it helps if someone has done some preparation, and they have a document around which the discussion can be centred. They also felt that having a document could be a useful catalyst. This was demonstrated very clearly in the observation of meetings, both co-located and distributed.

Three key aspects that would affect the selection of media used would be:

- Low set-up costs, that is, easy to set up and intuitive to use, so that the medium does not interfere with the communication itself.
- Speed of response. This is possibly as important as media-richness. Even if the medium is asynchronous, the possibility of a rapid response is important.
- The capability to share an artefact. This proved to be exceedingly important. Unfortunately the technology available needed a relatively high degree of expertise in order to use it.

### Ad Hoc Communication

Ad hoc or opportunistic communication was shown very strongly in the analysis of the CoP. It is part of the culture of the organisation. There are no offices. Everybody has cubicles with no doors in order to make it easier to "drop in" on a colleague. Coffee and biscuits are freely available around the building, and there is a central café-style area with a range of magazines and newspapers. People are encouraged to chat with their colleagues because informal interaction is felt to be important. Although ad hoc communication is a part of the culture, much of it comes about through proximity. Ad hoc co-located meetings can happen a lot more easily than distributed meetings. In fact, no ad hoc distributed meetings were seen. When meeting in e-media, the CoP members feel that the meeting is much more successful if it is planned. This does not mean, however, that ad hoc electronic communication does not take place; for example, this e-mail from Wayne: "I sent a couple of voice mails yesterday with not a lot in — 'Hi, I've heard about this. Thought you might be interested'."

Ad hoc communication does therefore take place between the cores but not often simple "for your information" communication. It does sometimes happen that technical and collaborative help is obtained from Palo Alto on an opportunistic basis.

However, as a result of proximity and time difference, opportunistic communication primarily takes place within the cores. As it is so important to the group, there is scope to try to improve this situation. Something that could help would be a system that would improve social awareness — having an indication of whether the prospective partner is at his/her desk and available to take calls.

## Culture

Culture was an aspect that was highlighted in Chapter IV as being an issue that affects work in the physically distributed environment. Its importance was confirmed in the analysis. Cultural aspects were felt on three levels — the national level, the organisational level, and the group level.

Culture at a national level impacted the work of the group in several ways. It can influence the medium that is selected for communication. If e-mail is used, the group is very careful about using humor as it has been found that the British humor did not translate well in e-mail. The importance of culture made the group feel it was very important to travel to visit the partner core on its home ground. Being in Palo Alto with the USIT staff helped the UK members understand the local culture better. They felt that as they got to know the Californian culture, they would be better placed to work with other Californians. In addition, they also gained experience of work practices within their partner core and could gain insights to their group culture — "the way things are done here."

The organisational culture influences very strongly the working of the group. The organisation has a strong oral and sharing culture, and staff members are encouraged to chat with their colleagues. Much of the communication is opportunistic, and therefore a lot of what the group does can be serendipitous.

The group culture can show differences between the cores; for example, it was pointed out that the American group, USIT, is much larger and can encourage staff to specialise, so the USIT group has a much larger number of wizards or gurus. UKIT is substantially smaller and its members each have to cover a much wider field. This generally means they do not have the *depth* of knowledge. This does not have to be a problem. On the contrary, it can be a positive benefit as the two sides can be mutually beneficial. In UKIT there is a wider group of people who have some knowledge about something and who can therefore be consulted about it, but if further knowledge is required there is a specialist available in Palo Alto.

## Face-to-Face Interaction

We noted in Chapter IV that even in some on-line communities (for example, SFNet) people reach the point where they need to meet face-to-face to further develop the relationships. We also noted that social processes (trust in relationships) are important in a CoP, and the question was raised as to how these might be affected in a distributed environment. Even though the CoP in the study was distributed, it was interesting to see the emphasis that was placed on face-to-face interaction for the development of the social issues.

The members felt that face-to-face interaction was important to the development of a good relationship without which the CoP could not function. They could recall two relationships (in WWIT, not in WWITMan) that had developed purely electronically but both of these were the result of a shared (non-work-related) interest and were felt to be very much the exception. It was felt that the development of a relationship needed "that bit extra. You can give some more details of your personal life, personal interactions," according to one case study respondent.

Although the group members felt the face-to-face interaction was important, they did not feel it was *absolutely essential*. They felt that collaboration could take place without face-to-face interaction, and that with the range of new media available, it is possible for a relationship to develop over a long period of time. However, they were also of the opinion that the development would be slower without face-to-face interaction and that there would be a limit or a boundary. As a result of their use of the video, they had considered this question very carefully and came to the conclusion that if you are going to work closely with someone, you *do* need to meet them. Mike felt that:

> *the big thing about actually travelling is that you actually get to meet people, you get to shake hands and you get to have a curry with them, you get to see where they live ... and understand much more the actual culture that they live in, which allows you to pick up a lot more on the relationship you've got with them, to make that work better. And people say that they'd like to do video-conferencing 'cause they feel they can get better in touch with you as an individual. I'd argue that they can't — it's an illusion. Actually, the best way to get in touch with someone is to actually go and see that person or have them come and see you and then once you've built that relationship ... then you can continue that relationship, using that as a basis, on either video or audio conferencing.*

The strong personal relationship appeared to carry the community through the periods of e-communication. Knowing each other gave them a greater feeling of unity and common purpose, or, as one of the respondents put it, "you need the personal relationship if you are to go the extra half mile for someone." The strong personal relationship was also felt to help with issues of identity — the members of the group *knew* who they were communicating with, even if it was via e-mail. Because they felt they knew their partners so well, they also had confidence in what they were receiving from them. This point of confidence also has a bearing on the legitimation. As members get to know each other, have confidence in each other, and trust each other, they gain legitimation in the eyes of each other. The trust and confidence that the members had in each other was evidenced in the fact that the UKIT members would trust USIT to test some of the UK systems for a millennium problem. They would be willing to do this because of the confidence they had in the US team — as a result of the relationship that had been developed. The UKIT members felt they knew the US team so well that they could trust them with the testing of their systems. The face-to-face interaction itself does not develop trust and confidence; rather, it facilitates the more rapid development of strong relationships that allow trust and confidence.

The group felt they were developing relationships using face-to-face visits and then trying to maintain them over e-media. This worked well, but there was an element of decay to the point where they would meet again face-to-face in order to refresh the relationship. They were keen to point out however, that the relationship did not decay to the same level each time; that is, there was an upward "trend curve" in the relationship. After a period of time they felt they reached a "comfort zone" where they were compatible with their colleagues. This would be the point at which the element of trust was present. They considered there to be a "hierarchy" of media that affected the speed at which this state could be reached, and at the top of this was getting to know people through personal visits. If a relationship were conducted solely through e-media, it would be restricted. It would be possible to get to know someone through the e-media, but it would take longer and there would be more misunderstandings. The feeling was that a cushion was needed — a basis on which the relationship can build. People need to meet physically and build up the relationship. It is not necessary to meet physically to collaborate. They felt that collaboration can take place perfectly adequately over e-media, but if more of a relationship is needed then meeting face-to-face can take it further, faster.

## Importance of Shared Artefacts

A most striking finding from the case study was the importance of shared artefacts. There were several shared artefacts in evidence — a knowledge base, minutes of e-meetings in the form of a chat log, and a planning document. The planning document was the most striking, and it proved to be more central to the operation than the group realised. Although the document was designed initially to help with the planning and coordination of the group, it was also deliberately used as a communication tool. In addition, the document played a number of other, unintended roles — it stimulated discussion, problem solving, and reflection, and acted as a catalyst to collaboration. The most interesting feature, however, was that it was designed *deliberately* to have this effect; that is, it was only literally a planning document, but it was also used as a way of ensuring participation, and was even designed with this use in mind — not merely as a planning document.

Another striking aspect of the planning document was its stimulative quality. It stimulated both discussion and collaboration. The planning document was used to drive meetings and also was the focus of meetings. During discussion around the artefact, it would often trigger other discussions. Issues would be raised and be discussed, but the document would remain the focal point, like an anchor, as discussions moved around it, away from it, and returned. Some of the issues raised for discussion were problems that were being experienced by one of the cores. In that case the members would apply their knowledge to the problem that had been raised. In some cases they could solve the problem there and then, or they could provide the name of a local expert who could help. Alternatively, one core might have already tackled the problem, and it would make arrangements to get together so one core could help the other.

The document also functioned as a catalyst for collaboration. In the same way as discussions were triggered, the members of the CoP, through discussion of the document, would come across areas where they could usefully collaborate. As in the above example, they might see areas where one side could help another with a problem. Similarly one core could possibly leverage from the other and thereby avoid having to "reinvent the wheel." Through discussion of the document contents they were able to identify areas where they could work together, that is, projects where they could usefully collaborate, or areas where one side had a guru who the other could use. In addition to identifying projects already listed on the document, ideas were stimulated as to further areas that would provide useful collaboration opportunities. The most obvious area for collaboration was that Dan in the US wanted to have the opportunity to examine the document more closely, with a view to combining the UK and US versions and making it a single document.

Other uses of an artefact were shown by other artefacts. In e-meetings the members noted actions on an "action list" in the chat log. This functioned as the minutes of the meeting, thereby providing a "history." More importantly, this means of providing the minutes gave the members more confidence in their accuracy as they were visible to all as they were being written. The members felt that this was a great improvement over the traditional method where, as one case respondent put it, "sometimes you think the guy that wrote the minutes was at a different meeting."

There was also an occasion where an artefact was used for demonstration, a sort of situated learning. This was an e-meeting where UKIT wanted to learn from what USIT had done with its Knowledge Base. Rather than simply telling UKIT about it, the people in USIT set up a meeting over e-media and demonstrated it and took the UK people through the system.

It was, however, the planning document that was most in evidence during the period spent with UKIT. It was not the artefact per se that was important, but the *process* of creating it and using it. This was illustrated by the fact that the UKIT had developed a planning document the previous year, and the document itself was seen as the aim. Once the document was finished, it was rarely, if ever, referred to again. The members had learned from this and were much happier with the current situation. Mike pointed out that they had realised eighteen months previously that they needed to go through a planning cycle. They created a document and then put it away. They learned from that, and now have a continuously rolling document and intend to revisit it monthly with the aim that it will be a mature document by the following year. This will be beneficial, not because they have a document but because of the continuous process.

The process of creating the document meant the members were interacting around the document and were applying their knowledge and expertise to its creation. As they applied their knowledge, so it came to be embedded in the document. For example, as Dave worked on the planning for the Year 2000 problem, his planning expertise was reflected in the contents of that section of the document. It did not appear to be the case, however, that the soft knowledge was captured in the document and then transmitted to the other group. Rather, it provided an opportunity for the sharing of knowledge through stimulating collaboration and interaction.

The process of creating the document provided a further interesting aspect: Although the initial aim of the document was as a planning tool, it was also intended to be used for communication with the members of the other core. It was interesting to see the use of the shared artefact to aid communication with distributed members and at the same time serve as a catalyst, focal point, and embodiment of soft knowledge. In aiding communication with the peers in the US, the document had to cross boundaries. It was therefore deliberately tailored for the purpose. This aspect was the subject of both formal and informal discussion within the UK core. They were able to tailor the document partly by using an existing document that had already been prepared by USIT. This meant they could adopt a similar structure. However, the members of the two cores had already developed strong relationships with their peers in the US and felt they knew them well. Knowing them meant they could tailor the document to their intended audience. The group also had a shared background and a shared language, which would help to reduce possible misunderstandings.

As the document was also intended to be used as a communication tool, it was therefore going to be deliberately used as a boundary object. In this case the boundaries it would have to cross were cultural and physical but were *within* the same CoP. Interestingly, the document was also used to communicate with the vertical teams, thus crossing the boundaries between groups but, in this case, not having to cross cultural or physical boundaries. The document was not only used to communicate with the members of the vertical teams — they also had input to the document. The team managers (Dave, Mike, and Stan) consulted their people in the early stages and incorporated their views in their initial documents, which were then melded to create the main document. We see here how the representations were represented across different states and media; for example, Dave received written input from his team via e-mail and on printed paper. Stan took the four documents and merged them. The resulting document was printed and discussed. Stan transferred it between his PC and his laptop computer for working at home. This was repeated several times and then the document was placed in NetMeeting for the e-meeting where it was discussed with USIT.

The planning document also provided a vehicle for the application of the softer side of knowledge. Softer knowledge was not captured and codified, but was applied to its creation and perhaps embodied some of the softer knowledge of the people who created it. It was when it was used that it fired discussion of issues and people talked about the issues and applied their knowledge to the problem that softer knowledge was applied. Thus the document became a catalyst and a vehicle.

# MOVING TOWARD STAGE TWO

We have spent some time with WWITMan, a distributed CoP, and we have had a look at the issues that arose from our time with them. We have seen many of the CoP characteristics and seen something of how they apply in the distributed world, but the two most striking themes to emerge from Stage One are:

- The importance of developing relationships; and
- The importance of shared artefacts.

The emergence of social issues (in the form of relationships) and shared artefacts maps on to the Participation/Reification duality described by Wenger (1998). The shared artefact is an example of reification, and the relationships that are developed between the community members encourage participation. It is important to note that the process of developing relationships and the artefact, and the process of working with the artefact underpin everything. The process of creating the artefact and working with it facilitate further participation (Figure 7).

*Figure 7: Mapping WWITMan to Wenger (1998)*

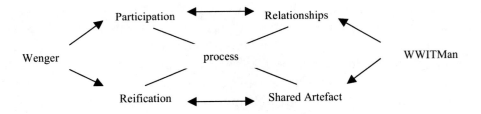

We have already learned a lot from our time with the UK core, but this is only part of WWITMan. As we are interested in the functioning of an internationally distributed CoP, we really need to spend some time with the US core, too. We will accompany the UK core on one of its regular visits to America to visit its colleagues in California, then we will be able to follow up on the insights and issues that arose from Stage One of our study. In particular, we want to pay close attention to the importance of the social issues in the form of developing relationships and the role of the shared artefact — for example, its stimulative roles, its role as a boundary object, how it is propagated across different media, and the knowledge it might have embedded in it.

# Chapter VI

# Stage Two — Visiting the American Core

*Chapter VI describes Stage Two of the case study. Here we participate in a visit made by the UK core of the CoP to visit its peers in the US. In Stage Two, we want to focus on the issues and insights gained from our time with the UK core. In particular, Stage One showed us the importance of relationships for sustaining a distributed CoP and the importance of a face-to-face element in the development of the relationships. In Stage Two, we can observe the face-to-face element between the cores. Stage One also showed us the importance of the development and use of a shared artefact in the form of the planning document. In Stage Two, we can follow the continued development and use of the planning document.*

## WWITMAN FACE-TO-FACE

In Stage Two of our study, our goal is to extend and inform the issues and insights that came out of our time with the UK core of our CoP. The two most striking issues that we found in Stage One were:

- the importance of the shared artefact (a planning document), and
- the importance of social issues in the form of the relationships that were developed in face-to-face situations.

In Stage Two, we want to pay particular attention to the face-to-face element of relationship development and the continued development and use of the planning document.

The vignettes in this section describe one of the regular face-to-face visits made at approximately six-monthly intervals between the cores of WWITMan. In this case it was the UK core's turn to visit its American colleagues. The period of the visit is outlined in Figure 1.

*Figure 1: Summary of Events in Stage Two of the Case Study*

| | Case Study Timeline Stage 2 |
|---|---|
| Wednesday | → UK core arrive in California<br>→ Robert (USIT colleague) joins them for dinner |
| Thursday | → Mike goes in early to support an e-meeting<br>→ UKIT members have 1:1 meetings with colleagues (not all from USIT, some from other project groups)<br>→ Lunch with Robert<br>→ Two pre-arranged meetings open to all members of USIT<br>→ Evening: UKIT members go for a meal with Robert |
| Friday | → Mike and Wayne go in early for e-meeting<br>→ Chakaka (from Japan) present<br>→ Stan and Dave check e-mails<br>→ Business Control Audit meeting<br>→ Wayne prepares presentation<br>→ Mike has informal meeting with his opposite number and a colleague<br>→ Stan has a number of 1:1 meetings with colleagues (both in USIT and other project groups)<br>→ Wayne and Dave go to Year 2000 meeting<br>→ Dave goes to a meeting to discuss cross geography systems management<br>→ Evening: UKIT go for a meal with Robert |
| Saturday | → Mike has arranged to meet a friend in the city<br>→ Rest of UKIT go out for the day with Robert<br>→ Evening, UKIT (except Mike), Robert and Chakaka go out for dinner |
| Sunday | → UKIT take trip down the coast<br>→ Evening: barbecue at home of Doug (one of wider USIT group) |
| Monday | → UKIT/USIT cores go to meeting with centre directors<br>→ Meeting to prepare for off-site<br>→ Stan has a 1:1 meeting about the room booker<br>→ UKIT core give presentation to full USIT<br>→ Stan has a 1:1 with a colleague<br>→ Leave for off-site |
| Tuesday | → Announcement made about company structure<br>→ CoP returns early from off-site<br>→ Evening: whole CoP out together for dinner |
| Wednesday | → UKIT core go in early (06.45) to set up coffee talk for a UK manager<br>→ WWITMan meet to discuss the organisational restructuring<br>→ Stan has a 1:1 with Graeme (was a member of wider USIT, now a member of CoP) |
| Thursday | → Mike has his own meetings to attend<br>→ Stan has some impromptu meetings<br>→ There is a range of pre-arranged meetings<br>→ Dave, Wayne and Robert attend a meeting with corporate IT |

*Figure 2: People in USIT*

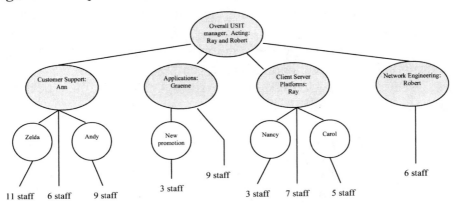

In this part of the case study many more people were involved. The main players are shown in Figure 2, which shows some of the people in USIT.

The four managers of USIT make up the US core of the WWITMan CoP. Some of them were already encountered in Stage One as they were contacted by their UK peers or as they participated in e-meetings. There is one notable difference between the first and second phases: Don has left the organisation, and has been replaced by Graeme. Graeme previously occupied the post "New Promotion" in Figure 2, so he was already a member of the wider WWIT group and was well known to all of the CoP members. Don's additional role as overall head of USIT is temporarily being shared by Ray and Robert.

The visit had been planned well in advance. Wayne and Robert had got together electronically to draw up a schedule. This had been followed by an e-meeting where other people had made suggestions. The schedule had been updated to take the comments into account and had then been placed on the intranet for further comment and for information. The schedule contains space for informal contacts and also a number of pre-arranged meetings. The planning document influences the schedule to some degree in that a number of the meetings are to cover topics that have been taken directly from the planning document. The purpose of the meetings is not to come away with action items (as is usual in the e-meetings) but to discuss and come together as a group.

## Arrival and Day 1

Wednesday afternoon, the members of the UK core of WWITMan arrive at San Francisco airport. They make their way through the formalities and go to collect the two rental cars that are waiting. On arrival at the hotel, the rooms are allocated and the core members separate to settle in, agreeing to meet in the hotel restaurant for the evening meal.

During the evening meal Robert calls at the hotel to see if they have arrived. Seeing them there, he joins them for the meal and spends the rest of the evening with them.

The following morning, Mike goes into the office early in order to support the e-meeting that is scheduled to take place with the UK location. Dave and Stan go in about 09.00 and go directly to the cubicle that is kept permanently available and equipped for visitors from the UK location. They spend some time checking their e-mail, discussing the ones that affect them both, and then Stan goes off to see some of his colleagues. He is keen to use the opportunity to have some one-to-one individual meetings and has planned several of these. This morning he plans to see three people. Some of the people he wants to see this week are directly relevant to his work, but others are more relevant to the other projects with which he is involved. In addition to the three planned meetings, he also manages an ad hoc chat with the lady who organises the USIT newsletter. Their chat results in the idea of UKIT adding a column, "What you should know when visiting the UK site." Meanwhile, Mike has returned to the hotel to catch up on some sleep as the e-meeting was cancelled. At lunchtime Robert takes Dave and Wayne to lunch at a local restaurant where they chat informally.

After lunch, there are two parallel meetings arranged—one on AV events and one on the web infrastructure. Specific people have been identified to attend each meeting, but the meetings are also open to anyone in USIT. Ray and Stan host the web infrastructure meeting while Mike and Robert host the AV events meeting. There are several people at the latter meeting, and Robert starts the meeting by having the attendees introduce themselves. Mike then shows a video about the electronic meeting room at the UK site. Occasionally, he stops the video to clarify a point. When the video finishes, Mike takes questions and Robert makes notes of issues on two flip charts. An hour before the meeting is due to finish, Robert stops the meeting, suggesting they step back from the fine detail of issues and take a wider view. He explains what he has been noting on the flip charts. Discussion continues. Towards the end, they feel that the meeting has been so useful that, despite the fact that the aim of the meeting was a "get to know you" meeting, they will make a list of action items after all. The main issue to come out of the meeting is the need for someone to fulfill a "producer" role at each site, as local knowledge is essential. Mike and

Robert agree to write up the contents of the meeting. Mike would also like the information to go to some people involved in a related project.

Meanwhile, Stan and Dave have been in the web infrastructure meeting with Ray, Graeme, Chakaka (who arrived this morning), and some members of Ray's and Graeme's teams. Again, although the intention of the meeting was not to come away with action items, it resulted in some decisions and recommendations. Stan has made notes that will be translated into a set of minutes.

That evening Robert arrives at the hotel to go for dinner with the UKIT people. They also look for Chakaka, but are unable to find her.

## Day 2: Friday

Mike and Wayne go into the office early for the e-meeting that was cancelled yesterday. Stan and Dave go in later and, as a first step, check their e-mails. All the UKIT people then go to a pre-arranged meeting about Business Controls with Graeme, Robert, and Carol (a member of Ray's team), and Chakaka. The topic for this meeting is one that has come from the planning document. Ray is supposed to be co-hosting the meeting with Wayne, but he is not there. They call him to see if they should start the meeting or wait for him. He's been detained and will arrive later, so he asks Graeme to take his part for him. As they work through the topic. Graeme makes notes on a PC. The notes are visible to all on a large screen. Similar to yesterday's meeting, some action items and areas for collaboration come out of the meeting. There is general discussion about the topic, and in some cases one core asks the other core for advice about how to tackle specific issues. The answers tend to take the form of stories: "What we do is …," "Do you remember when …?"

Towards the end of the meeting, nothing has been heard from Chakaka, so Robert asks her directly what the situation is in Japan. He is endeavoring to include her so that she does not feel on the periphery. Chakaka explains the situation and procedures in Japan. She has some printed comments on a sheet so Robert has copies made for all the participants.

After the meeting, Stan goes off to have some more one-to-one meetings about some of the different projects in which he's involved. Wayne, on the other hand, co-hosts another meeting that is about another topic from the planning document: the Year 2000 issue. His co-host is Doug Hall. Doug is a member of Graeme's team, and he is the USIT Year 2000 Manager. Dave, Chakaka, and Robert are also present. Wayne takes the points that were on the original schedule and writes them up on the board as an agenda. He then starts by bringing Chakaka into the conversation by asking her directly if there is anything she wants to discuss. She wants to talk about Y2K patches, so Wayne adds this to the agenda. Dave then brings everyone up-to-date regarding progress that has been made at the UK site. As he does so, Wayne makes notes on the whiteboard. Robert summarises the differences between the US and UK locations, pointing out that they still have "Chipmunks." This is a new term to the UK people so he explains that they are 98/36 workstations, Series 200 Models. Doug points out that they have been limited with contingency planning to some extent as they have had to wait for a document from Corporate IT. This document has now arrived, but there are a number of gaps in it. Wayne asks if Doug can forward the document to him. Ray arrives and Dave summarises what has been discussed. Doug reads from the corporate document that they (USIT) are considering closing all outside transactions for December 31, 1999, and switching off all non-critical applications. This is immediately criticised on business grounds by most of the people present, but it is Mike who immediately points out several technical reasons why the idea is unsound. Dave asks Ray what USIT will be doing about personnel. He suggests they might use contractors, but Robert points out that they would prefer to use their own personnel because of the experience and local knowledge they have that would not be available in a contractor. Doug proposes a USIT meeting to take this further, but the general feeling is that a WWIT meeting would be more beneficial. Wayne notes some action items, and the meeting closes.

After lunch, Wayne works on preparing a presentation, and Dave co-hosts another meeting based on a planning document topic. This topic is cross-geography systems management, and he is co-hosting it with Carol. Ray is also present along with three other members of USIT. Dave is the only UK member, here but he has made a point of speaking with one of his team, Nigel, back in the UK by phone before the meeting. They work through the five points that were on the schedule. Some problems are raised and issues discussed, and gradually they feel they are starting to move forward in the area. During the discussion, one of the USIT people feels the discussion has exposed a gap in his knowledge. Dave suggests it may be worthwhile talking with one of his team, Nigel, in the UK.

The final meeting of the day is also based on the planning document. It is about the computer networks in the company and is co-hosted by Robert and Dave. There are only two other people present: Chakaka and Kirnan (from

USIT). Robert introduces Chakaka and Kirnan. He then starts the meeting by referring to an illustration that Chakaka had given him about the Japanese network. Chakaka asks about the UK situation, and Robert uses an overhead projector (OHP) to show an overview of the Local Area Network (LAN) in the UK. He then describes the American LAN. The discussion then becomes very technical, and the meeting closes with Dave feeling that good progress had been made.

## The Weekend

Mike had made plans to visit a friend in San Francisco, and Chakaka has gone shopping, so Dave, Stan, and Wayne go for a drive into the country with Robert. That evening, Dave, Stan, Wayne, Chakaka, and Robert go for a meal. During the meal, the talk turns to the next joint meeting, which will be in the UK. Chakaka expresses disappointment that she will not be able to attend because of budgetary constraints. Wayne and Robert both want her included and immediately both say they will find some arrangement to enable her to travel.

On Sunday, Robert has commitments and Chakaka also has something she needs to do so they decide to meet up afterwards and go to the cinema. The UKIT team takes the rental car and drives down the coast. In the evening, the WWITMan team (and a few others) is invited to a barbecue at Doug's house.

## Monday

The WWITMan team is supposed to meet with centre directors at 09.00 but find the meeting is suddenly cancelled as the centre directors have been summoned to Head Office for a meeting there. Instead, WWITMan starts preparing for the two-day off-site session that is scheduled to be held at a remote location on the coast. Stan takes the opportunity to visit someone on Graeme's team who will be working with Gary (in Stan's team) on the room-booking system.

The main meeting of the day is a presentation by Chakaka and the UKIT people to all of USIT. Each of them talks a little about his or her roles and the roles of their teams. The aim of the meeting is simply to put names to faces, a "getting to know you" meeting. Dave, Wayne, and Mike all base their presentations, to a large degree, on their sections of the planning document.

Stan finishes off the morning by having another one-to-one meeting. Again, it is with a member of Graeme's team who expresses his appreciation of the support and knowledge of Gary and DaveW (on Stan's team) in the development of solutions. He's intending to meet up with Gary at a forthcoming conference.

After lunch, there are two meetings scheduled. Ray and Dave co-host the first one about security, and Ray and Stan co-host the second about messaging and directory services. In the evening, WWITMan members (along with an external facilitator) leave for the coast for the off-site. During the off-site, they want to brainstorm as a group and decide a long-term plan as to what they want to do over the coming three years. It is intended that this will be more a strategic plan than the tactical level planning embodied in the planning document. The aim is to create a strategic document for the group, probably over two or three iterations.

## Tuesday — The Announcement

Early on Tuesday morning, Stan goes for a walk along the coast. When he returns, the others are excitedly discussing a rumour of a major re-organisation. The group goes into overdrive, using all its teamworking skills and all the communication facilities available (mostly mobile phones) to find out more information. On hearing that the rumour is true, they decide that there is no further point in developing a strategic plan as the situation is so fluid, so they abandon the off-site and return.

That evening all of WWITMan go out for a meal together.

## The Final Two Days

At 06.45 the UKIT team goes into the office to set up a coffee-talk[10] for Bristol by a senior manager. The same talk is due to be presented in California at 09.00. After this, Stan meets with Graeme. They have met before and they have worked together electronically, but as Graeme has taken over from Don, Stan appreciates the opportunity to spend some time with him one-to-one and discuss who does what on the Applications Team. Then WWITMan meets as a full group to discuss how it will meet the re-organisation of the company. The overall head of WWITMan, Dan, is present and the WWITMan staff is priming him with the concerns and issues to raise at a senior level. There is a real sense of activity in the building — Robert himself has been in four meetings already this morning. Many issues are raised and discussed. Everybody applies knowledge or experience of some sort; for example, the legal aspects are touched upon, and some people have no knowledge in this field so are informed by those who do. At the end of the meeting, the attendees all feel happier simply for having done *something* and having something with which to move forward. The following day, Thursday, Mike has some one-to-one meetings arranged and Stan has an e-meeting scheduled. This is in fact a tutorial for "Eroom" administrators. DaveW from Stan's team is at the UK end. Stan follows this meeting by calling on some people for opportunistic chats. While all this is happening, Wayne, Dave, and Robert go and meet people in Corporate IT. This building is located a mere 200 yards away, and the UK people feel that there should be some scope for collaboration.

Dave leaves on the Thursday. Stan, Mike, and Wayne stay on for another meeting on Thursday afternoon and two on Friday morning. Friday afternoon, Stan, Mike, Wayne, and Chakaka all depart.

# ISSUES AND INSIGHTS

This second stage proves useful in several ways. It provides more insights into some of the CoP characteristics that we saw in Stage One and also provides evidence of more CoP characteristics. It throws more light on some of the issues that were raised in Stage One, and it also brings some new issues to the surface.

## The CoP
*War Stories*

There was more evidence of war stories in Stage Two. Most of these occurred in the meetings, but there were also examples evident in an e-meeting during the final session with the UK core after its return to the UK.

In the meetings, people were asking direct questions of others. The answers often took the place of stories. Stories were told about the network in Israel, about the system being under simulated attack, about the Americans' experience with ISDN — "What we do is ...." "What we've done is ..., Do you remember ...?" The listeners listened and applied their knowledge, leading them to understand, to transfer the story to their own situation, or to point out problems. The stories therefore often fired up further questions, issues, and discussion. People were therefore able to learn from hearing the stories and from further discussion about them.

*Newcomers*

Stage Two offered the opportunity to view a newcomer to the CoP. During Stage One of the study, Don was the manager of the Applications Team, but he had left prior to Stage Two. Graeme had been a member of the team but had been promoted to take Don's place, so he was now part of WWITMan. Most of the other members had already met Graeme either face-to-face or in e-media so he was already accepted by them. However, there were some aspects of the job to which he was new, so as far as the UKIT members were concerned, he still had to earn the trust for part of his role in WWITMan, and the relationship still needed to be develop. The visit helped move this aspect forward very quickly, as illustrated by Stan's comment after his visit:

> *Graeme was new, and I've known about him ... ever since I came to [the organisation], the first time I went to PA, but not in the role he's doing now, so that relationship needed to grow because he's now taken on supervisory control of the parallel operation. So I achieved success there in terms of growing that.*

*Evolution*

We have already heard how WWITMan had evolved from a bidding group into the CoP that is WWITMan. Stage Two showed how the CoP evolves further but also shows how the evolution is linked with the development of relationships.

Both Robert and Ray (US members) felt that WWITMan was still evolving and developing.

> *I would say it's still developing. I think it's going in that direction. (Ray)*

> *It's still a developing Community of Practice, if you will, in some ... respects, rather than an established Community of Practice. (Robert)*

The CoP continues to evolve as the relationships are developed. Stan explained how the relationship has developed to the point where the members are comfortable with each other:

> *The first time I went to PA it was chucking plastic at each other[11] ... and I don't do that any more. I don't need to go blow-by-blow*

*what everyone does. The atmosphere is so much more relaxed.
No one's trying to prove anything any more.*

Mike's experiences showed that the relationships should not be forced, but should also be allowed to evolve:

*... six months or a year ago I was very much in the "we should be working closer, let's work closer together" and just trying to find reasons to work closer together. I've gone about circle on that now ... if I end up having a friend-based relationship with either Robert or Ray, great. But I don't see myself in a business relationship with them in the way that I will with Graeme and Zelda ... This time last year I was all of trying to make it happen ... I was putting an awful lot of energy into creating relationships with everybody and getting frustrated that it wasn't happening with some people. Now I've grown through that ... because there's no need for me to have like a working relationship with those people.*

### Legitimation

The issue of legitimation has already surfaced in the example of the newcomer to the CoP. Stage One showed how relationships are important and the role they play in legitimation—as people develop strong relationships they also develop trust and confidence in each other. As they gain confidence and trust in someone, (s)he becomes an accepted and established member of the group. This also came through in Stage Two, as evidenced by Wayne's comment:

*...in the last two years we've gone through the process of the managers getting to know each other quite well and so we all recognise kind of how we work ... we've got to the point where we can predict how people are going to react to things ... we've got degrees of trust. All these kinds of things are in place so when we're meeting, the purposes of our meetings have moved on from build trust, build understanding. We've got that now so we're sort of spinning on to the next thing now which is to say "OK, so how do we get our teams to work?"*

Stage Two of the study also illustrated how legitimation is closely linked to the two elements of participation and peripherality. This was well illustrated through the experiences of the Japanese member, Chakaka. It was shown in Stage One how Chakaka is on a physical periphery as she is the single member in Japan. There is no time window when the two cores *and* Chakaka can participate together in an e-meeting. If Chakaka wishes to participate, it is 0200 for her. The language also causes a problem in an e-meeting as she has difficulties with the British accents. She therefore tends not to participate in e-meetings unless absolutely necessary and therefore can feel isolated at times. However, Chakaka is fully accepted as a legitimate member of the group and has a good relationship with the rest of the members — a relationship where the other members will "go the extra mile" to include Chakaka in the face-to-face situations and to help her participate. In the meetings when Chakaka is rather quiet, Robert is good at making a point of including her and getting her participation. When she says she will not be able to attend the UK meeting because of budgetary constraints, Wayne and Robert immediately say that they will find some way of getting her there — they *want* her to be present and participate. This is, however, more difficult when they are not in a face-to-face situation. Chakaka says she feels she is out on a periphery, but she is now copied in on the USIT e-mail loop, which makes her feel more included, more comfortable. She would therefore also like to be copied in on a UKIT loop.

## Distribution/Globalisation

Stage Two of the main study highlighted what the CoP members considered to be the greatest of the hurdles posed by working in a globally distributed environment — the time zone differences.

The time difference is an inherent problem for internationally distributed working, and this was seen in Stage One of the study. The issue was also raised in Stage Two and, interestingly, was generally held to be a greater barrier to the functioning of the CoP than physical distance. Although they felt face-to-face communication to be essential at regular intervals, it has also been shown that regular frequent interaction is important. Although Lipnack and Stamps (1997) showed that interaction decreases as proximity decreases, Stage Two of the case study demonstrated that temporal distance is a greater barrier than physical distance:

*Time zone is a problem. I either find it inconvenient to be at work at an early hour or I feel guilty about inconveniencing somebody at a late hour. (Ray)*

*I think ... if PA was in South Africa we would maintain a high level of communication. Because it doesn't matter in that instance that they're 8000 miles away. The fact is it is still 2.00 in the afternoon when it's 2.00 in the afternoon here. Having this one and-a-half-hour window, and it's a window that for them is the most difficult hour of the day. It's when they come in and pick up all their e-mails and problem reports ... and they're not really necessarily interested in talking about problems or projects. For the first couple of hours of the day you're fire-fighting, you're in fire fighting mode, you want to clean out your e-mail, clean out your voice mail and so on, so it's very difficult ... for them to be able to knuckle down to our level at that time of day and for us it's quite difficult sometimes ... if you can't phone them until half four, five o'clock. If you've had a hard day, it's the last thing you want to do. (Mike)*

## Communication/Collaboration

During Stage Two there were several more examples of the CoP members finding opportunities for working together on projects or identifying areas where members of their teams could usefully collaborate.

*Media*

As in Stage One, different people had different media preferences. Stage Two also supported the idea that people selected the media for the task they wanted to undertake and the context of that task. However, because of individual preferences, where one person might choose one medium, someone else might choose another. Where Stages One and Two differed was in the view that was held of video facilities. At the beginning of the case study, UKIT did not feel that having a video facility was important. In Stage Two, UKIT was much happier to have a camera to provide context. High fidelity video was not felt necessary — just something to provide context:

*I like NetMeeting for what it can do and I like being able to see. I don't rate high fidelity video in that sort of meeting. I don't necessarily think that you need high fidelity, high transmission rate, and high frame ratio. I think maybe that's going over the top, but you do need and you gain enormously from having an impression or image of what's happening at the other end. (Mike)*

The UKIT core members feel that having the camera provide a context has added a benefit to the meetings, as illustrated by Dave's comment:

*That's added something ... that's definitely an improvement. It's really ... more than anything else you see the commitment, you see people at least present. You know there's an element there of ... you're both making an effort on either side. On the end of just a polycom, a voice bridge, you're not really sure whether someone is still in the room or not.*

They were very clear that they did not see video as a replacement for face-to-face interaction, however. In that regard, Stan remarked:

*I had a good chat with Sandy. I'd never met her before. I've seen her on the video before but it's a totally different impression when you meet and we talk the same language so it was good.*

*Ad Hoc Communication*

Stage Two supported the importance of opportunistic communication, which we also saw in Stage One. The members of UKIT went to visit their colleagues with the express intention of using the opportunity for ad hoc communication, to encounter people in corridors, to be able to drop into their cubicles to say "Hi." This helps maintain relationships and can lead to opportunities for collaboration:

*I said, "Oh, that's interesting. My guy, Gary has been working on EHS[12] projects and he's done something very similar. What you're doing here is very complementary to what he's done." And then we went to talk with the EHS project sponsor and told her what we'd done, and they said "Oh, Corporate is doing something in this area," so when I came back I went back to Gary and I went back to Mary and said, "This is what I found out in PA. There's overlap here, there's stuff which you could use*

*on-site, and stuff that we've done which they could use," so ...
I was going away and trying to oil the wheels, put people in
contact. There's no way I could have done that without meeting,
and it was one of those "head round the corner" jobs. I think
those are great ones. (Stan)*

This was felt to be much easier in a face-to-face environment. When operating in a distributed environment, it is easier to get a pre-arranged meeting:

*There's a lot of pressures and you have to be very conscientious
and very fixed and very booking times to speak to people and
arranging meetings for people rather than having the informal
telephone contact with them. If I say to Robert, "OK, we need
to talk about this, let's have an hour on the phone starting at half
eight your time next Tuesday, we'll book it, we'll have it. I will
be here on the phone for an hour with him. No problem. But with
Wayne I can pop round and see him ... a different style of
communication there — formal versus informal. (Mike)*

The difficulty here was held to be temporal, rather than physical distance. Support for a distributed CoP would need to support ad hoc communication as suggested by the use of instant messaging software such as ICQ[13].

## Culture

During the analysis of the data from the study we looked for cultural issues as influencers (people who affect or constrain work), influences, and breakdowns (problems that interfere with work). In Stage One we saw that cultural issues can be problematic for a distributed CoP on three levels: national, organisational, and group levels. Stage Two extended this by highlighting another "breakdown" that caused problems for sustaining a distributed CoP: local issues. One example was Robert and Ray were sharing the job of Wayne's equivalent on a temporary basis in addition to doing their own full-time jobs. This meant that, in some cases, they were unable to give some tasks the attention they needed. It was also felt that, in general, local issues tend to appear more pressing and therefore take precedence over on-going CoP work:

*We put aside our day-to-day responsibilities to a large extent
when we have the team and that's where we work very effectively*

*as a team, but then we have to go back to our regular lives and when the phone is ringing constantly and there are three people in line standing outside my office to see me for the entire length of the day, and my meeting schedule means that I don't even have time to have lunch or go to the bathroom, then I don't have time to think about [the UK] in that context. (Robert)*

The local issues that obstruct the ongoing CoP work can therefore reduce participation. The local issues are overcome by a mix of having a task focus and by the motivation/desire that drives the CoP.

**It would need a focused task in order to break, like you say, the local dependency** ... *I think that, personally, I'm really keen on seeing the security stuff ... so that's probably why I'm more optimistic about the levels of communication because* **I've got the need there**. *I've personally got the desire and the need to support those programs and see them carried through. If I see the progress slowing down because of PA dependency, then I personally have the commitment to do something about it.* **I know them well enough** *(emphasis added). (Dave)*

## Relationships

In Stage One, the importance of forging strong relationships was identified by the highlighting of the face-to-face aspect. The theme of relationships also came out very strongly in Stage Two.

*Face-to-Face Interaction*

Stage One showed that, even though the CoP operates in a distributed environment, the members still consider face-to-face communication to be essential. This was supported in Stage Two, both for starting to develop a relationship and for maintaining it. For example, Ann had worked with Mike over e-media and had seen his face in a NetMeeting through video, but had not actually met him until she visited the UK for the previous visit. After her face-to-face meeting with Mike, Ann said:

*I don't feel that I knew him well. Well, I thought I knew him but not in the sense that, like after you have face-to-face contact that you really feel like there's strong teamwork feeling when you can work face to face ... last year was my first trip. I've worked with Bristol on and off, mostly over the phone, and mostly actually over e-mail and voice-mail because of the time difference. Although you are able to get information exchanged, you don't get that bonding ... really human bonding.*

Having face-to-face communication was also felt to be helpful with overcoming a language barrier. Chakaka had no difficulty with the American accent but found the British accents difficult. Robert said, "Face-to-face meetings help to bridge those language barriers a lot more than working at a distance meeting." This was not just the case with Chakaka but had also been found to be the case with other Japanese colleagues.

The opportunity to have face-to-face communication also resulted in several projects being resolved, completed, or at least given a boost. All of the UKIT people experienced this, and it was described by Mike as follows:

*We actually got to, we got some things done, which is ... things that we spent months and not getting very far on and then all of a sudden ... in two hours we have a common, complete understanding of the common goal and the common way of getting there. For a number of different issues that arose that have been around for a long time.*

Mike also expressed how having face-to-face communication highlights the difficulties of communicating across time zones:

*Every time we go there it emphasises to me that ... there is a limited set of stuff you can do on sort of videoconferences or audio conferences and that you need to get there and discuss things with people over breakfast and lunch and in the corridor or pop round their cube[14] and be free to be able to talk to people eight or nine hours a day instead of two hours a day.*

The visit of the UK core to the US provided further examples of how face-to-face visits can affect the relationships in a distributed environment.

### Relationship Decay
Stage Two confirmed that there is some relationship decay in periods of e-communication, but it was also emphasised that the relationship does not

decay to the same level each time — core members described it as having an upward trend curve. Robert described this as follows:

> *Basically, the wave is lifting everybody's boats higher than they were before ... where it was previously.*

The upward trend curve was supported by the fact that the relationship reaches a point where it can sustain the CoP through a period of e-communication. This was exemplified by Robert and Wayne's relationship, which has reached the "comfort zone":

> *Wayne and I were able to be flexible in the way we actually communicated. I mean he has my home numbers, I have his and ... he's left me a message and I'd respond to him the same day. If not, the next day. He'd call me at home and say "Why haven't you responded?" or something like that. I think it works quite well because of the nature of our relationship. I think, particularly with Wayne, there has been a considerable sort of exposure, personal exposure which has been helpful. (Robert)*

*Strengthening the Relationships*

We also saw other aspects of the relationship development in Stage Two. For example, it provided examples of how the members were growing the relationships they had with their colleagues. The UK team went to Palo Alto with the express intention of strengthening the relationships, of giving them a "turbo-boost." Mike said:

> *For me, personally, strengthening relationships and so on is really very important and every time I go there it really does help an awful lot.*

They did this not only in the meetings but also by using the opportunity for opportunistic meeting and enjoying joint social occasions, as described by Stan:

> *If you check on relationships, the Doug Hall stuff, being invited back to their houses, for dinner. I think that was really good. I mean ... there's obviously some relationship there. Every time*

*I go across, Doug and I and Lucy will go out for meals in the evening. We've done wine trips, and you may not communicate every week or every month after that but when you come back you just walk straight in and say, "Hi, how about going for a drink?" You don't need any preamble. The time distance becomes ... not always relevant.'*

Stan's relationship with Doug and Lucy is a good example of how the relationship can develop to the "comfort zone" even to the point of not needing so much interaction between visits.

### Spreading the Relationships

In addition to growing existing relationships, the two core teams were also taking the opportunity to spread the web of relationships, both for themselves and also for their vertical teams. In the first place, some of the meetings and the UKIT presentation to all of USIT were "get to know each other" exercises. The UKIT people were also making new contacts within USIT. This also happens in reverse:

*I've been to [the UK] a number of times now. Part of this is the network research for [the organisation] is done in [the UK] so I have a lot of established relationships there that relate to my responsibility here for networking and I suspect that some of the others don't have quite those same relationships outside of Wayne's team, but every time I go to [the UK] I become more familiar with the people and programs that are of interest to me. (Robert)*

However, most of the new contacts were ground preparation for spreading relationships through the wider WWIT group. The CoP members were all intent on setting up contacts between members of their teams:

*Since I came back ... I haven't had a chance to put, especially Karen, in touch with one or two people from Ann's team who she would, they would probably gain benefit from talking to each other in some fashion, be it just e-mail rather than telephone and e-mail. And similarly, Gordon would benefit from communicating with his direct equivalent over there. (Mike)*

In some cases, they were planning to send some of their team members abroad for face-to-face collaboration. In that regard, Wayne said:

*There were some specifics that have come out of [the visit] ...*
*some of the ones that strike me as most significant is that it's led*
*to arrangements for a number of exchanges of people in the*
*other direction, so we've got in April now, we're likely to see*
*four or five people come from PA to [the UK] but these are not*
*full managers ... four out of the five are going to be individual*
*contributors from the teams, engineers coming over.*

## Participation

In Stage One, we saw how participation was closely linked with the development of relationships. Stage Two provided us with more insights into the issue of participation, demonstrating how it might be achieved in a distributed environment.  In Stage One, the CoP members felt that the relationship deteriorates to some degree over a period of time and that there is a need for face-to-face contact to refresh the relationship.  Stage Two confirmed the need for face-to-face contact to refresh the relationship but also provided some pointers as to how participation and the maintenance of the relationship could be helped.

*Regular/Frequent Interaction*
Keeping in regular and frequent contact can help to maintain the relationship, as illustrated by Dave's comment:

*We don't regularly swap e-mail just for the sake of it.  But you*
*would maybe just have a regular telephone conversation for the*
*sake of speaking or hearing each other's voices and just coming*
*up-to-speed on certain things.  You wouldn't need to have an*
*agenda item, so every three weeks is something I would predict*
*would be the frequency of keeping in touch.*

However, the relationship needs to be there first, probably developed in a face-to-face environment.  The regular and frequent interaction cannot happen in isolation — it needs to have either a task focus or a willingness or motivation.  The motivation to keep in frequent contact is a result of the development of a strong relationship. This was shown in Stage One where Wayne had reached the stage in his relationships with some of his colleagues where their opportunistic communication had increased. Even with the motivation, local issues can hinder the interaction, therefore it needs to be made easy, hence the need to support social awareness. This means that a user can see at a glance that a colleague is at his/her desk. This does not need to be a video image, but something small such as an icon on the desktop (for example, ICQ, as mentioned earlier).

### Task Focus

Having a task focus aids participation as it helps overcome local issues that can hinder distributed participation. It gives more of a reason for having frequent interaction in cases where the relationship has not developed to a point where distributed opportunistic communication is more frequent.

Having a task to focus the interaction helps with the frequency of interaction that is necessary.

*If we've got very clear tasks to accomplish, then the activity will keep going ... the things like the ... Knowledge Base is a very clear task. We'll keep that going until it's finished. Event management ... as new events come up, we'll do those. (Wayne)*

Another example of this was shown in that WWITMan meets electronically as a group every month. As a result of the company restructuring, the group was going to have to work on its response to the new situation and was going to increase the meetings to fortnightly.

There were several examples, both within WWITMan and the wider WWIT group, of how having a task focus is helping relationship development. Some of these were part of the evolution of the group as WWITMan members encouraged people in their vertical teams to collaborate with their peers in the other country. One example was described by Carol:

*Alastair here and Al in [the UK] actually do have services that they are keeping synchronised and managing together so their communications are much more frequent ... and the same with Micky and DaveW over there, cause they're working on things that they have to keep synchronised.*

*Interest/Desire/Motivation*

An issue that came to the fore in Stage Two was the need for the members of a CoP to have a shared interest, a desire, and a motivation for the CoP to succeed. It became clear that all three aspects: regular and frequent interaction, a task focus, and the interest/desire/motivation were all necessary in varying degrees. They all had a role in the maintenance of relationships, in the growing of relationships, and in the extending of relationships to other people.

There is a cyclical aspect to the effects of these issues, for as the relationships develop so the motivation and interaction can become greater. This was exemplified by Robert looking after Chakaka during the weekend. They had developed a good relationship, and he was willing to go the extra mile to help her feel at home.

There was an agreement within WWITMan that there was an internal motivation and a general desire to make the CoP work. This was stated explicitly in interviews and was shown in the goals the group had for the planned off-site meeting where they were going to look together at developing a longer-term plan. "The intent," according to Wayne, "was there in the off-site to think as one group and develop a long-term vision. The fact it didn't happen was due to external factors."

But despite the external factors affecting the off-site meeting, the group demonstrated how it has become one unit by reacting as a single entity and working on a single unified response to the new circumstances.

One interesting episode demonstrated the importance of the desire to do something, and how it can overcome problems of distance. Wayne's description of it follows:

> *[UKIT] arranged meetings with Corporate IT — [USIT] wanted to come along. They were only 200 yards away and had never made the contact. We wanted to. We had a lot of questions to ask people about ... "What does this mean?" "Where are you going?" "How can we work with you?" All kinds of questions. And we initiated these meetings from [the UK] because ... we kind of assumed that in PA, because they're just up the car park, the people in [USIT] could just any day of the week ring them up and go down and see them and find out what's going on. Because we don't get that opportunity, we'd made some specific meetings there, and it was really very interesting that the folks from [USIT] were very keen to join the meetings, and when we*

*went to the meetings it became absolutely clear that ... these*
*people who [are] literally 200 or 300 yards apart don't know*
*each other, never talk to each other, know nothing about what*
*each other's actually doing and so ... it was quite interesting to*
*go to those meetings and I think ... the [UKIT] team acted as a*
*catalyst there to get those discussions going.*

## The Artefact

Having seen the importance of a shared artefact in Stage One, it became a central focus of Stage Two, but concentrated particularly on the development of the planning document. Figure 3 shows the overall development of the planning document.

*Figure 3:  The Artefact Timeline*

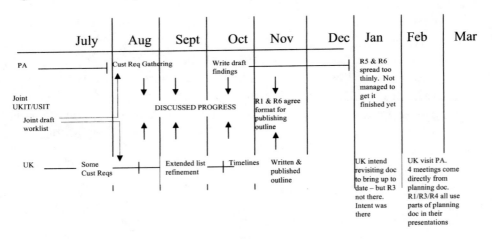

The current version of the document had changed considerably. It had started out as a UK document, but then the two cores wanted to see it as a joint document. However, the process has forked, and it is now regarded as a UK document rather than a PA document. This does not mean that the PA people were not involved. As the UK team has made changes to the document, it has passed it to PA for comment and put it on a server in PA, so the people there also have access to it. It has gone through several stages of refinement—there is a "July version," a "September version," and an "October version." The September version has a lot of notes on it, as the UK team started to do a list refinement. They used the document to help them make a transition — by the September version, they were in a position to differentiate between items that were site specific, joint or "leverage" (that is, one side keeps the other informed). They finally came out with ten or eleven different areas where they could group workloads together.

Since then Wayne has also printed the published outline for distribution and has put it on the intranet for the PA people to comment and improve. The outline is intended to be a boundary object and states Part X is PA-relevant, Part Y is UK-relevant and Part Z is joint. The intention is to review timelines and the document on a monthly basis and update it so the document evolves. The key issue, however, is the *process*. The UKIT team learned from the process of the creation, and the document has provided a focus for this. By the time of the visit, Wayne wanted an iterative way of keeping the plan up-to-date and was inviting comments from PA. Between December and the following February (the visit), UKIT had not had chance to revisit the document, as Dave had been away from work; however, the intent had been there. The document was, however, clearly to be used in the visit to PA:

- Several meetings were based on topics extracted directly from the document.
- Wayne, Mike, and Dave all based their presentations on the document.
- Mike, at least, had taken the document with him with the intention of using it in face-to-face communication.

The US team confirmed what we saw in Stage One and agreed that the planning document was stimulative, that it drove meetings, that it helped with planning and coordination, that it was used as a communication tool, that it was propagated across different states and media, and that it crossed boundaries. Robert also pointed out that its use in e-meetings was helpful in cases of linguistic difficulty:

> *What the NetMeeting added is, my gosh, if we can see the document and we can point and then you add audio to that, you are not just looking at a piece of paper and talking back and forth. You've sort of improved the level of communication there quite a bit ... And if you talk to the people who are working between PA and Japan, they've found the same thing to be true*

*dramatically. Because when they were using just audio, you'd have a much worse language barrier between English and Japanese than you do between English — American English and British English. They find that, "Ok, I hear and I partly understand what someone in Japanese or English is saying here, but I can see it on the screen in crystal clear print in English," and I think that — you'd have to check to be sure but I think I've discerned that — they, the Japanese, say they are better able to read English than they are to hear it and understand it, you know as you're increasing your competency levels. So when they can see it as well as hear someone, the actual communication and therefore useful work that happens is more effective and more work gets done so things move along more quickly with less confusion, less people diverging because they didn't really understand what was being said.*

In Stage Two, we also saw other examples of artefacts being used in the CoP. Ray and Wayne had together created a schedule to coordinate the visit, and action item lists were created. Stan wrote a note-form account of the visit for his team and accompanied this with a PowerPoint presentation. None of these artefacts fulfilled all of the roles of the planning document, but they provided further examples of some of them.

What we saw primarily in Stage One was the articulation work of the community. Stage Two, on the other hand, highlighted even further social issues and their importance — trust, friendship, confidence. In this successful CoP, there is only a vague distinction between work and friendship as they build strong relationships to sustain the distributed CoP. It can be seen how the culture of the managers in the community is that friendship is the way to achieve work.

In the case study, we have investigated and explored the inner workings of a successful CoP in detail. This has highlighted a range of issues that appear to be important, or even essential, to the functioning of a distributed international CoP. In particular, the social issues (relationships, motivation, trust, identity) and shared artefacts have emerged as key points. What we need to do now is to explore these issues in the context of other CoPs in order to confirm (or otherwise) their importance.

## Chapter VII

# A Look at Other CoPs

*In this chapter we aim to take the issues that have been raised in the main study and explore them in the context of other CoPs. As we now have a much tighter focus, we do not have to spend so much time living with these CoPs but can use open-response structured interviews with key members of the CoPs. In these CoPs, the practice was not the work of the members but ran alongside their everyday work.*

## INTRODUCTION

Our purpose in this final short study is to explore the two main issues of a shared artefact and face-to-face communication/relationships in two other CoPs:

- The Environmental Sustainability Community (ESC); and
- Educational Excellence Alongside Work (EE-AW).

Both of these communities differ from WWITMan in that WWITMan's practice was the everyday work of its members. The practices of ESC and EE-AW are *extra* to the everyday work of the members.

## The Environmental Sustainability Community

The ESC is a group that has a shared interest in environmental issues. It was driven initially by a small group of individuals who obtained support from its organisation to run a conference for interested parties. This was attended by people from all over the organisation and also by people from outside the organisation. There was a hard core of volunteers who invited people who might possibly be interested. The attendance was approximately 130 and was very successful. The organisation has continued to support the community by funding one person to be involved full-time and allowing other people to work on it alongside their normal work.

There has been no major meeting since the conference, so the community is distributed to a much greater degree than WWITMan. It does not have the range of communications media available to WWITMan and therefore is restricted to the intranet and e-mail.

There is an active core of members who drive the community, which now numbers approximately 130. It has an intranet site maintained by a member of the active core. The active core is co-located to a degree. Members are not all in the same building but the majority is at least in the same town, with two members in a neighboring town. Other people are restricted to the intranet and to the mailing list. Participation and access are formalised to some degree, as some people are on an "everything" mailing list, which means they receive all the community e-mail. Others are on a "newsletter" list, which means they receive a newsletter giving a summary of the community's communications.

*Figure 1: ESC Degrees of Participation*

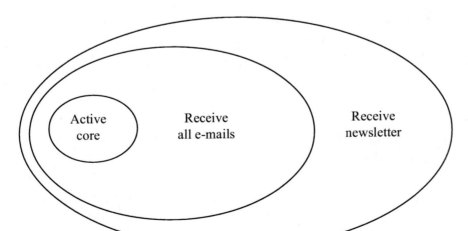

*Figure 2: ESC Physical Layout*

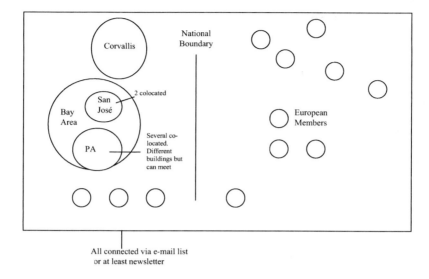

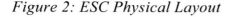

The people who are not members of the organisation but who attended the conference are not on the mailing lists for reasons of company confidentiality. Any communication with those people is undertaken on a one-to-one basis.

Figure 2 shows the physical layout of the ESC. The active core is located in California's Bay Area with most of the core members being located in Palo Alto. Two others are a short distance away in San José. There is also a branch in Corvallis (Oregon) where there are several members who participate in community discussions and also talk between themselves. Everybody else tends to be linked by e-mail or newsletter. The people in the Bay Area are recognised as the 'core'.

## Education Excellence Alongside Work (EE-AW)

EE-AW had been in existence about fifteen months and had been started by two people interested in education. They had pulled together a group of like-minded people to explore how the organisation could be involved in education in a different way. The organisation already donates regular large amounts of money to the educational system, but EE-AW is trying to see how products can also be matched to the educational needs. As part of this, scientists from the group go into schools and work as guest teachers. The group is supported by the organisation by the unwritten rule that people can use about 10% of their time for "undirected research." Like ESC, EE-AW is too distributed to be able to have people together on video or audio conferences, so communication tends to be by e-mail. Also like ESC, there is an active core of seven or eight people, referred to by the community as the "fanatic core." The active core is spread over two locations in Palo Alto. The members of the active core refer to the wider community as the "extended family." Members of the extended family occasionally call on the active core if they are in Palo Alto and will sometimes join meetings as peripheral members.

The name of the community is intended to be evocative of a children's story and, according to an EE-AW respondent, "has the nice characteristics that if we ever say it to anybody, their first impression is to giggle and that's always a good thing because it's interesting. It's new to the mind."

*Figure 3: EE-AW*

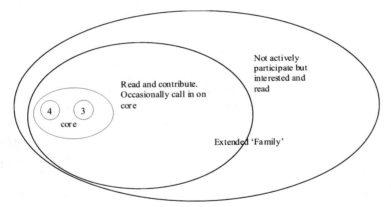

## ISSUES AND INSIGHTS

The two groups in question, EE-AW and ESC, were distributed to a far greater degree than WWITMan, did not have access to the wide range of communications tools seen in WWITMan, and had the practice of their communities extra to the everyday work. However, what we saw was in line with what we had seen in WWITMan, with the added dimension of viewing them from the point of view of a different type of CoP. In particular, it might be viewed as surprising that the social, human factors came out even more strongly as these groups were even more distributed that WWITMan.

## The CoPs

As with WWITMan, ESC and EE-AW both exhibited a range of CoP factors. As suggested in Chapter III, they did not display *all* of the characteristics identified in the model in Figure 3.

*Stories*

Respondents from both communities emphasised the importance of stories in the community communications. For one of the ESC people, this was a matter of personal style as she is renowned as a storyteller, but other members of the active core consciously considered the use of stories in their communications. They made use of them in the active core in the creation of the presentation that was being designed to communicate with physically distributed members. According to an ESC respondent, "That's one of the most important things we were thinking about as we were doing the slides was having good stories and examples. We want to make this real for people"

EE-AW also consciously used stories in its communication, saying it has lots of war stories and that as it talks more and more, the stories propagate out through the community. The stories were about the CoP itself and as they spread through the CoP they contributed to the feeling of membership, of a common bond. Two respondents gave an example of one of their "stories" — about how some of them attended a conference:

*Respondent 1:* Our trip to Vancouver. That's one of our stories.
*Respondent 2:* Ah, true.
*Respondent 1:* We tell what they told us and what we saw when we were there. We actually took a digital camera along and got five or six pictures that we used in one of the presentations.
*Respondent 2:* We wrote a big trip report on it, you know maybe a nine-page trip report.
*Respondent 1:* So that was part of the story. Partly it illustrated, if you will, and —

*Respondent 2:* And it was a shared bond.

*Newcomers*

The situation regarding newcomers in EE-AW and ESC is rather different from WWITMan. WWITMan is a very small CoP, and people join for a specific purpose, as there is a formal structure to the group even though it is a CoP. EE-AW and ESC are both much larger, and anybody who is interested can join either group.  Recruitment to EE-AW has tended to be through informal contact. Some people joined ESC as a result of attending the initial conference. Since then it has been more ad hoc and informal, both through physical contact and via the Web (www).

> *Well, sometimes it's word of mouth.  Sometimes somebody will have heard from somebody else that there's this group or somebody will be forwarded an e-mail that was sent to the distribution and they'll get back to us and say 'oh how do I get on this list?' Sometimes people are just browsing the web and they'll find our page and there's a web form where people can sign up directly and be added to the mailing list ... I'm always impressed, when I get a new member from [the organisation] Singapore. I just think that's really neat, that they could find us, just by looking, because they cared. (ESC Respondent)*

As the practice of the two CoPs is different from the everyday work of the members, a newcomer to either would not have to learn technical domain knowledge. Membership was determined by motivation and desire. Each member will be able to contribute something different.  Therefore, what newcomers have to learn will be softer elements, for example, the ways of speaking in the electronic forum, what issues have been raised already, etc. They will also need to learn who is who in the community; for example, there are major contributors whose names occur more frequently, and who are regarded as being the "active core."

*Evolution*

Both CoPs had come into being by an internal motivation and interest on the part of the people who founded the CoP; that is, the CoPs were not started by an external body. Since then the two CoPs have continued to change and develop, both as they settle down in their early stages and as they continue to develop. In one of the interviews, an ESC member observed that they (the members) were not in a position to force the pace with what they wanted to do, but had to work gradually, evolving and changing people's attitudes as they develop over time.

EE-AW has noticed a more dramatic change as it develops — as its focus has shifted, there has been a change in the male/female ratio of members, as related by an EE-AW respondent:

*We've had quite a lot of group change from January a year ago to where we are now. People early on you know dropping in, saying "Is this for me? Mmm no." When we changed to more of a hardware focus, we shifted from an almost entirely female group to an almost entirely male group, and that's been fascinating ... and now that we're broadening, well this thing has gone on for, since last January, so it's been going on for a while but we've really picked up more men ... in about August when we started picking up, well we got our thoughts crystallised enough as to what we actually want to do. We'd gotten out of the really vague and extraordinarily part-time exploration of what we wanted to do to more concrete. We recruited some team members. We got more of a hardware focus and suddenly it's, you know, it's this whole male energy thing, and now that we have broadened back out to encompassing the whole thing, not just the hardware piece but the other couple of pieces, now we've got some female members joining back in.*

## Community Identity

This refers to a feeling of identity as opposed to the development of individual identity within the community. Both communities have given themselves names. This creates a feeling of identity among the members who see themselves as belonging to the group. In particular EE-AW was very careful with the selection of its name.

## Legitimation

The legitimation in each of the two communities under discussion appears to be directly related to interest and participation. A shared interest binds the members and, as one of the members expressed it, "We know who's in our tribe" — an example of the softer aspects of their knowledge. The different degrees of participation legitimate the membership of the core or extended family. There is an active core that is recognised by all members of the community as being "the core." This was demonstrated particularly well by one member of ESC's active core:

*I'm one of the people who crops up all the time, and it's because I've sort of become a centre, a point of contact for folks, and in some ways I've become a filter for the mail that goes out, although what people don't realise is that I don't actually filter anything. They see a lot, people forward me messages, and I ask them, "Can I send this to the group?" Every message I get I ask, "Can I send this to the group?" and they say, "Go ahead." So I forward their message to the group, and then someone else says, "Oh, well if I want to send something to the group maybe I have to go through her to do it." So I think there's been a perception from some people that I have to send out messages, and it's hard for me to know, and it really is hard for me to gauge, being one of the people who sends out a lot of messages, but I also receive a lot of messages. It's hard for me to tell how other people who maybe aren't doing the same job I am perceive it. I sort of suspect from the way that people contact me and want to meet with me when they're in the area or send me their opinions, I suspect they view me as a leader because of that, because I send out all this mail. They think, "Oh, she must be somebody."*

### Participation and Peripherality

Although ESC and EE-AW are more distributed than WWITMan, the peripherality is not seen as a physical peripherality as was the case in WWITMan. The peripherality is seen more in the degrees of participation, as demonstrated by the remark of one EE-AW respondent: "There are some people in — I guess you'd call it our extended family — who read all of the e-mail flying by who decide to drop in every once in a while for other specific things."

In both ESC and EE-AW, there were noticeable degrees of participation. EE-AW has 40 people on the mailing list and not all are heavily active. The members of the active core sometimes consciously decide what information should be restricted to the central core and what should be issued to the "extended family." This decision is made based on what they consider might be a boredom factor for the wider group. The ESC central core has also reached the point where it has had to distinguish between degrees of participation in the wider group, as related by an ESC core member:

*In the past week we've come up with this need to distinguish certain levels of participation within the 130 people. It's the strangest thing, this hadn't been an issue at all, but suddenly we started getting a lot of conversation going, two or three threads at a rate of two to three mailings per day, and for some people, this is too much. So we've just sent out a notice this morning inviting people to choose their level of participation, which we hadn't previously had to do, but we've now distinguished. There's a monthly newsletter as a level of participation, and there's a "get all the memos, be involved in all the discussion threads ongoing" as a level of participation, and I think the degree to which the community is split into those two categories, we don't know how it'll go yet but there's certainly members of each.*

## Distribution

As the two communities are distributed to such an extent, they suffer from the problems of distribution such as proximity and time zones. The time zone restricts the use of the phone and restricts the effectiveness of e-meetings as their members are scattered to too wide a degree. According to one EE-AW respondent:

If we hold meetings the time differences constrain somewhat when we can do some of our work. Like the group in Australia that we talk to, their day starts at 1:00 p.m. our time. And so we have to worry about those issues. We also have actually another person in Bristol, England, who's been working with us and so if we want to have him part of the conversation, either we have to do it early morning or he has to call in from at home.

ESC does not regard it as a problem, for most of the work is done in an active core. Participation by other members tends to be restricted to contribution to e-mail discussions. At other times people from the extended group may call in when they are in PA, in which case the distance problems are overcome.

Both groups do recognise the difficulties that a lack of proximity brings. They regard co-location as being with people they see every day. Although there are members of the active core in a neighboring town who can attend meetings and participate on a face-to-face basis, there is still a feeling that one and one-half miles hinders spontaneous ad hoc communication, which is where a lot of work is done.

As the two communities are so widely distributed and suffer the distance and time problems, it poses the question as to how they manage to survive without the range of media available to WWITMan. In the first place, ESC see the distribution as an opportunity not just a problem. An ESC respondent explained:

*It's giving them a chance to bubble up a grass roots movement: The more people you have, the faster it will bubble to the surface, so the problem is it bubbles slower with fewer people who are distributed so they, you know you're always trying to unlock the door and go how can we get this to bubble up a lot faster?*

### Active Cores

Although both ESC and EE-AW are distributed CoPs with members all over the world, they still have a similar structure to WWITMan as they both have cores. These active cores can be people who participate the most, for example, there might be a hard core of contributors to an e-mail list. This is the case with ESC, but there is also another type of active core, evident in both ESC and EE-AW. This type of core does more than just contribute more to e-mail lists. This type of core has also been noticed by Wenger and Snyder (2000) as being a group that does much to maintain a CoP in a distributed environment: "Typically, it has a core of participants whose passion for the topic energizes the community and who provide intellectual and social leadership" (p. 141).

In both communities participation is the key to membership of the active core. This tended also to be enabled by proximity — the active core tended to be in relatively close proximity, if not co-located. The proximity has not caused the core to emerge, but it has enabled it. Proximity enables more frequent ad hoc interaction, face-to-face meetings are easier, and, as a result, closer relationships can be developed. Stage Two showed that relationships are developed more easily through face-to-face interaction, and the ESC and EE-AW respondents fully agreed with this. Therefore, the close relationships tended to be within the cores, and it tends to be easier to be a member of an active core when there is more opportunity for face-to-face interaction. As a result, people who are just outside of the co-location will call in when they can to meet members of the core. Due to budgetary restrictions, they cannot travel as often as they would like, but if they have to travel for another purpose, they will make a visit to meet core members as one leg of the trip, or if they are in PA, they will make a point of calling in.

The relatively close proximity of the active core members also means that having meetings is easier. The ESC core has a regular monthly meeting, and EE-AW holds core meetings as necessary.

*Fanatic core plus occasional extended members. Well, we have set meetings, that are ... usually called by me if it's the group which is "Oh boy! We've got enough on our plates. Let's get together and talk about it again," 'cause there's a lot that flies by on e-mail and voice mail when we aren't meeting, but ... when there's enough that we have to talk about, I'll call a meeting first to get together.   (EE-AW Respondent)*

## Communication
*Media*

Neither ESC nor EE-AW has the benefit of the range of media that is available to WWITMan. As a result, they tend to rely on the telephone and voice mail, fax, e-mail, and the Internet. For wider distribution, e-mail and the Internet are the primary media. As with WWITMan, respondents expressed preferences for different media and expressed that their choice of media would depend on the task being undertaken and the context in which it was undertaken. MS NetMeeting and video conferencing were not regarded as being viable alternatives for two reasons:

(a)  the group is too widely dispersed to use NetMeeting or video conferencing satisfactorily; that is, they did not feel that they had sufficient people at a site to justify the use of such media; and
(b)  the set-up costs of NetMeeting and video conferencing are currently too high, that is, the systems are not easy enough to use.

## Social Issues
*Face-to-Face Interaction*

The respondents in EE-AW and ESC were in agreement that face-to-face interaction is important, or even essential, for the development of relationships or maintaining the momentum. As one ESC respondent explained:

You may communicate or exchange ideas, but in terms of actually forming some joint plans and goals, and sharing each others ideas so you get some synergy between, you know, really building on each other's ideas, I think that you really need the face-to-face for that, at least occasionally, then you can start doing some of it separately. But unless you get the few face-to-faces in between, I think you lose the focus or lose the intention.

In the case of ESC, the community did begin with a face-to-face event, the conference, and one of the respondents, at least, said she felt the benefit of having met people at least once, but, in general, the wider distribution of these communities makes it difficult to have face-to-face interaction. The benefits of face-to-face communication were therefore felt primarily within the active cores.

*You need a couple doses of more intense interaction. My experience is that we, spending that one day working on the slides, will probably hold together our team for much better and much longer than several one-hour meetings. (ESC Respondent)*

*Motivation/Interest/Desire*

The motivation/interest/desire was encountered in WWITMan as being something that helps maintain the community. In the case of ESC and EE-AW, this becomes even more important, or even critical. One ESC respondent expressed this issue as follows:

*I think this is one of those issues where people's souls and hearts believe in this issue, and so that's what's keeping people going, too. It's a real core belief, and almost a feeling of urgency that something has to be done and why doesn't everyone else see this, and therefore we need to make it more clear, I mean I'm quite a zealot I suppose.*

The shared passion, common interest, and motivation fuel the community and keep it going. They help maintain the momentum and carry the community over the difficulties of distributed working. The motivation, desire, and passion made up a strong recurrent theme with all the respondents from ESC and EE-AW. In fact, both CoPs came into being as a result of a common interest, and anybody who wishes to be a member will have the shared interest. If someone does not have the motivation, they will leave; therefore; the membership consists of motivated and committed people. One EE-AW respondent explained:

*In my experience, this has been the most harmonious group I've ever worked in which has been really wild and I think it's because, you know, nobody's assigned to do this so we found*

*each other and we have this common passion really for education,
and you know, if people decide they have a problem with what's
going on they dropped out.*

## Task Focus

As the two communities are widely distributed and communicate mainly via the World Wide Web and e-mail, it would perhaps be expected that having a task focus might not help as much as in the case of WWITMan. This was indeed true for the wider community, but the active core found that having a joint task did help in that it pulled the individual members together, gave them impetus, and improved participation:

*If there's a specific task, for example, in our communications
team, putting together the final version of a slide set required all
day. We got a sit here together and pound it out meeting, and
we can't do it over the phone 'cause we have to have these
visuals. (ESC Respondent)*

The fact that the effect of a task focus is not as widespread as in WWITMan is overcome by the very strong motivation, interest, and desire of the members.

## Regular, Frequent Interaction

This was not really a possibility for the wider groups in EE-AW and ESC. It was only possible within the active cores; however, one of the ESC members made an observation that emphasised the importance of regular, frequent interaction where possible:

*I have a staff that sits at three different sites, you know within
the south San Francisco Bay area, but one of the things that I've
noticed, ever since we instituted Monday morning conference
calls where we just talk — not even about anything work, what's
going on, what's the calendar, who's doing what — is that if we
don't have the conference call, if we have them people always
complain about having to be in the conference call, but if we
don't have them everybody suddenly starts feeling disconnected.
And it isn't the fact that we don't need to see each other real
time, we can even realise that someone is dozing on half the
conference call, sleeping or you know, they're not totally there,*

*but somehow just having that chance to know that you could interact really seems to keep the group together.*

## A Shared Artefact

*Uses*

As ESC and EE-AW were so different from WWITMan, it was interesting to note that shared artefacts still played an important role in the communities. As with WWITMan, there was one particular artefact that came to our attention and that played a variety of roles, both intended and unintended. In each CoP the artefact in question was a slide presentation (for example, PowerPoint). The slide presentations were intended as communication tools, but the community members also found that, like the planning document in WWITMan, they played other roles:

- they were stimulative (they were expressly designed to ignite something in the receiver);
- the slides also drove meetings (in the active core);
- during work on the slide presentations and during the use of them, issues arose from the process and were discussed;
- the slides caused people to reflect; and
- finally, the slide presentations were a catalyst for collaboration in that everyone took something away to work on.

In particular, the groups found that having the presentations helped maintain the momentum of the group — they added a task focus to the active core.

*Boundary Object*

As with WWITMan, the active core used the softer aspects of its knowledge to design an artefact as a communication tool. In this case, it was explicitly intended to cross the CoP boundaries to communicate with people outside the CoP. The slide set was e-mailed to some people, and it was placed on the intranet site so it was available to anybody within the organisation who might be interested. However, it was felt very strongly that although the presentation could stand by itself, it was preferable for it to be used in conjunction with real-time communication by a community member. It was primarily intended for community members to walk non-members through it, possibly guiding interpretations:

*... [it is] intended to be presented at talks rather than someone just reading it. Needs a presenter, someone from the community for guidance. (ESC Respondent)*

It was not likely that the community member would be a member of the active core. The presentation was being designed so that any member of the community could take it in order to "spread the word" as (s)he wished. Having a member of the community work with the presentation helps maintain the participation/reification balance.

This supports Wenger (1998) who makes the same point: "In order to take advantage of the complementarity of participating and reification, it is often a good idea to have artefacts and people travel together. Accompanied artefacts stand a better chance of bridging practices" (pp. 111-112).

*Representation Propagation*

In both of the communities the slide sets were propagated across different media and states. ESC's slide set was initially created as a first pass by a member in San Diego. He then e-mailed it to another active core member in Palo Alto who refined the slides and used them in a meeting. She got some feedback and refined them again. The creation of the slide presentation was providing a task focus and encouraging participation even though the members were not meeting. However, the members of the active core then decided it would be a good idea to have a standard set of slides that could perhaps accompany a video. Having this task focus enabled them to set aside a day where the core could get together and work on them. They expected to complete the task in two hours but, according to one ESC respondent, found that:

*By the end of the day we'd looked at every slide and decided what sort of things we wanted to be different, assigned somebody to do every one of them, and then people took the assignments to go somewhere. So we set some guidance, you know, this is what should be on the slide, this is what should be here, this is the information we need to gather and it needs to go here, and so the people who took the notes took that away and are working, or actually I think have done all their slides now.*

Having spent the whole day discussing the slides and the issues that arose from the slide set, they made some changes and different people took parts of the presentation away to work on. At the time of the case study, the slides were almost due to be finished, but it was not anticipated that the presentation would remain static. It was intended that it would continue to develop and that at a later stage it would have gone through further iterations.

EE-AW's active core also works on its slide shows. However, EE-AW also tends to include more people via e-mail from the wider family. Occasionally someone will want to participate so much he or she will make a journey to meet the active core:

> *We have a few people who occasionally throw in stuff, like we have the person in Atlanta who ... threw some stuff in and she decided to come out here by herself ... to be present for a presentation that we had with an external vendor that wants to work with us and then had some brief conversations with a number of us while she was out here. She came out on Friday and then went back some time during the weekend. And then Steve throws in stuff from time-to-time and other people do too, so the community is mostly quiescent, but if we touch on an area of their expertise and their knowledge then they'll, sort of it lights up a little bulb, and they send us some stuff and then they're quiescent again until we cycle around to that area again. Like displays is an issue that we've talked about a lot, or battery life or things like that. So as we touch on those issues, people who are following that technology throw in some comments about what the state of that technology is. (EE-AW Respondent)*

Although the participation in the creation of the slides is extended to some members of the wider "family" the bulk of the work is still undertaken in the active core. Individual members will work on a section, mail it to a central person who will collate all of them. Thus the slide set will undergo a number of iterations.

As in WWITMan, the members of both communities felt that they learned a variety of things from working together on creating the slide presentation; for example, they learned about communication and presentation skills from each other. Just as seen with WWITMan, the benefit is not simply from having an artefact, but it comes from the *process* of creating and using it.

# SUMMARY

These two CoPs (ESC and EE-AW) were different from WWITMan in that they were more distributed and the practice was extra to the everyday work. However, it was interesting to note that all three CoPs exhibited very similar characteristics, especially in respect of the active cores, how proximity and face-to-face interaction further enable participation, and the importance of a shared artefact. The process of creating and using the artefact was emphasised, and this was further illustrated by the fact the artefact was being designed to be used as a cross-boundary communication tool, not by itself but with a CoP member, thus attempting to retain a participation/reification balance.

## Chapter VIII

# Lessons Learned

*In this final chapter we summarise briefly our journey from KM to our CoP and draw out lessons that can be learned from the issues that have arisen and the insights we have gained. We also consider what practical implications they might have.*

## OUR JOURNEY SO FAR

In this book we have explored the inner workings of a distributed international Community of Practice (CoP). In order to reach that point we first explored the field of Knowledge Management (KM) to set the context for the study. In doing so, we noted that a large part of KM focuses on the capture-codify-store approach and did not consider less structured knowledge that does not lend itself so well to this cycle. We did, however, note that less structured knowledge is receiving increasingly more attention, but the predominant approach to its "management" appears to be to try to convert it to a form where it can be captured.

Feeling that perhaps a different approach was required, we used the terms "soft" and "hard" knowledge and explored the notion of soft knowledge in some detail, as the management of hard knowledge is already well established. This led to the conclusions that dealing with soft knowledge in isolation is problematic and that knowledge should be viewed as a duality, with all knowledge being both soft and hard, with the balance varying. Harder aspects of knowledge would be easy to capture and codify while the softer aspects would be difficult (or impossible) to capture.

Observing that CoPs are groups where the softer aspects of knowledge are created, nurtured, and sustained, we refined our definition of a CoP, noting that shared artefacts might be an avenue worthy of exploration and embarked on our study to explore how a CoP functions in a distributed international environment. In doing so, a number of issues came to the surface, and we gained some valuable insights. But what can we learn from them?

# WHAT HAVE WE LEARNED?
## The "Sharing" of the Softer Side of Knowledge

In Chapter III we explored the softer aspects of knowledge from three different viewpoints, Distributed Cognition and boundary objects, Common Ground, and CoPs. Examples of all three viewpoints were in evidence in the case study, suggesting that the answer as to how the softer side of knowledge may be shared lies somewhere between the three. However, the main viewpoint that was supported was Wenger's (1998) reification/participation duality.

One of the questions that was raised in Chapter IV regarded the form that the artefact might take; that is, what might be in such an artefact? In the study, we saw a strong example of an artefact and how it was used. We were also interested in the possible proportions of the reification/participation duality. It was suggested that in a distributed environment sustaining participation may be more difficult and therefore reification would play a greater role. In the study, we saw that this was not necessarily the case. Artefacts were strongly in evidence and were more important than the groups had realised — they played a more central role than was expected and played a variety of roles that the CoP members had not previously recognised. Participation was shown to still be important, perhaps as necessary as in co-located groups. This was shown by the efforts made by the members to facilitate participation by designing the artefact for participation, by arranging regular face-to-face visits, and even, to some degree, formalising participation by making collaboration with peers in other locations one of the group's stated objectives. The case study demonstrated how maintaining participation might be achieved. We will discuss the issues of participation and reification separately. We saw in Stage One of the case study that the two most important aspects had been shown to be:

(a)   the use of a shared artefact, and

(b)   the development of strong relationships.

We also saw in Figure 14 that these mapped onto Wenger's duality. In Stage Two and the other two CoPs, we gained further insights as to how this works and how it overcomes the problems of working in a distributed environment.

### Reification

The duality was very visible in the main case study and was seen initially in examples of shared artefacts such as stories, procedures, documents, and slide presentations. The artefact that provided the best example was the planning document. It was particularly noticeable that this artefact played many roles over and above those for which it was originally intended. A key role played by the planning document was its role as a catalyst. It had stimulative effects, stimulating debate, raising issues and problems for discussion and solution, and acting as a catalyst for collaboration. It acted as a catalyst (as opposed to a vehicle) for the group members to apply their domain and soft knowledge for planning, for reflection, for discussion of issues, and for solving problems. The shared document was not essential to their work, but it played more roles more importantly than they had previously realised. This particular planning document has undergone a further iteration and still plays a major role in their work.

The other roles played by the planning document led to the most interesting insight into the work of this community. It was not the literal meaning of the planning document that was important but rather its role as a facilitator of participation. Furthermore, people were designing it with this role in mind as opposed to its literal role. They were designing a planning document but were using the softer aspects of their knowledge of the community to design the artefact to do something else (which had little connection with planning). This also sheds further light on the question raised in Chapter III as to why the softer aspects of knowledge cannot simply be made hard. It was shown in Chapter III that the Distributed Cognition view of knowledge is predominantly hard and suggests that softer knowledge could be made hard. The Distributed Cognition interest, therefore, would be in the artefact itself, and it would look for knowledge embedded in the artefact. The example of the planning document shows the soft knowledge that is going on around the artefact in order to make it work. Wenger's (1998) view suggests that the participation aspect of the duality is essential and has been overlooked in Distributed Cognition. The findings of the main case study support Wenger's view very strongly: it is not the artefact (reification) per se that is important for the community. The members learn and develop knowledge with each other by the *process* (participation) of creating the artefact and working with it. The process provides a link between reification and participation — it provides a means of participation, and it is through this that members are able to grow their knowledge. This was exemplified in the CoP by the previous unsuccessful attempt to create a planning document. In the current situation, the development of the document was ongoing, allowing continuous participation in the process. The document thus provided a concrete example of the essentiality of considering both sides of the duality and demonstrates how members of a CoP can use documents to make the CoP work.

The planning document also demonstrates how the traditional KM view fails in only viewing the harder aspects of knowledge. The document is a planning document and looks like a planning document, but it is used as something else. When considering the document alone, full understanding of the document would not be possible; it would simply appear to be a planning document — the participation is also essential. If it was observed from a traditional KM viewpoint, a practitioner would consider it easy to reproduce, missing the point that both the reification and participation are necessary

*Participation*

Even though the CoPs were distributed, it was clear that participation was as important, if not more so than in co-located CoPs. The difficulty is in how to achieve and maintain an adequate level of participation. This was illustrated by the fact that the time distance was perceived to be more of a problem than physical distance, showing that interactivity was more important to the members than visibility. The interactivity contributes perhaps to a greater feeling of participation.

Sustaining the participation is an area where the social issues in a CoP play a major role. It was through the social issues that the distributed CoPs managed to maintain the participation element.

It was clear that the motivation to work as a CoP must be present. The members must have that desire, motivation, and will to work towards the common purpose, to learn, and to share. The motivation is one of the factors that sustains the group through the periods of e-communication; that is, it is easier to maintain participation in an electronic environment if the members are motivated to do so. If the motivation is internal, it is even stronger.

All members of the CoPs who were involved in the study emphasised the importance of developing strong working relationships and the importance of face-to-face communication in developing these relationships. Having shared interests (as well as the interest in the community) helped develop the strong relationships, as did regular frequent interaction. During the periods of e-communication, it was found in WWITMan that the relationship can decay somewhat, but when the relationship developed to a "comfort level" where the relationship reached more of a "friendship"' footing, then the participants were more ready to indulge in regular and frequent communication. The development of a strong relationship meant the members were more likely to maintain the interaction and participation when working in a distributed environment.

Relationships are extremely important to a CoP. Not only do they aid participation, but legitimation in a CoP comes about through the development of relationships. This helps in the development of identity, confidence, and trust in the CoP. This is shown in the "war stories": war stories were a part of all three of the CoPs in the case study, and Orr (1997) talked of how war stories "amuse, instruct and celebrate the tellers' *identity* as technicians" (emphasis added). When the war stories are taken out of context, the identity is lost and hearers cannot have the confidence in them that they would otherwise have had. This provides further support to the view expressed in Chapter III that softer knowledge cannot simply be made hard — each side of the duality has no meaning without the other.

In the earlier stages of the development of a relationship, when regular, frequent interaction is not so high on a person's agenda, having a task focus can help. If people have a project or a task on which they must collaborate, then they will have to be in more frequent contact. If the motivation is there, too, then the relationship can start to develop.

The task focus can also help when local issues get in the way of the joint work, that is, when people are so busy with local issues that they have little time for considering CoP members who are in other locations (Figure 1).

The planning document itself provided an excellent example of the need for participation. It became clear that the artefact in itself was not as important as the *process* of creating it and working with it. People could share in the experience. It provided participation. This experience and what is learned from it are something that cannot be captured, codified, or stored.

Having a task focus can help increase the interaction. It also provides an area for participation. As people work together, the relationship evolves and is hastened by face-to-face interaction where people grow existing relation-

*Figure 1: Overcoming Difficulties*

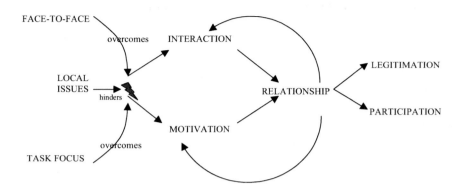

ships and try to extend the web of relationships to include new people. The task focus can help sustain the relationships through e-communication, and face-to-face interaction can boost the relationship, but fundamental to all of this is the motivation that must be present. The CoP members must have the desire for the CoP to function. This shows the importance of the human, or social, aspects (Figure 2), which must not be forgot.

*Figure 2: The Importance of the Human Aspect*

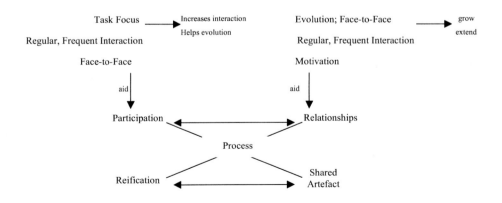

The importance of developing the strong relationships to the "comfort zone," that is, to nearer a friendship footing, shows that the inner workings of a CoP are about friendship. The case studies have shown that the capture-codify-store approach is not relevant to a CoP — what we can see at the heart of the CoP is friendship and trust. This has implications for KM, for it shows that it is no longer about managing *knowledge* as such, but about the human aspect of this process. It shows a need to put people back into the KM agenda, a turn to the social rather than the cognitive or, as Nardi and O'Day (1999) would express it, putting the "heart back into work." Humans are, after all, cleverer than computers — humans have the softer aspects of knowledge, too.

## Completing the Duality

Taking the diagram in Figure 2, we can add in soft and hard knowledge to complete the diagram as shown in Figure 3.

*Figure 3: Participation/Reification Mapped to Soft/Hard*

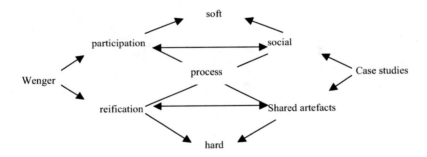

Figure 3 is intended to show that knowledge as a soft/hard duality (as described in Chapter III) maps onto the participation/reification duality. Reification, in the form of the shared artefact, needs the social aspects, too, in order to share the softer knowledge. The degree of softer knowledge depends on the degree of participation or social aspects. If the emphasis is on reification then there will be more of an emphasis on hard knowledge. The important part is to maintain a correct balance for the community.

## Are We Really Sharing the Softer Aspects of Knowledge?

The findings from the case study suggested that the softer aspects of knowledge are not so much shared as created, generated, and sustained. The shared artefact in the form of the planning document did not serve as a vehicle for sharing softer knowledge but as a focus for the application and creation of knowledge. It had, for example, Dave's planning expertise and Y2K experience embedded in it. This knowledge was not *shared* through the planning document, but in working with the planning document, other members had a focus to which they could apply their knowledge. This could also be seen in the different ways the artefact functioned as a catalyst to interaction and participation. It sparked discussion of problems and issues and the members of the community learned from their participation in this process. The planning document also highlighted opportunities for collaboration that provided further opportunity for learning and for generation of new knowledge. This perhaps indicates to us that the softer aspects really aren't *shared*. It is more the case that people learn from one another and are given the opportunity to develop their own softer knowledge. The parts that are shared are the harder aspects, and the softer aspects are developed through interaction, situated learning, and experience.

## Supporting CoPs

What we have seen in the study has supported Wenger's use of the participation/reification duality, as it mapped very well to the new environment. In doing so, we applied the theoretical duality and demonstrated in practical terms how a CoP would map this to its own practice. We have looked closely at the inner workings of an internationally distributed CoP, providing an insight into how such a CoP works. The study has shown that this is essentially about friendship and other social issues rather than specifically about knowledge. This raises the question as to how such things are managed. Clearly, they are not managed in the way KM as a discipline thinks of management. What is seen when we look inside the CoP is how central participants nurture these friendships. This is essentially a human activity at the level of practice, not at the level of the organisation or technology.

### Structure

It would appear that distributed CoPs in organisations are different structurally from the "virtual communities" that are found on the Internet, but such "virtual communities" are not the focus of this book. The focus of this book is on CoPs that exist in commercial organisations. The CoPs in the studies showed a major difference between the virtual Internet communities and the distributed organisational communities: one example of a virtual Internet community that was described as a CoP was a community that had formed round a MUD (Conkar & Kimble, 1997). The difference between such a CoP and those that were the focus of this book was that, in the case of Conkar and Kimble (1997), the medium was the practice; that is, the community existed only to use the medium. In the organisational CoPs, the practice of the CoPs is mediated by the medium. The case studies demonstrated a noticeable difference in structure between the two types. Whereas the Internet community was "virtual," that is, totally distributed, the organisational CoPs that were encountered were not virtual, but had "active cores" which, in the case studies, were also co-located. Although the initial aim was to explore the knowledge sharing in a distributed Community of Practice, the studies showed an interesting point regarding the structure and development of the groups. From this we can hypothesise that the development or evolution follows the lines:

1.  Communities of Practice seem to evolve, either from nothing or from an official grouping, as a result of the way the members work.
2.  The Community of Practice may then create a link with other people at other locations who do similar work. These people will possibly be members of other Communities of Practice.
3.  This situation can develop even further, in that the Community of Practice might create links with a group of others in another area, possibly abroad, who are involved in similar work and who also function as a Community of Practice. We are then left with a possible situation as shown in Figure 4.

*Figure 4: Community Structure and Evolution*

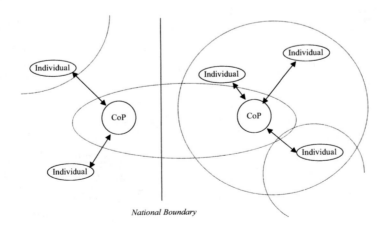

National Boundary

Figure 4 shows the links between a Community of Practice and other individuals who then may become members of the community but not be co-located. It also shows that members may be members of other Communities of Practice and that there may be links developing between Communities of Practice. To some extent this mirrors the networks of organisations developing in the globalised environment, as described by Castells (1996).

These stages of development show us some differences between a Community of Practice in the real world and one in a VE. It also shows that the structure of the CoP in the distributed environment is not totally distributed — there are co-located cores.

As the organisational CoPs had cores with links to other members (or other cores — see Figure 4), it extends the notion of peripherality. The peripherality in Lave and Wenger's (1991) groups was more a social periphery, as newcomers worked on the periphery and gradually moved to full participation. It was couched in terms of legitimacy of membership and practice. While this is undoubtedly true in the distributed group we saw in the study, physical and temporal peripherality were also factors that mediated the practice and the quality of interaction. In particular, physical and temporal peripherality provided further barriers to the functioning of the CoP in that they provided barriers to access; for example, the Japanese member did not have as much access to other CoP members as she would have liked. These barriers were tackled by the big effort that was put into sustaining the CoP — this involved a lot of work in designing the boundary object (the planning document), having meetings about meetings, and arranging the technology.

A further key difference is in the terms of identity. Identity is a central issue for the CoP as described by Wenger (1998) and is developed through participation and engagement. It is more than merely thinking in terms of being a member of a community (as, perhaps, is more the case in the fully virtual community); rather, it is constant negotiation of "ways of being" in the context of that CoP. Therefore, it can be seen how important it is that the members of the CoP work so hard to maintain participation, even going to the lengths of working hard to arrange the face-to-face visits.

*Practical Issues*

The members of WWITMan were experiencing a number of problems that affect teams, groups, and communities that are operating in a distributed international environment. These problems were the usual ones of differences in culture and language, time and distance. They also encountered the problem of relationship decay. As they met, they developed a relationship, but during the period of e-communication, they found they experienced a degree of relationship decay. Organisations supporting distributed CoPs would need to consider the following points, which are practical applications of the participation/reification duality as expressed in the terms of social factors and shared artefacts:

1.    First, the participants must be motivated and have the desire to make the community work. In addition to this, it is very helpful if the CoP exists in an organisational culture that *encourages* sharing, collaboration, and communication. If the culture is wrong, the CoP will struggle.

2.    Strong relationships are essential, but it is important to let them develop and evolve. Working *too* hard to make relationships will probably fail.

3.    An initial or early face-to-face meeting will probably give the relationship development a good start. In some cases, organisations have run an initial conference from which CoPs have developed. The first face-to-face does not need to be as grand as a conference, however. Simply getting like-minded and interested people together for a seminar or workshop would be a good start. Initially, there might need to be some structure to the discussions. It might also be necessary to continue with some structure, but the importance of the relationship development underlines the need for some unstructured social contact, too.

4.    Some occasional face-to-face meetings (if possible) will keep boosting the developing relationships and will help them move further, faster to enable the participants to reach the "comfort zone" more quickly.

5.    Regular, frequent interaction is important. This will come more easily once the comfort zone has been reached, and in the early stages will be encouraged by having a task focus.

6.    Having a task focus keeps people interacting, increases the frequency of communication, and provides the participants with something in common.

7.    It is important to facilitate the community's existence by the provision of ICT, but the following points regarding ICT are important considerations:

•    Asynchronous and real-time communication should both be supported.

•    A shared space for sharing artefacts during remote meetings or collaboration is very important.

•    An intranet can help with the "harder" side; that is, it can provide shared storage of documents, images, and other files that are used by the CoP. It can also provide discussion forums and message boards.

•    The media should be simple to use (that is, the medium should not obstruct the message). This includes video conferencing, which does not necessarily have to be a full videoconference suite. Cheap cameras with lower quality images can provide context and be perfectly adequate. They are also easier and cheaper to use than a videoconference suite, which also has to be booked in advance.

- There should be some functionality to help community members be aware of the presence of others so that remote ad hoc communication can be made easier.
- There should be a choice of media so that people can use the medium they feel most suitable for the task in context — this will be the medium they feel is most appropriate for the task, depending upon the sensitivity or the urgency of the message. Choice will also be affected by context; for example, the medium with which the user feels most comfortable, the time of day, the likelihood of the communication partner being available, and the number of intended recipients.

Software to support communities is now appearing on the market; however, it is important that, when appraising any community software, the principle behind the software should be "connection not collection."

The communities in the case study all found it helpful to have a shared artefact. This can be a range of things: documents, stories, procedures, slide shows, etc. The nature of the artefact will depend to some extent on the practice of the community. The most common ones seen during the case study were a planning document and slide shows, and all were used for communicating across boundaries. It is worth remembering that the shared artefacts were most effective in crossing boundaries when a community member was involved. The *process* of creating and working with the shared artefact is most important — more so than the artefact itself.

- Working on the artefact together can be part of the group's task focus.
- Working with it helps foster regular frequent communication.
- The process of working together on an artefact may stimulate collaboration in other areas.

If the CoP is distributed, it is also important to use the softer aspects of the members' knowledge, to recognise that the artefact will function as a boundary object and to bear this in mind during the design of the artefact. The members of WWITMan considered themselves to be part of a single CoP spread over a distance. The boundaries that the planning document had to cross were not, therefore, CoP boundaries but physical and cultural ones. It crossed boundaries *within* the CoP. However, participation, in the form of the relationships that had been developed, assisted the members in designing the document to function as a boundary object. This also exemplifies the softer aspects of knowledge — it is what the members know about the document and about the members in the other core that they use in designing the document to ensure participation. These are the softer aspects of knowledge.

The shared artefacts in the case studies were particularly interesting in that they played different roles from those for which they were primarily intended. In particular, they acted as catalysts for collaboration. This in turn encourages more interaction and participation and helps the relationship develop further.

## The Last Word

As KM practitioners have gradually come to recognise the importance of unstructured knowledge, CoPs have begun to receive attention, and there have been a number of attempts to "implement" them. Some practitioners have tried to formalise them — in some cases, organisations have been known to allocate members to a group and inform them that they are a Community of Practice with a specific brief. Further difficulties are encountered if the CoP has to operate in a distributed environment. These difficulties are further exacerbated when the distribution crosses national boundaries. However, as CoPs become increasingly recognised as important, and business becomes more global, the need for international CoPs will grow. The insights gained from WWITMan, ESC, and EE-AW should help practitioners become aware of the problems and issues involved, but more importantly, they show that practitioners need to change their views of the organisation when planning KM initiatives:

**Redundancy of Knowledge:** When planning outsourcing and downsizing, redundancy of knowledge was regarded as negative. The error of this view was seen when important knowledge was lost as people left the organisation. In a CoP, members learn from each other, and there is some sort of knowledge redundancy "built in" to the social distribution of knowledge. This helps maintain the knowledge base in the CoP as members leave and provides a buffer against the problem of knowledge loss. This was seen in WWIT when the members deliberately placed people in their teams together to learn from each other and when the Lotus Notes "guru" was going on holiday.

**A Different View of the Organisation:** The time spent with WWITMan showed us the importance of CoP members "going the extra mile" for each other. This refers to the social relations, the development of member identity, trust and confidence. It could be seen in the way the CoP members worked hard to sustain the community. They organised trips and documents in order to organise and develop their social relations. Practitioners therefore need to explore where the social relationships are and how they can be supported rather than looking at the organisation in terms of where the information is and how it flows (which would be the "traditional" approach). This also applies to document design. It is important to recognise the importance of what goes on around a document during its design and use. When analyzing documents in use, it is not only the document itself that is important, but also the softer aspects of the knowledge that has been applied to it. Widening this view further, it can also be applied to the company itself. The company can be seen as an adaptive and self-generative organisation. The KM practitioner, therefore, when planning a KM initiative needs to look beyond the organisation as stores and flows of information (as would be the case in a capture/codify/store approach) and explore the social networks that exist in the organisation. (S)he needs to concentrate on assisting groups and communities in developing and sustaining these strong relationships if the whole knowledge is to be created, nurtured, and retained.

The importance of social issues, shared artefacts, and the process of working with shared artefacts gives us a practical example of the importance of Wenger's (1998) participation/reification duality. We can also see that it is possibly not exactly a *sharing* of the softer aspects of knowledge as much as a nurturing and creating. It is clear that the CoP members work hard at the management of softer knowledge — of prime importance is the human work, as opposed to the capturing, codifying, and storage ability of computers. The importance of computers is their support of the human work. The importance of the softer aspects, the participation, suggests that the traditional KM view has been too restricted and that the rush to implement technological solutions follows a false trail without consideration of the softer aspects of knowledge.

# References

Aadne, J. H., Krogh, G. von & Roos, J. (1996). Representationism: The traditional approach to cooperative strategies. In G. von Krogh & J. Roos (Eds.), *Managing Knowledge. Perspectives on Cooperation and Competition* (pp. 9-31). Thousand Oaks, CA: Sage.

Adler, A. & Henderson, A. (1994). A room of our own: Experiences from a direct office share. In B. Abelson, S. Dumais, & J. Olson (Eds.), *Proceedings of CHI 94* (pp. 138-144).

Alavi, M. & Leidner, D. E. (1997). *Knowledge management systems: Emerging views and practices from the field* (Tech. Rep. No. 97/97/ TM). Cedex, France: INSEAD.

Allee, V. (1997). *The Knowledge Evolution. Expanding Organizational Intelligence.* Burlington, MA: Butterworth-Heinemann.

Argyle, K. & Shields, R. (1996). Is there a body in the net? In R. Shields (Ed.), *Cultures of Internet* (pp. 58-69). Thousand Oaks, CA: Sage.

Barnatt, C. (1997). *Challenging Reality.* Chichester, UK: John Wiley & Sons.

Berg, M. (1997). Formal tools and medical practices: Getting computer-based decision techniques to work. In G.C. Bowker, S. Leigh Star, W. Turner, & L. Gasser (Eds.), *Social Science, Technical Systems and Cooperative Work* (pp. 301-330). New York: John Wiley & Sons.

Breslow, H. (1997). Civil society, political economy, and the Internet. In S.G. Jones (Ed.), *Virtual Culture* (pp. 236-257).

Bromberg, H. (1996). Are MUDs communities? Identity, belonging and consciousness in virtual worlds. In R. Shields (Ed.), *Cultures of Internet* (pp. 1-10). Thousand Oaks, CA: Sage.

Bruner, J. (1990). *Acts of Meaning.* Cambridge, MA: Harvard University Press.

Buckingham Shum, S. (1998). Negotiating the construction of organizational memories. In U.M. Borghoff & R. Pareschi (Eds.), *Information Technology for Knowledge Management* (pp. 55-78). Berlin: Springer. [Reprinted (1997). Negotiating the construction and reconstruction of organizational memories. *Journal of Universal Computer Science,* 3(8): 899-928.]

Button, G. & Sharrock, W. (1994). Occasional practices in the work of software engineers. In M. Jirotka & J.A. Goguen (Eds.), *Requirements Engineering. Social and Technical Issues* (pp. 217-240). New York: Academic Press.

Carroll, J., Laughton, S. & Rosson, M. (1996). Network communities. In M. Tauber (Ed.), *Common Ground. Proceedings of CHI 96* (pp. 357-358). Vancouver, Canada.

Castells, M. (1996). *The Rise of the Network Society.* Malden, MA: Blackwell.

Chao, G. T. (1997). Organizational socialization in multinational corporations: The role of implicit learning. In C.L. Cooper & S. E. Jackson (Eds.), *Creating Tomorrow's Organizations* (pp. 43-57). New York: John Wiley & Sons.

Chen, L. L-J. & Gaines, B. R. (1998). Modeling and supporting virtual cooperative interaction through the World Wide Web. In S. Rafaeli, M. McLaughlin, & F. Sudweeks (Eds.), *Network and Netplay* (pp. 221-242). Cambridge, MA: MIT Press.

Cicourel, A. (1990). The integration of distributed knowledge in collaborative medical diagnosis. In J. Galegher, R.E. Kraut, & C. Egido (Eds.), *Intellectual Teamwork. Social and Technological Foundations of Cooperative Work* (pp. 221-242). Hillsdale, NJ: Lawrence Erlbaum Associates.

Clark, H. (1996). *Using Language.* Cambridge, MA: Cambridge University Press.

Cohen, D. (1998). Toward a knowledge context: Report on the first annual U.C. Berkeley forum on knowledge and the firm. *California Management Review,* 40(3): 22-39.

Cole, M. (1996). *Cultural Psychology*. Cambridge, MA: Belknap Press.

Conceição, P., Gibson, D. & Shariq, S. (1997). Towards a research agenda for knowledge policies and management. *Journal of Knowledge Management,* 1(2): 129-141.

Conkar, T. (1999). *'CLIMATE' for multiview*. Doctoral Dissertation. University of York.

Conkar, T. M. & Kimble, C. (1997*). CLIMATE - Developing a framework for the requirements analysis of virtual environments*. (Technical Report No. YCS 291). University of York, Department of Computer Science.

Conklin, E. J. (1996). *Designing organizational memory: Preserving intellectual assets in a knowledge economy.* Retrieved on March 27, 1997 at: http:www.zilker.net/business/info/pubs/desom/body.htm.

Cook, S. D. N. & Seely Brown, J. (1999). Bridging epistemologies: The generative dance between organizational knowledge and organizational knowing. *Organization Science,* 10(4): 381-400.

Danet, B., Ruedenberg, L. & Rosenbaum-Tamari, Y. (1998). Hmmm...Where's that smoke coming from? In S. Rafaeli, M. McLaughlin, & F. Sudweeks (Eds.), *Network and Netplay* (pp. 41-76). Cambridge, MA: MIT Press.

Davenport, T. & Klahr, P. (1998). Managing customer support knowledge. *California Management Review,* 40(3): 195-208.

Davenport, T. & Prusak, L. (1998). *Working Knowledge. How Organizations Manage What They Know*. Cambridge, MA: Harvard Business School Press.

Dawley, D. D. & Anthony, W. P. (1998). *Email use and information overload at a state agency: A qualitative case study.* Paper presented at the Conference on Management and Organizational Cognition: Implications for Entrepreneurship, Decision Making and Knowledge Management, May, Stern School of Business, New York University.

Deans, P.C., Karwan, K., Goslar, M., Ricks, D. & Toyne, B. (1991). Identification of key international information systems issues in US-based multinational corporations. *Journal of Management Information Systems,* 7(4): 27-49.

Dearden, A. & Wright, P.C. (1997). Experiences using situated and non-situated techniques for studying work in context. In S. Howard & G. Lindgaard (Eds.), *INTERACT '97. IFIP TC13. International Confer-*

*ence on Human-Computer Interaction* (pp. 429-436). London: Chapman Hall.

Drucker, P. (1992). The new society of organizations. *Harvard Business Review,* (September/October): 95-104.

Dyrkton, J. (1996). Cool runnings: The contradictions of cyberreality in Jamaica. In R. Shields (Ed.), *Cultures of Internet* (pp. 49-57). Thousand Oaks, CA: Sage.

Fahey, L. & Prusak, L. (1998). The eleven deadliest sins of knowledge management. *California Management Review,* 40(3): 265-276.

Fernback, J. (1997). The individual within the collective: Virtual ideology and the realization of collective principles. In S.G. Jones (Ed.), *Virtual Culture* (pp. 36-54). Thousand Oaks, CA: Sage.

Fields, R.E., Wright, P.C., Marti, P. & Palmonari, M. (1998). Air traffic control as a distributed cognitive system: A study of external representations. *Proceedings of ECCE-9, the 9th European Conference on Cognitive Ergonomics* (pp. 85-90). Roquencourt: EACE Press.

Finerty, T. (1997). Integrating learning and knowledge infrastructure. *Journal of Knowledge Management,* 1(2): 98-104.

Fish, R., Kraut, R., Root, R. & Rice, R. (1992). Evaluating video as a technology for informal communication. In P. Bauersfeld, J. Bennett, & G. Lynch (Eds.), *CHI 92 Conference Proceedings* (pp. 37-48). Monterey, CA.

Geus, A. de (1997). The living company. *Harvard Business Review,* (March/April): 51-59.

Gill, J. & Johnson, P. (1997). *Research Methods for Managers.* London: PCP.

Glazer, R. (1998). Measuring the knower: Towards a theory of knowledge equity. *California Management Review,* 40(3): 175-194.

Goguen, J. A. (1997). Toward a social, ethical theory of information. In G.C. Bowker, S. L. Star, W. Turner, & L. Gasser (Eds.), *Social Science, Technical Systems and Cooperative Work: Beyond the Great Divide* (pp. 27-56). Hillsdale, NJ: Lawrence Erlbaum.

Goldstein, D. (1993). Computer-based data and organizational learning: The importance of managers' stories. *Journal of Organizational Computing,* 3(4): 417-442.

Halverson, C. (1994). *Distributed cognition as a theoretical framework for HCI: Don't throw the baby out with the bathwater — the importance of the cursor in air traffic control* (Tech Rep no. 9403).

University of California, San Diego, CA.  Department of Cognitive Science.

Hargadon, A. B. (1998). Firms as knowledge brokers: Lessons in pursuing continuous innovation. *California Management Review,* 40(3): 209-227.

Hicks, M., Wright, P. & Pocock, S. (1998). A distributed cognitive perspective on civil aircraft failure management system design. In D. Harris (Ed.), *Engineering Psychology and Cognitive Ergonomics* (pp. 101-110). Aldershot, UK: Ashgate.

Hinds, P. & Kiesler, A. (1995, July/August). Communication across boundaries: Work structure, and use of communication technologies in a large organization. *Organization Science,* 6(4): 373-393.

Hollan, J. & Stornetta, S. (1992). Beyond being there. In P. Bauersfeld, J. Bennett, & G. Lynch (Eds.), *CHI'92 Conference Proceedings* (pp. 119-125). Monterey, CA.

Holtshouse, D. (1998). Knowledge research issues. *California Management Review,* 40(3): 277-280.

House, N. A. van, Butler, M. H. &  Schiff, L. R. (1998).  Cooperative knowledge work and practices of trust: Sharing environmental planning data sets.  In *CSCW '98, Proceedings of the ACM 1998 Conference on Computer-Supported Cooperative Work* (pp. 335-343).

Huang, K. (1997). Capitalizing collective knowledge for winning execution and teamwork. *Journal of Knowledge Management,* 1(2): 149-156.

Hutchins, E. (1990). The technology of team navigation. In J.R. Galegher, R.E. Kraut, & L. Egido (Eds.), *Intellectual Teamwork: Social and Technological Foundations of Co-Operative Work* (pp. 191-220).  Hillsdale, NJ: Lawrence Erlbaum.

Hutchins, E. (1995a). *Cognition in the Wild.* Cambridge, MA: MIT Press.

Hutchins, E. (1995b).  How a cockpit remembers its speeds. *Cognitive Science,* 19: 265-288.

Hutchins, E. & Klausen, T. (1991). Distributed cognition in an airline cockpit. In Y. Engeström & D. Middleton (Eds.), *Cognition and Communication at Work.* Cambridge, UK: Cambridge University Press.

Interrogate the Internet. (1996). Contradictions in cyberspace: Collective response. In R. Shields (Ed.), *Cultures of Internet* (pp. 125-132). Thousand Oaks, CA: Sage.

Ives, B. & Jarvenpaa, S. L. (1992). Global information technology: Some lessons from practice. *International Information Systems,* 1(3): 1-16.

Jones, S. (1998).  Media use in an electronic community. In S. Rafaeli, M. McLaughlin, & F. Sudweeks (Eds.), *Network and Netplay* (pp. 77-94). Cambridge, MA: MIT Press.

Jones, S. G. (1997). The Internet and its social landscape. In S.G. Jones (Ed.), *Virtual Culture* (pp. 7-35). Thousand Oaks, CA: Sage

Junnarkar, B. & Brown, C. (1997).  Re-assessing the enabling role of information technology in KM. *Journal of Knowledge Management,* 1(2): 142-148.

Kaniclides, A. (1997). *Critical factors in executive information systems implementation.* Doctoral Dissertation. University of York.

Karimi, J. & Konsynski, B. R. (1991). Globalization and information management strategies. *Journal of Management Information Systems,* 7(4): 7-25.

Kidd, A. (1994). The marks are on the knowledge worker. In B. Adelson, S. Dumais, & J. Olson (Eds.), *Proceedings of CHI '94* (pp. 186-191).

Kogut, B. & Zander, V. (1992).  Knowledge of the firm, combinative capabilities and the replication of technology. *Organization Science,* 3(3): 383-397.

Kristoffersen, S. & Rodden, T. (1996). Walking the walk is doing the work — Flexible interaction management in video-supported cooperative work. In M. Tauber  (Ed.), *Proceedings of CHI '96* (pp. 171-172).

Krogh, G. von (1998). Care in knowledge creation. *California Management Review,* 40(3): 133-153.

Krogh, G. von & Roos, J. (1995).  A perspective on knowledge, competence and strategy. *Personnel Review,* 24(3): 56-76.

Krogh, G. von  & Roos, J. (1996). Introduction. In *Managing Knowledge* (pp. 1-8). London: Sage.

Krogh, G. von, Roos, J. & Slocum, K. (1996). An essay on corporate epistemology.  In G. von Krogh & J. Roos (Eds.), *Managing Knowledge. Perspectives on Cooperation and Competition* (pp. 157-183). Thousand Oaks, CA: Sage.

Laudon, K. C. & Laudon, J.P. (1995). *Essentials of Management Information Systems.* Prentice Hall.

Lave, J. (1991). Situating learning in communities of practice. In L.B. Resnick, J. Levine, & S. D.Teasley (Eds.), *Socially Shared Cognition* (pp. 63-82). Washington, DC: American Psychology Association.

Lave, J. & Wenger, E. (1991). *Situated Learning. Legitimate Peripheral Participation.* Cambridge, UK: Cambridge University Press.

Leonard, D. & Sensiper, S. (1998). The role of tacit knowledge in group innovation. *California Management Review,* 40(3): 12-132.

Li, F. & Williams, H. (1999). Organizational innovations through information systems: Some lessons from geography. In L. Brooks & C. Kimble (Eds.), *Information Systems – The Next Generation. Proceedings of the 4th UKAIS Conference* (pp. 471-485). York, UK.

Lindstaedt, S. (1996). Towards organizational learning: Growing group memories in the workplace. In M. Tauber (Ed.), *Proceedings of CHI '96* (pp. 53-54).

Lipnack, J. & Stamps, J. (1997). *Virtual Teams.* New York: John Wiley & Sons.

Mackay, W., Malone, T., Crowston, K., Rao, R., Rosenblitt, D. & Card, S. (1989). How do experienced information lens users use rules? In K. Bice & C. Lewis (Eds.), *CHI '89 Proceedings* (pp. 211-216).

Mambrey, P. & Robinson, M. (1997). Understanding the role of documents in a hierarchical flow of work. In S.C. Hayne & W. Prinz (Eds.), *Group '97 Proceedings of the International ACM SIGGROUP Conference on Supporting Group Work* (pp. 119-127). Phoenix, AZ.

Manville, B. & Foote, N. (1996). Harvest your workers' knowledge. *Datamation,* (July 6).

Martin, D., Bowers, J. & Wastell, D. (1997). The interactional affordances of technology: An ethnography of human-computer interaction in an ambulance control centre. In B. O-Connaill, H. Thimbelby, & P. Thomas (Eds.), *People and Computers XII: Proceedings of HCI '97* (pp. 263-280). New York: Springer-Verlag.

McLaughlin, M. L., Osborne, K. K. & Ellison, N. B (1997). Virtual community in a telepresence environment. In S.G. Jones (Ed.), *Virtual Culture* (pp. 146-168). Thousand Oaks, CA: Sage.

Mitra, A. (1997). Virtual commonality: Looking for India on the Internet. In S.G. Jones (Ed.), *Virtual Culture* (pp. 55-79). Thousand Oaks, CA: Sage.

Nardi, B. (1993). *A Small Matter of Programming.* Cambridge, MA: MIT Press.

Nardi, B. & Miller, J. (1991). Twinkling lights and nested loops: Distributed problem solving and spreadsheet development. *International Journal of Man-Machine Studies,* 34: 161-184.

Nardi, B. & O'Day, V. L. (1999). *Information Ecologies: Using Technology with Heart.* Cambridge, MA: MIT Press.

Ngwenyama, O. K. & Lee, A. S. (1997). Communication richness in electronic mail: Critical social theory and the contextuality of meaning. *MIS Quarterly,* 21(2): 145-167.

Nonaka, I. (1991). The knowledge creating company. *Harvard Businesses Review,* (November/December): 96-104.

Nonaka, I. & Konno, N. (1998). The concept of "Ba": Building a foundation for knowledge creation. *California Management Review,* 40(3): 40-54.

O'Dell, C. & Jackson Grayson, C. (1998). If we only knew what we know: Identification and transfer of internal best practices. *California Management Review,* 40(3): 154-174.

O'Dell, C. & Jackson Grayson, C. (1998). *If We Only Knew What We Know: Identification and Transfer of Internal Best Practices.* Houston, TX: American Productivity and Quality Center.

Orr, J. (1990). Sharing knowledge, celebrating identity: War stories and community memory in a service culture. In D.S. Middleton & D. Edwards (Eds.), *Collective Remembering: Memory in Society* (pp. 169-189). Beverly Hills, CA: Sage.

Orr, J. (1997). *Talking about Machines: An Ethnography of a Modern Job.* Ithaca, NY: Cornell University Press.

Pearce, J. L. (1997). The political and economic context of organizational behavior. In C.L. Cooper & S. E. Jackson (Eds.), *Creating Tomorrow's Organizations* (pp. 29-41). New York: John Wiley & Sons.

Polanyi, M. (1967). *The Tacit Dimension.* London: Routledge and Kegan Paul.

Poltrock, S. & Engelbeck, G. (1997). Requirements for a virtual collocation environment. In S. Hayne & W. Prinz (Eds.), *Group '97 Proceedings of the International ACM SIG Group Conference on Supporting Group Work "The Integration Challenge"* (pp. 61-70).

Porter, D. (1997). Introduction. In D. Porter (Ed.), *Internet Culture* (XI-XVIII). London: Routledge.

Porter, M. E. (1985). *Competitive Advantage: Creating and Sustaining Superior Performance.* The Free Press.

Powell, W. (1998). Learning from collaboration: Knowledge and networks in the biology and pharmaceutical industries. *California Management Review,* 40(3): 228-240.

Rafaeli, S. & Sudweeks, F. (1998). Interactivity on the Nets. In S. Rafaeli, M. McLaughlin, & F. Sudweeks (Eds.), *Network and Netplay* (pp. 173-189). Cambridge, MA: MIT Press.

Rice, R.E. (1987). Computer-mediated communication and organizational innovation. *Journal of Communication,* 37(4): 65-94.

Rivera, K., Cooke, N. & Bauhs, J. (1996). The effects of emotional icons on remote communication. In M. Tauber (Ed.), *Proceedings of CHI '96* (pp. 99-100).

Robinson, M. (1991). Electronic mail and postmodern organization. In M. Nurminen & G. Weir (Eds.), *Human Jobs and Computer Interfaces.* New York: Elsevier Science Publishers.

Robinson, M. (1997). As real as it gets... Taming models and reconstructing procedures. In G. C. Bowker, S. L. Star, W. Turner, & L. Gasser (Eds.), *Social Science, Technical Systems, and Cooperative Work: Beyond the Great Divide* (pp. 257-274). Hillsdale, NJ: Lawrence Erlbaum Associates.

Robson, W. (1994). *Strategic Management and Information Systems: An Integrated Approach.* Pitman Publishing.

Rogers, Y. & Ellis, J. (1994). Distributed cognition: An alternative framework for analyzing and explaining collaborative working. *Journal of Information Technology,* 9(2): 119-128.

Roschelle, J. (1996). Designing for cognitive communication: Epistemic fidelity or mediating collaborative inquiry. In D. Day & D. Kovacs (Eds.), *Computers, Communication and Mental Models* (pp. 15-27). London: Taylor and Francis.

Rudy, I. A. (1996). A critical review of research on electronic mail. *European Journal of Information Systems,* 4: 198-213.

Rulke, D., Zaheer, S. & Anderson, M. (1998). *Transactive knowledge and performance in the retail food industry.* Paper presented at the Stern School of Business Conference on Managerial and Organizational Cognition, New York.

Sachs, P. (1995). Transforming work: Collaboration, learning and design. *Communications of the ACM,* 38(9): 36-45.

Sandusky, R. J. (1997). Infrastructure management as cooperative work: Implications for systems design. In S.C. Hayne & W. Prinz (Eds.), *Proceedings of the International ACM SIG Group Conferences on Supporting Group Work* (pp. 91-100).

Seely Brown, J. & Duguid, P. (1991). Organizational learning and communities of practice. *Organization Science,* 2(1): 40-57.

Seely Brown, J. & Duguid, P. (1996, July/August). Universities in the digital age. *Change: The Magazine of Higher Learning,* 28(4): 10-19.

Seely Brown, J. & Duguid, P. (1998). Organizing knowledge. *California Management Review,* 40(3): 90-111.

Seely Brown, J. & Solomon Gray, E. (1998). The people are the company. *Fast Company.* [On-line]. Available at: http://www.fastcompany.com/on-line/01/people.html. September 9, 1998.

Sellen, A. (1992). Speech patterns in video-mediated conversations. In P. Bauersfeld, J. Bennett, & G. Lynch (Eds.), *CHI92 Conference Proceedings* (pp. 49-59). Monterey, CA.

Shade, L. R. (1996). Is there free speech on the Net? Censorship in the global information infrastructure. In R. Shields (Ed.), *Cultures of Internet* (pp. 11-32). Thousand Oaks, CA: Sage.

Shields, R. (1996). Introduction: Virtual spaces, real histories and living bodies. In R. Shields (Ed.), *Cultures of Internet* (pp. 1-10). Thousand Oaks, CA: Sage.

Star, S. L. (1989). The structure of ill-structured solutions: Boundary objects and heterogeneous distributed problem solving. *Distributed Artificial Intelligence,* 2: 37-54.

Star, S. L. (1995). The politics of formal representations: Wizards, gurus, and organizational complexity. In S.L. Star (Ed.), *Ecologies of Knowledge. Work and Politics in Science and Technology* (pp. 88-118). Albany NY: SUNY Press.

Star, S. L. & Griesemer, J. R. (1989). Institutional ecology, "translations" and boundary objects: Amateurs and professionals in Berkeley's Museum of Vertebrate Zoology, 1907-39. *Social Studies of Science,* 19: 387-420.

Stewart, T. A. (1996). The invisible key to success. *Fortune.* [On-line]. Retrieved on April 4, 1996 at: http://pathfinder.com/@@V3AagAUAZyq OEYKS/fortune/magazine/1996.960805/edg.html.

Sumner, T., Domingue, J. & Zdrahal, Z. (1998). *Enriching representations of work to support organizational learning* (Tech Rep No KMI-TR-60). Knowledge Media Institute, The Open University.

Sveiby, K. (n.d.). *What is Knowledge Management?* Retrieved on October 10, 1996 at: http://www2.eis.net.au/~karlerik/KnowledgeManagement. html~CaptureStore Tacit. Revised version retrieved on January 21, 2003 at: http://www.sveiby.com/articles/KnowledgeManagement.html.

Symon, G., Long, K. & Ellis, J. (1996). The coordination of work activities: Cooperation and conflict in a hospital context. *CSCW,* 5: 1-31.

Tang, J. & Rua, M. (1994). Montage: Providing teleproximity for distributed groups. In B. Adelson, S. Dumais, & J. Olson (Eds.), *Proceedings of CHI 94* (pp. 37-43).

Teece, D. J. (1998). Research directions for knowledge management. *California Management Review,* 40(3): 289-292.

Thu Nguyen, D. & Alexander, J. (1996). The coming of cyberspacetime and the end of the polity. In R. Shields (Ed.), *Cultures of Internet* (pp. 99-124). Thousand Oaks, CA: Sage.

Vasconcelos, J. (1999). *The creation of collaborative knowledge towards an organizational memory: An ontological approach.* Qualifying Dissertation, University of York, UK, Department of Computer Science.

Vicari, S., Krogh, G. von, Roos, J. & Mahnke, V. (1996). Knowledge creation through cooperative experimentation: In G. von Krogh & J. Roos (Eds.), *Managing Knowledge. Perspectives on Cooperation and Competition* (pp. 184-202). Thousand Oaks, CA: Sage.

Voiskounsky, A. E. (1998). Telelogue speech. In S. Rafaeli, M. McLaughlin, & F. Sudweeks (Eds.), *Network and Netplay* (pp. 27-40). Cambridge, MA: MIT Press.

Walsh, J. P. (1995). Managerial and organizational cognition: Notes from a trip down memory lane. *Organization Science,* 6(3): 280-321.

Watson, N. (1997). Why we argue about virtual community: A case study of the Phish.Net Fan Community. In S. G. Jones (Ed.), *Virtual Culture* (pp. 102-132). Thousand Oaks, CA: Sage.

Wenger, E. (1998). *Communities of Practice, Learning, Meaning and Identity.* Cambridge, UK: Cambridge University Press.

Wenger, E. C. & Snyder, W. M. (2000). Communities of practice: The organizational frontier. *Harvard Business Review,* 78(January/February): 139-145.

Wheatley, M. J. (1992). *Leadership and the New Science.* San Francisco, CA: Berrett Koehler.

Wilbur, S. P. (1997). An archaeology of cyberspaces, virtuality, community, identity. In D. Porter (Ed.), *Internet Culture* (pp. 5-22). London: Routledge.

Williams, T. (1994). Information technology and self-managing work groups. *Behaviour and Information Technology,* 13(4): 268-276.

Witmer, D. F. & Katzman, S. L. (1998). Smile when you say that. In S. Rafaeli, M. McLaughlin, & F. Sudweeks (Eds.), *Network and Netplay* (pp. 3-11). Cambridge, MA: MIT Press.

Zhang, J. & Norman, D. A. (1994). Representations in distributed cognitive tasks. *Cognitive Science,* 18: 87-122.

Zickmund, S. (1997). Approaching the radical other: The discursive culture of cyberhate. In S.G. Jones (Ed.), *Virtual Culture* (pp. 185-205). Thousand Oaks, CA: Sage.

Zwass, V. (1992). *Management Information Systems.* WCB.

# Endnotes

1   CBR is a form of AI but instead of using 'classical' rules, the system's expertise is held (or embodied) in a library of past cases. Each case holds a description of the problem. It will also record the solution or the outcome. If a user has a problem (s)he matches their problem against the cases in the case base and retrieves similar cases. These are then used to suggest a solution. The solution is tried and revised where necessary. This new case will then be entered as a new case to the case base.

2   Some people consider a knowledge base to be part of an expert system and that it contains facts and rules which are needed for problem solving, however, the term is now more widely used to mean that it is a searchable electronic resource (which may simply be a database) which is used for the dissemination of information, often via the Internet or an intranet. It may be accessible to the public. An example is the Microsoft knowledge base which is available on the Microsoft support site. As problems arise and are solved they are written up and entered into the knowledge base. Any Microsoft user can access the site and type in their problem query. The system should then return a number of possible solutions — all without the need to contact a technician.

3   A data warehouse is a consolidated view of enterprise data. The data will have come from a variety of sources (production and transaction data). The data warehouse will therefore contain a wide variety of data. The data are optimised for reporting and analysis and are designed to support management decision making. As the data are from a variety of sources but are optimised they present a coherent picture of business conditions at a single point in time. It is easier to run queries over data which have been warehoused than over data which are in several different locations and systems.

4   alidade: special telescopic sighting device

5   An intranet is an internal network which is contained within an organisation. It can be used for collaboration, to share files and use websites as it typically uses Internet protocols and looks like a mini, private version of the Internet.

6   The full list of CoP characteristics offered by Wenger (1998, pp. 125-126) is:
There are sustained mutual relationships. They do not have to be harmonious — they may be conflictual
There are shared ways of doing things together
There is a rapid flow of information and also a rapid propagation of innovation
Introductory preambles are non-existent. It is as if conversations and interactions are simply continuing an on-going process
Problems to be discussed are set up very quickly
When members offer a description of who 'belongs' there is a lot of overlap in the different descriptions
The members know what each other knows, what they are able to do and how they can make a contribution 'mutually defining identities'
The appropriateness of actions and products is easily assessed
There are specific tools, representations and other artefacts
There is a shared background — stories, insider jokes
The members have their own language in the form of jargon
There are certain styles which indicate membership
A certain view of the world which comes out in 'a shared discourse'

7   Interdisciplinary working group, meeting bi-weekly in order to examine and discuss the implications and impact of the Internet. The group consists of members from diverse backgrounds including students, system operators, computer consultants, professors.

8    A MUD is a multi-player, interactive, social experience, managed by a computer. They are now accessed via the Internet but were around before the Internet when they were accessed by telnet. They are inventively structured and often take place in a theme, such as an old castle. They were originally a form of text-based on-line game where the players engaged in combat, puzzles and adventure. The player logs in and adopts a character. Many MUDs are still text-based but some now use a Virtual Reality environment. Even though the players' characters can be seen, the focus is still on the textual exchanges between the players who are logged in. There are many MUDs each with its own rules, name, character, 'feel'.

9    Avatar: an interactive representation of a human in a virtual reality environment

10    Coffee talk: essentially a communication meeting for all of the employees in a business entity (usually a business unit within the organisation) with a general manager. They are management driven in that they are scheduled by the general manager and are a primary vehicle for him/her to share "strategic" information about the business, for example the progress being made, the direction it is taking. They also include a lot of more general information such as the introduction of new employees, visitors from other locations, upcoming events, employee reward and recognition. Although the general manager leads the meeting it is usual to have a number of speakers covering specialist topics, for example IT issues, Research and Design projects. One of the useful facets of the coffee talk is the way it acts as a place to "legitimise" things, for example if a speaker needs the organisation's support to do something or to introduce a new policy then it can be presented at the coffee-talk, after previous discussion with the general manager. Thus the message automatically has the support of the general manager.

11    Stan means that for his first visits he was well prepared with OHP slides and that they had to make a lot of formal presentations

12    EHS (Environmental Health and Safety)

13    ICQ is an Internet instant messaging Tool which enables quick and easy communication with a user-defined list of contacts. This can include quick messages, chat, e-mail, file transfer. Importantly, there is a window on the desktop (which can be minimised) which shows by virtue of color which of the user's contacts are logged onto their machines and whether they are available for contact or not. A fuller description is available in Moody, G.

(1998, July 2). Searching for a Net Community Computer Weekly, p. 47.

[14]    cube = cubicle. Open plan offices.

# Abbreviations

| | |
|---|---|
| *AI* | Artificial Intelligence |
| *APQC* | American Productivity and Quality Center |
| *AV* | Audio Visual |
| *CBR* | Case-Based Reasoning |
| *CD* | Contextual Design |
| *CIO* | Chief Information Officer |
| *CMCs* | Computer-Mediated Communications |
| *CoP* | Community of Practice |
| *CPU* | Central Processing Unit |
| *CSCW* | Computer-Supported Cooperative Work |
| *DC* | Distributed Cognition |
| *EE-AW* | Educational Excellence Alongside Work (CoP in Final Study) |
| *EHS* | Environmental Health and Safety |
| *ESC* | Environmental Sustainability Community (CoP in Final Study) |
| *HP* | Hewlett-Packard |
| *ICTs* | Information and Communication Technologies |
| *IRC* | Internet Relay Chat |
| *IRM* | Information Resource Management |
| *IS* | Information Systems |
| *IT* | Information Technology |
| *ISDN* | Integrated Systems Digital Network |

| | |
|---|---|
| *KM* | Knowledge Management |
| *KMS* | Knowledge Management System |
| *LAN* | Local Area Network |
| *LPP* | Legitimate Peripheral Participation |
| *MOO* | Object-Oriented MUD |
| *MS* | Microsoft |
| *MUD* | Multi-User Dungeon |
| *NT* | Windows network operating system developed by Microsoft |
| *OCR* | Optical Character Recognition |
| *OHP* | Overhead Projector |
| *PA* | Palo Alto, California |
| *PC* | Personal Computer |
| *SSADM* | Structured Systems Analysis and Design Method |
| *UKIT* | UK IT Support Team in Case Study |
| *USIT* | American IT Support Team in Case Study |
| *VE* | Virtual Environment |
| *VR* | Virtual Reality |
| *WWIT* | World Wide IT Group in Case Study |
| *WWITMan* | Management team of WWIT |
| *Y2K* | Millennium Compliance Problem |

# Appendix Section

## APPENDIX 1: THE METHOD

It is perhaps worth spending some time describing the method that was used for the study as it proved particularly useful in the detailed exploration of the inner workings of a CoP and could well prove useful in general CoP work. For the study, I adapted Beyer and Holtzblatt's (1998) Contextual Design method, as it provides support in the handling and analysis of the large volume of rich data created by ethnographic approaches. It is a multi-layered approach to understanding work, including cultural and social views. This would appear to be a useful tool in gaining an improved understanding of CoPs.

## CONTEXTUAL DESIGN

Contextual Design is broadly ethnographic in its approach and falls ideally between participant and non-participant observation so that the researcher is not completely immersed in the work yet is more than a mere observer. The method was primarily developed for work analysis and redesign and provides a structure for data collection but also offers models for working with the data and clear steps for how to move from the rich data to design issues. It provides a structure, models, and steps; however, these are not a rigid, restrictive framework but are intended as a support (Beyer & Holtzblatt, 1998):

*How to get data about the structure of work practice ... how to make unarticulated knowledge about work explicit ... and how to get at the low-level details of work that have become habitual and invisible ... These problems suggest an open-ended, qualitative approach that brings us in contact with the customer's real work[1] (p. 37).*

Contextual Design moves from qualitative data to themes and models to work redesign. It is intended to be a multi-disciplinary team effort and goes through seven clearly defined stages:

1.  Inquiring and collecting data;
2.  Interpretation session;
3.  Work models;
4.  Affinities and model consolidation;
5.  Work redesign;
6.  User environment design; and
7.  Prototype evaluation.

The first four of these stages were used for exploring the interactions of WWITMan.

The Contextual Design method is based on Beyer and Holtzblatt's (1998) experiences in the field, but it has its roots in ethnography and the development of Grounded Theory (Glaser & Strauss, 1967), which has recently been used in Information Systems research (Howcroft & Hughes, 1999). In the development of Grounded Theory, data is collected. The researcher then develops conceptual categories from the data, followed by the collection of more data to expand on and inform the categories already created. The theory develops from the data itself (Frankfort-Nachmias & Nachmias, 1996). This procedure uses an ethnographic approach and develops the categories as research is proceeding, starting with an in-depth study and being followed by subsequent studies, not necessarily to the same depth, being used to inform the findings that have already been developed. These subsequent studies tend to be searches for confirmation or elaboration. Contextual Design adds to the development of Grounded Theory as Glaser and Strauss (1967) emphasised the need for a codified procedure for analyzing the data in order to convey credibility. Although a purely ethnographic approach would not use frameworks, the models in Contextual Design provide additional support to the researcher and go some way to addressing some of the difficulties outlined above and provide the researcher with a method that can be followed.

The advantages of using Contextual Design are several. The data gathering is ethnographic in form, allowing the researcher to see the work, practice, and interactions of a CoP in context. The method provides a range of models to handle the data, using and extending standard techniques for handling qualitative data, but also employing five different types of models designed to gain a full understanding of the practice being observed. I intended using the method as a framework and adapting it as necessary.

For the initial stages of the study I used a slight adaptation of the method. This involved the gathering of data using Contextual Design methods. The models were used but were adapted as necessary. Contextual Design is essentially a team-based activity, but I tackled this by involving other colleagues and interested parties to provide different perspectives. The fact that I was working primarily alone on the study did have benefits, as it meant I had a detailed view of the whole data set. Contextual Design is intended to involve the interviewees (customers) in the process as much as possible. It was not possible to do this according to Contextual Design principles, so I made use of the "Challenging Assumptions" stage of Dearden and Wright[2] (1997), which takes propositions back to the respondents. Time and cost constraints meant that the case study could not be longitudinal and therefore took the form of two shorter periods (snapshots) with the CoP. Stage One formed the first of these two periods.

The study of the CoP was also supplemented by smaller studies of other CoPs. This follows the principles of the Discovery of Grounded Theory (Glaser & Strauss, 1967) on which Contextual Design is partly based, and provided expansion and confirmation (or otherwise) of the issues that arose from the study of the CoP. In summary, I spent Stage One with part of the CoP. After examining the issues that arose from my time with the CoP, I went back and spent more time with them to focus on any issues that arose. Finally, I undertook shorter studies with other CoPs where I could focus purely on key issues arising from the study of the main CoP. Due to access and time limitations, and the fact that I now had a much tighter focus, open semi-structured interviews were used with these other CoPs.

# STAGE ONE DATA COLLECTION

The data collection is based on ethnography, but it falls between participant and non-participant observation. The researcher goes through a one-to-one contextual interview with the subject as (s)he works. The role of the researcher is similar to that of an apprentice to the subject's master. The researcher is more than observer in that (s)he must question what is happening and the "master" must talk through what is happening. Contextual Inquiry is based on the four principles of context, partnership, interpretation, and focus.

- Context: To get as close as possible to physical presence. It allows the gathering of ongoing experience and concrete data.
- Partnership: The role is actually more than apprentice-master. The researcher and the subject are collaborators in understanding the work. In particular, the interviewer/interviewee, expert/novice, and guest/host roles are to be avoided.
- Interpretation: It is not sufficient to collect data. Interpretation is necessary to make a hypothesis about what the data means. If the method were being followed through to design, the hypothesis would have an implication for the design that could result in a design idea.
- Focus: A clear focus steers the direction of the contextual inquiry and allows the researcher to keep the conversation on track. The project focus must be defined in advance. This allows the researcher to find suitable sites to visit, suitable people to talk to, and which sort of tasks to observe.

The structure of the contextual interview is as follows:

1. The conventional interview.
   The first stage is to get to know the subject. This is helped by running the first stage of the contextual interview along conventional lines. The researcher introduces him/herself, explains focus, promises confidentiality, and asks for permission to record. This stage takes approximately 15 minutes.
2. The transition.
   This takes approximately 30 seconds and involves the interviewer explaining the rules for the contextual interview — that is, the customer works while the researcher watches and interrupts if there is something unclear or particularly interesting.
3. The contextual interview.
   The subject works, the researcher watches, and, as an apprentice, asks questions, analyzes artefacts, makes notes, and drawings.

4.    The wrap-up.
Using the notes made, the researcher goes over what has been observed and gives the customer a final chance to correct and expand on issues that were raised.

I used contextual interview with the four UK members of WWITMan. Contextual Design asks for a focus statement. This is a statement of what is being sought and implies what the interviewer should look for. The focus statement for the case study was: "How people share knowledge, learn, and solve problems in a community that operates in a distributed environment." Before the Contextual Interview proper, I had an unstructured interview with the manager of the group. The aim of this interview was to set the CoP in context by finding out:

- the structure of the group,
- its background and history,
- its role in the wider context of the organisation,
- the KM technologies in place in the organisation,
- locations of community members, and their roles,
- when people meet,
- other groups with which people are involved, and
- what problems are experienced.

The contextual interviews were with the four UK members of WWITMan. A whole day was spent with Wayne, one half-day session each with Dave and Mike, and two, separate half-day sessions with Stan. The contextual interview format was followed closely:

- The short traditional interview to find out background information about the respondent.
- The transition to explain the format of the contextual section.
- The contextual section. The format for this was followed as per the prescribed method. The work was observed, questions were asked, and notes were made. However, the focus in Contextual Design is on the whole work picture, whereas the focus for this case study was rather more specific. This resulted in the collection of some data that turned out to be irrelevant for this particular study. This was a minor point, for the contextual interview yielded a large amount of relevant, rich data.

- The wrap-up. In this case the wrap-up was also used to broach some areas that it was felt had not been satisfactorily covered. This generally turned out to be the respondent's use and impressions of communications media that had not been observed.

# STAGE ONE ANALYSIS

At this stage there was no apparent need to adapt the method much. The data had been collected using the contextual interview and so, for Stage One, the data were analyzed using Contextual Design techniques. These are outlined below.

## The Interpretation Session

The interpretation session is the first main stage of analysis. This is an important stage because under normal circumstances Contextual Design is intended to be a team activity. A variety of interviewers will have interviewed a range of users, and it is important for all members of the team to gain a shared understanding of all the customers. The aims of this session are:

- To get better data — people question the interviewer who therefore remembers more than if (s)he were working alone.
- To create a written record of customer insights.
- To have effective cross-function co-operation. The interested parties in the project are likely to come from a range of functions.
- To obtain multiple perspectives on the problem — as each team member brings a different focus.
- To develop a shared perspective — through discussion.
- For team members to have true involvement in the data — data is revealed interactively rather than through a presentation.
- To make better use of time — questions would still have to be asked of the interviewer. The interpretation session brings all the questioning together.

The members of the team are intended to play different roles in the interpretation session. The interviewer talks the rest of the team through his/her interview. Some members of the team are creating the work models. One member notes insights and observations. There is also a member whose role is to ensure the meeting stays on track. Any other members of the team are expected to actively participate by asking questions, offering insights and interpretations, and suggesting ideas.

The interpretation session could clearly not be run as a team session in this study as I was primarily working alone. This did not prove to be a major problem as all the interviews had been recorded and transcribed, and were supported by detailed handwritten notes made during the interviews. This meant that the interview recall was very good without the need for prompting and questioning. Working through the data, I was creating the different models and recording insights and observations. The effect of this was that it gave me an intimate knowledge of the data. The major disadvantage was that by working alone there was no possibility of extra insights that might have been offered by other team members.

## The Work Models

The second stage of the analysis is to create five work models. The work models are created in the interpretation session and are each intended to represent one aspect of work for design. They were developed over time based on the experience of the design problems encountered by Beyer and Holtzblatt (1998). Although the final aim of the case study was not to design a system, the models were all used for the first part of the study as a means of handling the large amount of rich raw data and providing further insights.

### The Flow Model

The Flow Model is concerned with how people divide up responsibilities among roles, and how they co-ordinate with each other while they do the work. In other words, it is used to explore distributed co-ordination. The Flow Model models communication flow and distinguishes between:

- Individuals who do the work.
- The responsibilities of the individual (or the role).
- Groups — these are people who have common goals.
- Flow — communication between people. This might be verbal or it may be in the form of artefacts.
- Artefacts — both physical and conceptual.
- Communication Topic, for example, asking for help.
- Places — where people go to and from to get the work done.
- Breakdowns — problems in communication or co-ordination.

It was anticipated that this model would be particularly relevant for the case study, in particular its emphasis on communication, distributed coordination, and artefacts. A Flow Model was created for each of the CoP members to show the communications observed during the time spent with that person. An example is shown in Appendix 2.

*The Sequence Model*

The Sequence Model is designed to model the ordering of work tasks, that is, what triggers the task, what the steps are in the task, and what is the intent behind the work. It is based on the principle that the actions that people take reveal the strategy they are employing and what is important to them. If a system were to build on these aspects, it could improve the work. It is essential to see the intents (both explicit and implicit) behind the work. Simply automating the tasks will cause a system to be rejected if the intents are not catered to.

The Sequence Model shows:

- Intents: What the sequence is intended to achieve.
- Triggers that cause the sequence of actions.
- Steps, that is, what actually happened.
- Order. This aspect is shown using loops, branches, and arrows to connect the steps.
- Breakdowns or problems in executing the steps.

At first glance, it was felt that this model appeared to be less relevant than the Flow Model but could provide useful insights into interactions between people, both co-located and distributed. A range of Sequence Models was created from the transcripts, covering both contextual interviews and meeting observation. An example of one of the Sequence Models is in Appendix 3.

*The Artefact Model*

People create and adapt artefacts to use in the course of their work, for example forms, documents, lists, and spreadsheets. The structure of an artefact can show the conceptual distinctions of the work. The Artefact Model is designed to show the structure and the information content.

It shows:

- The information that is presented by the artefact.
- The parts of the artefact.

- The structure of the parts.
- Annotations that show the informal use.
- The Presentation. This might be the use of color, white space, or layout.
- Other conceptual distinctions such as past/present/future.
- Usage, for example, when the artefact was created and how it is used.
- Breakdowns — problems when using the artefact.

The use of artefacts in a distributed Community of Practice was a particular focus in the case study, and it was felt that the Artefact Model would be a particularly useful way of exploring the use of the artefacts. An Artefact Model was created for each of the physical artefacts that were collected during the course of the investigation; however, particular attention was paid to the planning document. Unfortunately the Artefact Model did not prove to be as useful as anticipated, as it is more suited to everyday artefacts that people use regularly in their work. This was not the focus as such in WWITMan, and the artefacts that were relevant to the focus were created during the work. The planning document proved to be of particular interest, and it was the process of creation and its use in interactions that were more relevant than the artefact itself.

### The Cultural Model
The cultural context of the work is of immense importance. If a system does not take into account the culture of the people it is intended to support, it will not be successful. The cultural context includes the organisational policies, national culture, how people see themselves, the formality of the organisation, and laws, rules, and regulations.

The Cultural Model, however, has a more restricted view of culture and represents:

- Influencers, that is, people who affect or constrain work.
- The extent: To what degree the influence affects the work. This is shown by overlap of components on the diagram.
- Influence on the work, and the direction of the influence.
- Breakdowns: the problems that interfere with the work.

Cultural aspects have a large bearing on work that is carried out by distributed international groups. Therefore, it was anticipated that the Cultural Model would also be of particular relevance. One single Cultural Model for the CoP was created during the course of the study, rather than one for each member. The resulting model was very large, hence a small section of it is reproduced in Appendix 4 as an example.

*The Physical Model*

The fifth and final model is intended to represent the physical environment and how it either enables or supports the work (or, indeed, how it hinders the work). The reason for this is also geared towards system design; that is, any system that is designed will have to live within that environment. It must therefore take into account the constraints, otherwise it will cause problems for the users.

The Physical Model shows:

- Places — where the work takes place.
- The physical aspects of the environment that limit the space, for example, walls, desks, and other large objects.
- Usage and movement — how people move within the space.
- Tools, hardware, software, and communication.
- Artefacts that are created and passed around.
- Breakdowns that show how the physical environment interferes with the work.

As the group being studied was part of a distributed group, it was not felt that the physical model would contribute a great deal to the study, and this proved to be the case as the immediate environment was modeled for each respondent. However, it may have been useful to have created a higher level model of the environment to show the problems the group encounters when operating in the distributed environment. Such a model could have demonstrated the differences in mode of operation when interacting with colleagues on site and when interacting with distant colleagues. These aspects, however, were brought out through the other models and the Affinity, but a high level physical model to show this would also have been useful.

## Consolidation and the Affinity Diagram

After the creation of the models, the next step is to consolidate. Beyer and Holtzblatt (1998) describe this as "the inductive process of bringing all the individual data together and building one Affinity diagram and one set of models that represent the whole customer population" (p. 154).

To create an Affinity, all the insights and observations that have been recorded during the interpretation session are organised into hierarchies in order to show common issues and themes. It is an inductive process and is done by placing a note on the wall, and then adding any others that the researcher feels fit with it. If a note doesn't fit with any on the wall, a new category is started. When the notes are all allocated they are organised into hierarchies by grouping together and providing meaningful names. In a normal contextual enquiry, the Affinity diagram would be based on a large number of notes and would therefore be a team activity.

When the Affinity has been created, all the data are arranged clearly and present the issues. The researchers then "walk" the Affinity; that is, they "read" the wall. Reading the notes raises further issues that might need to be addressed in further interviews or it might lead to the creation of ideas. The intention is for anyone to be able to walk the Affinity — researchers, customers, and outsiders. It is intended to be a collaborative activity. As WWITMan's organisation was many miles distant, it was impractical for the respondents to visit; therefore, my

*Figure 1: The Affinity*

departmental colleagues were invited to walk the Affinity and provide their insights and feedback.

Having created and walked the Affinity, the work models had to be consolidated. The aim of consolidation is to move to one set of models representing the study population. Therefore, each set of models is combined to create one.

*The Flow Model*

The Flow Model consolidation is intended to show the communication patterns that underpin the business of the study population. Consolidating the Flow Model moves from individuals to the roles played by those individuals. I hoped that this would provide insights into the interactions within the CoP and also show the roles undertaken by the members in sustaining the CoP.

The first step is to create a complete list of responsibilities for each individual. Undertaking this process may also bring previously overlooked responsibilities to light. Having listed the responsibilities, roles can be identified. The stages that were followed in consolidating the Flow Model were adapted from Beyer and Holtzblatt (1998) to cater for the tight focus and population of the study, which would be smaller than that of a normal Contextual Design exercise.

*Step One:* Generate a complete list of responsibilities for each individual.
*Step Two:* Examine the flows to see if they suggest any other informal roles.
*Step Three:* Look for roles and name them.
*Step Four:* Combine the people into roles.
*Step Five:* Combine the roles into another flow model and bring in flows from the original flow models.

Examples of these stages and a section of the consolidated Flow Model are shown in Appendix 5. Consolidating the Flow Model proved to be a useful exercise. Four main roles were identified, and although not all four were totally relevant to the focus of the study, the model and the process of creating it led to insights into the data and the situation of the study group.

*The Sequence Model*

It was doubtful whether the consolidated Sequence Model would be particularly relevant, as its purpose is to examine a particular task. The CoP in the study did not have particular repeated tasks, and the focus of the study was more on interactions. However, the process proved to be much more useful than expected and led to a number of further insights about the work of the community.

Whereas the consolidated Flow Model shows the interaction between roles, consolidating the Sequence Model demonstrates the structure of a task and the strategies used. Different people will approach work in different ways, and the consolidation of the model helps identify common structures. To consolidate the model, there are six steps:

1.   Using the Sequence Models, the researcher needs to identify a number of sequences that address the same task and that would possibly consolidate well. This was done by reading through the sequences, marking with a pencil, and basically coding the sequences.
2.   In the selected sequences, activities are identified. The end point for the first activity is marked in each sequence.
3.   The triggers are matched across the sequences — these may start at different points.
4.   The sequence steps within the first activity are matched, with any omitted steps being added in to make matching easier.
5.   The actual steps are abstracted with any breakdowns being added at this point.
6.   When the end of the sequence is reached, the intents are added.

Sequences were chosen to show:

- Collaboration
- Arranging meetings
- Having a meeting
  (a) Co-located management team
  (b) Distributed WWIT
  (c) (a) and (b) combined
- Identifying collaboration
- Noting action to be taken
- Planning
- Customer service
- Clarification
- Discussion of issues

- Technical
- Problem solving/improving
- Making improvements based on knowledge/expertise/experience
- Getting help
- Solving a technical problem

The consolidated Sequence Model for "Identifying Collaboration," along with the notes that were made, is shown in Appendix 6 as an example.

*The Artefact Model*

I had initially expected that the Artefact Model would perhaps be the most relevant to this study because of its interest in reifications in the form of shared artefacts. This turned out, however, to not be the case, and the consolidation reinforced this point. The aim of consolidating the Artefact Models is to demonstrate how people organise their work and structure it from day to day. This did not work in this case, as the CoP in question does not have a regular, representative weekly routine, and the purpose of the central artefact (the planning document) could not show in its structure how the members organised the work, as it was not that sort of artefact. Holtzblatt and Beyer (1998) explain that people's tasks have similar structure, and therefore the intent and usage of artefacts will also be similar. However the only similar artefacts revealed by the study were:

(a)   different drafts of the planning document; and
(b)   two copies of a chat history, one that had been formatted by hand and one that had not been formatted at all.

The selection of Artefact Models is decided by the project focus; for example, if the project is to develop a personal organiser, then the artefacts of interest would have calendar functions. In the research study, the focus was more on how artefacts were used in interactions than on the work itself. Therefore, the emphasis was on a different type of artefact, and it was the Affinity, the Flow Model, and the Sequence Model that proved to be more revealing.

The steps for consolidating the Artefact Models are:

1.   Take the Artefact Models and group them according to the roles that they play.

2.   Identify common parts in each artefact, and the intent and usage of each part.
3.   Identify breakdowns and common structure and usage within each of the common parts.
4.   Build a generic artefact to show all the common parts, usage, and intent.

For Step One, the most important artefact within the project focus was felt to be the planning document, and possibly also the online minutes. It did not appear to be beneficial in any way to consolidate the different drafts of the planning document. It also did not seem possible to do Step Two unless it was for the planning document drafts, and this did not seem to be worthwhile. Therefore, I did not do any consolidation of the Artefact Models. I felt it preferable to find a different model to explore the usage of the artefact. This took the form of a time line that was created after later iterations of the planning document (Figure 3, Chapter 6).

*The Physical Model*

One of the aims of consolidating the Physical Models is to make the researchers aware of limitations imposed by the physical environments. The effectiveness of the models was, however, limited by the fact that they only represented the immediate physical environment. It would have been better had I created a higher level model to demonstrate the limitations imposed on the CoP by the distance to their colleagues in California.

There are only main two steps in consolidating the Physical Models:

1.   To separate the models into types of spaces. Beyer and Holtzblatt (1998) note that a set of models will usually represent a whole site or several sites, focusing on the buildings and the relationships between them. Some models may also focus on individuals' spaces and specialised spaces.
2.   To catalogue common large structures and organisation. Beyer and Holtzblatt suggest that, for example, telephones, calendars, and address books gathered in one corner of the desk in several models indicate a common theme of communication and co-ordination. Movement is identified if it is relevant to the project focus.

The consolidation phase indicated that the initial Physical Models had not been created well enough and that a better range would have produced more insights in the consolidation. For example, it would have been useful to have created models showing the different sites and the specialised spaces (video suites, AV rooms with polycoms), whereas the models only showed the individual work spaces that were perhaps slightly less relevant to the project focus. The workspaces were all very similar and were indicative of the culture of the organisation in that they were open cubicles in order to encourage informal ad hoc communication. Each cubicle had a range of communication media suggesting the importance of communication and finding people. The movement on the models was only really relevant in cases of co-located work. Although the focus was more aimed at distributed working, the co-located work showed the importance of informal ad-hoc, serendipitous communication. Despite the difficulties posed by the initial error of emphasis in the creation of the models, the process did show two useful insights:

1.    It needs to be made easy to locate people in Palo Alto and lower the set-up difficulties in talking to them.
2.    The individual workspaces are open, so that colleagues can drop in to talk informally. This was an immensely important part of the co-located environment, and it would be beneficial if they could move towards this in the distributed environment. This indicated that a useful avenue to follow would be to increase the awareness of a person's presence at his/her desk, or awareness of his/her availability.

*The Cultural Model*

I had anticipated that the cultural model would be particularly useful in increasing understanding of the functioning of a CoP in the international environment, as it would record and show the cultural aspects that help sustain or hinder a community.

As with the other models, the Cultural Models are normally created separately, that is, a Cultural Model for each contextual interview. However, during the course of the study so many aspects were being repeated that one single model was created. By the end of the interviews, the result was a Cultural Model that was already well consolidated. Therefore, consolidation was not undertaken as a separate stage for this model. The creation of the Affinity had thrown light on some aspects and to reflect this, some parts of the Affinity were added in to the model for illustrative purposes.


# Extra Stages

An important aspect of the Contextual Design method is communication with the customer or, in this case, the people participating in the study.

Adjustments had already been made to reflect the fact that I was working mainly alone rather than as part of a design team, and further adjustments had to be made in this stage. Beyer and Holtzblatt (1998) suggest that the "customers" should be invited to the design team's room to walk the Affinity and for the work models to be used as communication tools.

It was not possible for the members of the group to visit; therefore, a series of propositions were drawn up from the insights created during the process of making the Affinity and consolidating the work models. The propositions and some of the consolidated models were presented to the members of the CoP in two separate meetings in order to elicit feedback and inspire further discussion of the issues. This process was used to confirm, or otherwise, the insights that had been made and to further inform the Affinity. The propositions were designed to encourage discussion, with some of them being made deliberately contentious. The propositions were presented one at a time, but are shown in a list in Appendix 7.

The feedback from the two meetings was then used to further inform the Affinity and the insights that had been extracted from the Affinity and the model consolidation. Linking the categories produced the web of possible relationships shown in Appendix 8.

## STAGE TWO AND THE EXTRA COPS

The purpose of the second stage of the study (and the extra CoPs) was to expand on and inform the initial insights. Glaser and Strauss (1967) observe that the fuller coverage comes at the beginning of the research as categories and themes emerge. Subsequent studies do not need such full coverage as the aim is to gather more data pertinent to the themes and categories that have emerged, generally looking for confirmation or elaboration. To this end, Glaser and Strauss point out that earlier stages will take a fuller approach, such as reading documents, interviewing, and observing at the same time. Later stages can be more focused with shorter interviews and more direct questions. This was the approach that I took with Stage Two of the study and with the extra CoPs. The Contextual Design tools were not as applicable for the second stage, as the focus was tighter than in Stage One. In Stage Two and with the extra CoPs, the focus was not on the whole work but on the use of artefacts and the importance of relationships and face-to-face communication. Additionally, Contextual Design focuses on regular work with the overall aim of designing a system to support the work. During Stage Two of the study, the regular work had been at most suspended, or at least interrupted for the period where the two cores were together. Therefore, the tools used for data gathering and analysis tended to be a mix of Contextual Design techniques and interviews.

## Data Collection

The greater part of the study was spent observing the members of WWITMan in meetings and interacting together. It was not possible to follow a Contextual Interview Model with the researcher playing the role of apprentice. Rather, the observation was simply observation. However, there was also the opportunity to speak with the three established American WWITMan members, the Japanese member, and with Carol, a member of the Client Server team. In the interviews with these people, an open semi-structured interview seemed to be the most suitable approach. This took the highlighted issues from Stage One and tackled them directly but still allowed for flexibility to pursue other relevant avenues that might arise. The interview schedule (Appendix 9) was intended purely as a guide for the interview and was not intended as a script. To finish the interview, a subset of the propositions that had been presented to the UK core was presented and discussed. The interview also offered the opportunity to refer the respondents back to the meetings for clarifications and explanations. Detailed notes were made during the meeting observations, and all interviews were recorded.

Following the period spent in California, I spent a further period with the UK core to ascertain what effect the American visit had had. This period also consisted of observation and interviews that were annotated and recorded.

## Analysis of Stage Two

The first stage of the analysis, as with Stage One, was to transcribe the interview transcripts. The coding of the transcripts followed the pattern in Stage One; that is, notes were made as the transcripts were read, as if it was being done in a Contextual Design interpretation session. These notes were then added to the Affinity, for example, creating a new category or being added to an existing category.

The Contextual Design Models were then explored to see if they could be of use. Physical Models had not been drawn for the American core; however, Physical Models had been drawn for the meetings.

The Artefact Model in Stage One had not proved to be as useful as had been expected. Additionally, only one new artefact had been retrieved from Stage Two — Stan had made notes and a PowerPoint presentation to present to his Informatics Team. Therefore, the Artefact Model was not used in Stage Two.

A Cultural Model was not created for Stage Two. The Cultural Model that was created in Stage One seemed to be sufficiently comprehensive, and the few points that arose in Stage Two fitted better in the Affinity.

The Flow Model proved to not be relevant in Stage Two for a number of reasons:

- The focus was much tighter than in Stage One, which took a broader view of the work in general.
- The everyday work was suspended in view of the visit of the UK — and, like the UK core, there is no such thing as a "representative week."
- The consolidated Flow Model of Stage One had highlighted the importance of collaboration in the role of the CoP members. This became one of the propositions that was presented to the UK core. A subset of the propositions was also presented in the interviews in Stage Two, and this seemed to cover the Flow Model aspects satisfactorily.

In Stage One, meetings were seen where:

- the UK and the US cores were distributed, and
- the UK core was co-located.

In Stage Two, the UK and US cores were co-located; therefore, Sequence Models were created for the meetings to see if they showed anything different.

As one of the focus points of Stage Two was the use of shared artefacts and the Artefact Model had not proved useful, a different approach was needed. A tracking approach seemed to offer a way forward. The main artefact in evidence was still the planning document and so an artefact timeline was drawn to show the planning document's development up to the visit to America and then its use in America.

# EVALUATION

Although Contextual Design is primarily aimed at a systems design environment, for the purposes of this study, Contextual Design provided a methodological framework that suited the aims of the study and that allowed the easy handling of a mass of qualitative data. This was an interesting application of the method and resulted in some interesting insights. In general, the method proved to be practical and useful, but showed that there were some areas that needed to be adapted.

The data gathering techniques worked exceptionally well for the purposes of KM research when focusing on CoPs. It is not surprising that this stage worked so well, for it has its roots in ethnographic procedures. In later stages when the focus became tighter, the contextual inquiry techniques were too exploratory and more focused questions were needed alongside. This, too, was not unsurprising, as Contextual Design also has roots in the Discovery of Grounded Theory (Glaser & Strauss, 1967), which observes that data should be gathered iteratively in order to inform the findings of previous iterations. The iterations become more focused and the questioning tighter.

Contextual Design provided five models and an Affinity with which to handle the mass of ethnographic data. These models are intended to be the beginning of a work re-design process, but in the case of this project, they were used for the analysis of the qualitative data. The analysis of Contextual Design data is intended to be a team activity. In the case of this study, I was working alone. This did not prove to be a disadvantage as it meant I obtained a comprehensive view of the data. In order to avoid too narrow a view, however,

(a)   colleagues and interested parties were brought in to "walk the Affinity" and to provide different insights, and

(b)   a set of propositions was created to take back to the interview respondents. I could then use the feedback to the propositions to provide further insights to the Affinity and models and provided a form of validation.

Taking these two steps overcame the limitations imposed by working alone.

The Affinity is a standard qualitative technique that sorts the data into themes and categories and as such was an essential stage in the process, providing a number of insights.

It had initially been expected that the Artefact Model would be a useful model as the research was exploring the use of artefacts in a CoP. Unfortunately, it did not prove to be useful as it focused on the structure of an artefact with a view to embodying this in a system. For example, it would explore the structure of a calendar and how people used it, in order to use those insights in a personal information management tool. A better picture of the use of the artefact in the CoP was obtained by creating a different model, in the form of a timeline, to track the creation, iterations, and use of the artefact. This provided a picture of the development of the planning document over time and its use in the community. It showed the people involved, some of the work that went into its preparation, the number of iterations, where it was used, when it crossed the boundaries between the cores, and also how it was stored and displayed (for example, used in a meeting or placed on the intranet for comment). As the planning document became something of a focus, the timeline provided a means of pulling all the data about its development and use into one model. It did not, however, show the application of the softer aspects of people's knowledge. This understanding was built up through the use of the timeline, the Affinity, and the Flow Model. For the purposes of planning KM issues, it would be useful to further develop the timeline model to include more details on the development and use of an artefact by the CoP members.

The purpose of the Flow Model was to abstract the work done by the members of the CoP into roles. It was also helpful in mapping some of the movements of the planning document. This worked well and provided a number of insights into the working of the CoP.

The Sequence Model also worked well in that it provided a means of representing the actions taken, suggesting reasoning behind the actions, and steps taken to accomplish an action. This provided a number of insights into how the CoP accomplished some of its tasks.

The Cultural Model was satisfactory to the extent that it provided a visual representation of the impact of culture on the CoP. The notion of culture in the model, however, is restricted to issues (and people) that hinder work and enable it and breakdowns in the process. Culture in the broader sense, that is, national, organisational and group cultures, was not addressed but was a theme that came out strongly in the Affinity. A useful development would be to further develop the Cultural Model to cater for a less-restricted notion of culture.

The model that contributed the least was the Physical Model. This may be partly due to the fact that, although it was used properly as per the method, it was not adapted sufficiently. The model was created as directed, but it became clear during the analysis stage that the model would have benefited from being broadened to reflect the wider context of the CoPs operation, as opposed to the immediate physical environment of each member. The Physical Model was used to record the immediate physical environment of the members. This provided no insights at all, other than to emphasise the importance of ICT. It would perhaps have been preferable to record the wider physical environment and illustrate the difficulties of the distributed environment.

Once all the models and the Affinity had been created, they were "read," and any insights or findings recorded. These were then used as a focus for the next stages, which in turn further informed the findings to increase the understanding of the situation. The timeline was not used at this stage, being developed at the beginning of Stage Two of the main case study in order to bring the development of the planning document up-to-date.

Using the Contextual Design as a methodological basis worked very satisfactorily from a practitioner point of view. It must be emphasised, however, that it was only satisfactory as a basis, and that the method had to be adapted by:

- adding an extra stage of creating propositions with which to return to the respondents;
- changing the Artefact Model;
- using structured, open-response interviews in the later stages [In the later stages, the only models that were used were the Sequence Model and the adapted Artefact Model (timeline). It was not felt that the other models would add anything extra at this stage.]; and
- extending the Physical Model to reflect work in the distributed environment.

Further improvements that could be made to the method for use in investigating work from a KM standpoint with a view to developing a KM initiative would be:

- Further developing the Artefact Model to reflect the application of people's softer knowledge.
- Adapting the Cultural Model to reflect a richer definition of culture.
- Developing a model to reflect the social networks of the organisation. The Flow Model does this to some extent but translates the flows into work roles. A model to map the social network in an organisation would be particularly useful. It could be mapped in stages or smaller units and consolidated to cover a wider group.

It must also be borne in mind that the focus of this project was an organisational CoP that operates in a distributed international environment. It is unlikely that the method would have proved so effective in exploring the interactions of a totally virtual community.

# REFERENCES

Beyer, H. & Holtzblatt, K. (1998). Contextual design. San Francisco, CA: Morgan Kaufmann.

Dearden, A. & Wright, P.C. (1997). Experiences using situated and non-situated techniques for studying work in context. In S. Howard, J. Hammond, & G. Lindgaard (Eds.), Proceedings of INTERACT '97. IFIP TC13, International Conference on Human-Computer Interaction. London: Chapman Hall.

Frankfort-Nachmias, C. & Nachmias, D. (1996). Research methods in the social science, 5th ed. London: Arnold Publishing.

Glaser, B.G. & Strauss, A. L. (1967). The discovery of grounded theory. New York: De Gruyter.

Howcroft, D. & Hughes, J. (1999). Grounded theory: I mentioned it once but I think I got away with it. In L. Brooks & C. Kimble (Eds.), Information systems — The next generation. Proceedings of the 4th UKAIS Conference, (pp. 129-141). York, UK.

Patching, D. (1990). The political and economic context of organisational behavior. In C. L. Cooper & S. E. Jackson (Eds.), *Creating Tomorrow's Organisations* (pp. 29-41). John Wiley and Sons.

# ENDNOTES

1   Customer: as the overall aim of Contextual Design is the creation of a computer system, respondents/subjects are referred to as customers.

2   One approach to tackling the problem of handling a wealth of ethnographic data was used by Dearden and Wright (1997) who used a mix of situated and non-situated approaches. The study reported by Dearden and Wright (1997) was subject to time constraints (22 person days) and was intended to analyse the 'quality of fit' between the work undertaken by a specific group of office workers and the IT system which had been put in place to support the work.

The time constraint of the study meant that time could not be lost handling large amounts of ethnographic data. Dearden and Wright (1997) therefore used an ethnographic technique (contextual inquiry) for observing the work in context after having had a training session to quickly learn the procedures and terminology in use. As the focus of the work was well-defined it was possible for them to use non-structured techniques such as semi-structured interviews and rich pictures as used in soft systems analysis (Patching, 1990). The understanding of the work was validated by the use of three techniques:

- Model building: this forces the researcher to work through his or her understanding of the situation.
- Challenging assumptions: the researchers returned to the organisation and presented groups of interviewees with a number of propositions or assumptions, some of which were deliberately contentious, in order to encourage debate.
- Wish Lists: The researchers made suggestions and created a 'wish list' from open-ended questions in the interviews. The wish list was then presented to the groups of interviewees (who did not know which were suggestions made by the researchers and which had come from the interviews) in order to obtain more 'wishes.' The final list was put into groups and then displayed for discussion.

The mix of situated and non-situated techniques, using models to handle some of the data, appeared to work very well for Dearden and Wright (1997) allowing them to undertake the research, handle the data and report within a short time scale.

# APPENDIX 2: EXAMPLE FLOW MODEL*

*Figure 1: Example Flow Model*

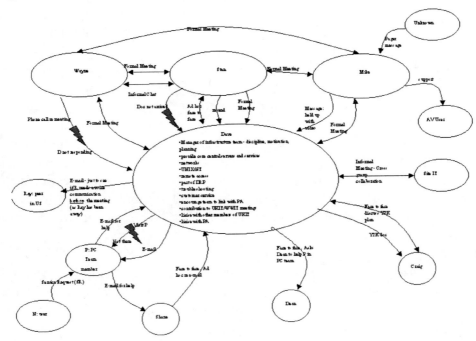

*Figure 2: Example Flow Model — Detail*

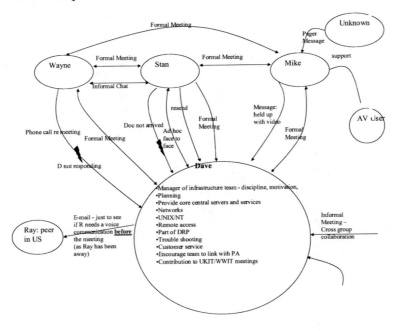

# APPENDIX 3:
# EXAMPLE SEQUENCE MODEL

*Figure 1: Example Sequence Model*

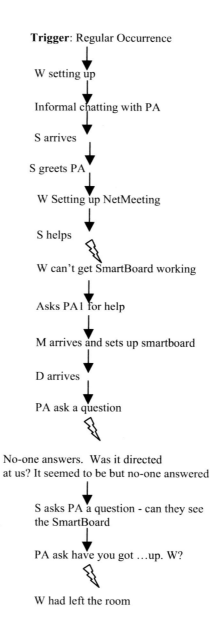

**Intent**: formal meeting

**Trigger**: Regular Occurrence

W setting up

Informal chatting with PA

S arrives

S greets PA

W Setting up NetMeeting

S helps

W can't get SmartBoard working

Asks PA1 for help

M arrives and sets up smartboard

D arrives

PA ask a question

No-one answers. Was it directed
at us? It seemed to be but no-one answered

S asks PA a question - can they see
the SmartBoard

PA ask have you got ...up. W?

W had left the room

*Figure 1: Example Sequence Model (continued)*

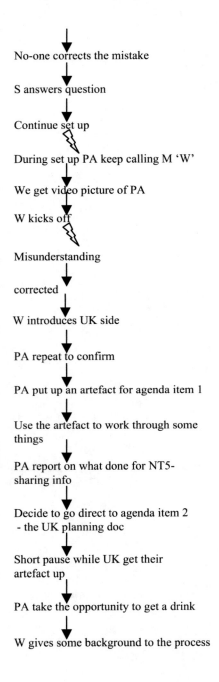

No-one corrects the mistake

S answers question

Continue set up

During set up PA keep calling M 'W'

We get video picture of PA

W kicks off

Misunderstanding

corrected

W introduces UK side

PA repeat to confirm

PA put up an artefact for agenda item 1

Use the artefact to work through some things

PA report on what done for NT5-sharing info

Decide to go direct to agenda item 2
 - the UK planning doc

Short pause while UK get their artefact up

PA take the opportunity to get a drink

W gives some background to the process

*Figure 1: Example Sequence Model (continued)*

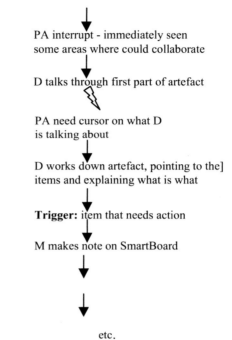

PA interrupt - immediately seen
some areas where could collaborate

D talks through first part of artefact

PA need cursor on what D
is talking about

D works down artefact, pointing to the]
items and explaining what is what

**Intent:** note an action item                **Trigger:** item that needs action

M makes note on SmartBoard

etc.

# APPENDIX 4:
# EXAMPLE OF CULTURAL MODEL*

*Figure 1: Example of a Cultural Model*

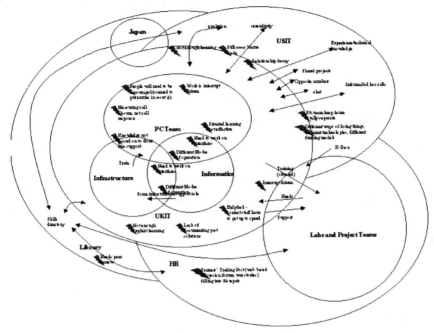

*Figure 2: Example of a Cultural Model — Detail*

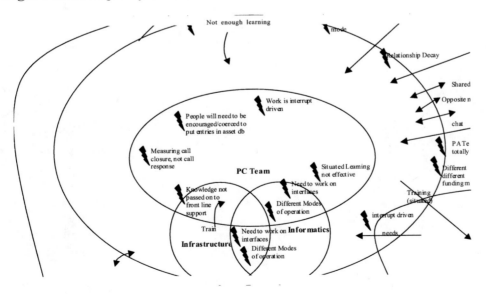

# APPENDIX 5:
# EXAMPLE OF CONSOLIDATED
# FLOW MODEL*

In Step One, a complete list of responsibilities was generated for each individual. Roles were then created and named. The example below shows how this was done for W.

---

**W: Manager UKIT**

- Provide tools, infrastructure, support for distributed international working
- Liaise with other areas in Labs (e.g., Internet telephony)
- Oversee the three teams in UKIT
- Budget responsibilities
- Lead team meetings
- Advisory (e.g., meeting with Bea and Stan)
- Liaise with PA/coordinate

---

**Roles:**

*Manager*
Oversee the three teams in UKIT
Budget responsibilities
Lead team meetings
Personnel matters
Personal evaluations

---

*CoP Collaborator*
Liaise with PA/coordinate
Arrange WWIT meetings with PA
Look for opportunities for collaboration/leverage

---

*Technical*
Provide tools, infrastructure, support of distributed international working

---

*Collaborator*
Liaise with other areas in labs
Advisory

When all of the roles and responsibilities had been created for each of the CoP members, they were combined into one consolidated Flow Model.

*Figure 1: Consolidated Flow Model — Detail*

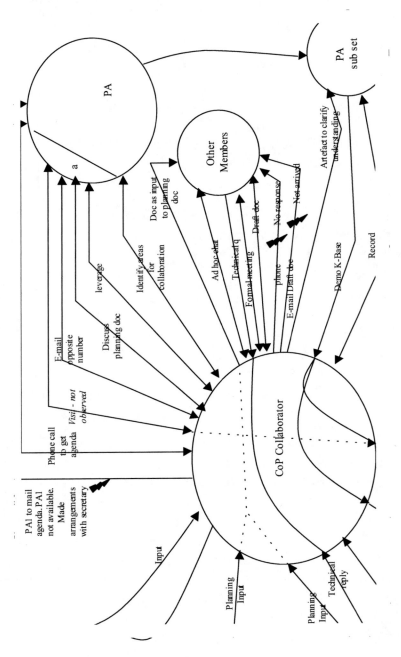

# APPENDIX 6: EXAMPLE OF CONSOLIDATED SEQUENCE MODEL

## Identifying Collaboration

M2; M2 — i.e., both examples that have been selected are from an electronic meeting

These two examples come from the second distributed meeting. There were other (less explicit) examples, but some of them were related secondhand and not seen directly, for example:

- S said that when he was abroad he dropped in on one of his colleagues with whom he had a good relationship, saw a project, and thought, "That would be good in the UK."
- W said that the possible collaboration with the Internet Telephony Unit came about because someone from PA happened to see a demo and thought, "We want to use that."

These were both serendipitous, but there were also occasions in the co-located meetings where it was expressed that more cross-team cooperation was needed. Here they were recognising a need and suggested ways for cooperation/collaboration.

There are two examples. One is general — "several areas where we can collaborate" and just highlights the possibilities. The second is very specific — "what we have here is ... and what we need to do is ... and this is who could do it." This happened on several occasions in the meeting — this one has been selected as being representative.

The people who act on the need will learn from their collaboration, but what about sharing the knowledge (if relevant) with other members of the group? If they create something — some of their knowledge will be embedded in it.

Another interesting point — they do not select people just from the CoP to work on these actions, but also bring in people from WWIT (the wider group).

## Appendix 6: (continued)

| Activity | M2 | M2 |
|---|---|---|
| Use artefact | Trigger: PA scans trough artefact on screen while WD talking about it | Trigger: discuss items on artefact |
| See possibility for collaboration | PA stop WD – seen several areas where we might collaborate | During discussion of artefact realize it would be suitable for collaboration |
| Refine possibility | | Define need |
| | | Suggest people to action this |
| Note collaborative action | | Note action item |
| Move on | | Move on |

| Activity | Abstract Step | M2 | M2 |
|---|---|---|---|
| Use artefact | Read artefact | Trigger: PA scans trough artefact on screen whilst WD talking about it | Trigger: discuss items on artefact |
| See possibility for collaboration | Notice area where could work together | PA stop WD – seen several areas where we might collaborate | During discussion of artefact realize it would be suitable for collaboration |
| Refine possibility | Discuss feasibility | | Define need |
| | Identify personnel | | Suggest people to action this |
| Note collaborative action | Record action to be taken | | Note action item |
| Move on | Move on | | Move on |

| Activity | Intent | Abstract step |
|---|---|---|
| Use artefact | Communicate with colleagues* | Read artefact |
| See possibility for collaboration | Work together to<br>• Learn<br>• Leverage<br>• Share | Notice area where could work together |
| Refine possibility | Work out initial detail of collaboration | Discuss feasibility |
| | Create partnership/team to work on this | Identify personnel |
| Note collaborative action | Have history | Record action to be taken |
| Move on | Identify further possibilities | Move on |

*Key point to come out of this is the artefact that is stimulating collaboration.*
*\* In this case, the artefact was being used as a communication tool.*

# APPENDIX 7:
# PROPOSITIONS USED IN STUDY

The only thing representative about the week was that it was unrepresentative.

A CoP cannot be created, only facilitated.

*From the Flow Model: Collaboration:*
The major part of your role is collaboration
    Within UKIT
    Directly with PA
    Identification of areas for USIT/UKIT collaboration

*From the Flow Model: CoPs:*
Only some groups are CoPs:
    USIT/UKIT Management teams together are a CoP
    Subgroups are not CoPs
    WWIT is not a CoP
    PC Team, Infrastructure team, Informatics — are not CoPs

There is evolution — WWIT may become a CoP

*From the Flow Model: Media:*
You consciously choose the medium you use for communication.

You get communications breakdowns in the media.

The selection of the wrong media does cause problems.

Relationships do not grow electronically — you have to meet the people face-to-face first.

*From the Flow Model: Distribution/Internationalisation:*
The short time window is a problem.

You need regular and frequent interaction — this lessens as one moves out of physical proximity.

Being aware that your communication partner is at his/her desk would not be of noticeable benefit.

Because you work with PA, you now have access to more expertise.

You ask PA for help with technical problems and collaborative projects.

Sometimes asking for help is not pre-planned — you just pick up the phone.

*From the Flow Model: Learning and New Knowledge:*
The easiest things for people to learn are technical things. It is harder to learn how things get done.

When something is finished you don't take stock and ascertain what you've learned from it.

*From the Flow Model: Ad Hoc Communication:*
A lot of your ad hoc communication is a result of physical proximity.

*From the Sequence Model: Media:*
Fast response and a shared artefact are of more use than bandwidth.

Getting to know the PA people has happened through visits and not at all through e-media.

Getting to know the people well has helped with issues of trust and confidence.

Knowing who you are talking to is sometimes a problem in e-media. The fact that you know the people so well does not help at all.

Your communication media need:
- To be easy to set up and use
- To have a fast response
- To have shared artefact

*From the Sequence Model: Gurus/Experts:*
When you turn to a guru for help you let him/her do it — you don't learn from him or her.

When an expert leaves, the knowledge is easily replaced.

Having two people working at the same job (e.g., backups) is a waste of resources.

If you haven't got an expert in UKIT, you are stuck.

*From the Sequence Model: Learning and New Knowledge:*
You use your shared knowledge to create new knowledge.

Learning is dependent on serendipity.

Spending time with a mentor is valuable but doesn't often happen.

There is scope for facilitating more learning from each other in the group.

You do learn from and act upon past experience — your own and PA's.

As a group, you have recognised that you need to learn more effectively.

*From the Sequence Model: Ad Hoc Communication:*
Ad hoc communication is a key element of your communication.

Ad hoc communication takes place:
• Electronically
• Within formal settings
• Drop-in

Ad hoc communication provides opportunities for:
• Collaboration (even distributed)
• Sharing information
• Technical queries
• Discussing issues/problem solving

*From the Sequence Model: Knowledge Management Issues:*
Breakdowns
• Loss of knowledge
• Duplication of effort

Needs
- To share knowledge
- Spread the load

*From the Sequence Model: Use of the planning document:*
The Planning Document was more important than you realised.

The Planning Document was used for:
- Communication with PA

The Planning Document was used for:
- Communication with your teams

The Planning Document was used for:
- To include input from your teams

The Planning Document was used for:
- Planning

The Planning Document was used for:
- Stimulating discussion

The Planning Document was used as a:
- Collaboration catalyst

The Planning Document was used for:
- Driving meetings

The Planning Document was used for:
- Flagging up issues, problems and technical issues

The Planning Document was used for:
- Applying knowledge from Bristol and PA to solve problems and technical issues

*From the Cultural Model: Media:*
You and your colleagues are happy in e-media but get to know each other better face-to-face. Part of this is a cultural thing — you can understand the culture better.

*From the Cultural Model: Gurus/Experts:*

Cultural difference: US has experts (people more focused on specific topics). Bristol has to go for "Jack of all trades" approach — this can actually be beneficial.

Time is a problem — it is easier to grab the guru and get him/her to solve the problem than to learn about it and do it yourself.

*From the Cultural Model: Ad Hoc Communication:*

Ad hoc communication is part of the culture of the organisation.

# APPENDIX 8: WEB OF POSSIBLE RELATIONSHIPS FROM THE AFFINITY*

*Figure 1: Web of Possible Relationships from Affinity*

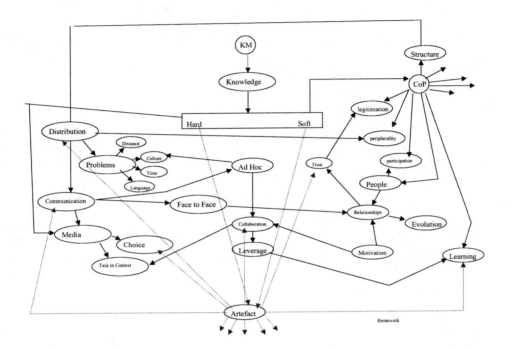

# APPENDIX 9:
# INTERVIEW GUIDE FOR STAGE TWO

## 1:1 Sessions with USIT Members

How useful did you find the process of creating the planning document with UK?

Artefact use. These were my impressions from the observations. What are your opinions?

a)  Discussion document:
    *Does the document serve to drive a discussion? Is it a focus of discussion?*

b)  Collaboration catalyst:
    *Does working with a shared document highlight areas for further collaboration?*

c)  Planning:
    *Do you ever use a joint document for planning?*
    *Do you create a planning document?*
    *What is of most use — the process of creating the document, or the actual finished product?*

d)  Reflection:
    *Does using/working on a shared document cause you to reflect (as a group) on what you are doing?*

e)  Demo:
    *Do you ever use any shared artefacts to demonstrate anything to anybody — e.g., how to do something?*

f)  Problem solving:
    *Does working on a document, or going thorough a document flag up any possible problems that you then turn your minds to as a group?*

g)  History (minutes):
    *Do you record minutes of meetings?*
    *How do you do this?*

h)  Clarification of understanding:
    *Do you ever use the shared document to clarify understandings?*

i)  Communication tool:
    *Do you use a shared document as a communication tool?*

j)  Boundary object:
    *Does your shared document cross any boundaries?*
    *What boundaries does it cross?*

k)  Interpretation:
    *Do different people get different interpretations of things that are in the document?*
    *Is this a good or a bad thing?*
    *Explain.*
    *How do you cope with different interpretations?*

l)  Representation propagation:
    *How does the document get created?*
    *What input is there?*
    *Vertical*
    *Horizontal*

Your opinion on the importance of face-to-face interaction.

What media do you use?

Likes and Dislikes?

You have your own version of the planning document. How does that tie in with the UK one?

What aspects have to be taken into account when creating the boundary object?

In the development of the artefact, they came together at certain points for co-ordination points. What is the purpose of these?

A contribution we are making is to look at the process of constructing an artefact — analysis will look at these processes.

# APPENDIX 10:
# INTERVIEW GUIDE FOR EXTRA COPS

## Part A: Background

1.    What is the structure of the group — who is where?
2.    How did the group come into being?
      (evolution)
3.    How is the group progressing now?
      (evolution)
4.    What is the work of the community?
5.    What difficulties are there in operating in a distributed environment?
6.    And what benefits?
7.    Are people members of different groups?
      (marginals)

## Part B: Media

Looking for importance of face-to-face interaction, what media are used for doing different tasks.

1.    How do you solve problems?
2.    How do you contact colleagues in other locations?
3.    What media do you use in the course of your work in the community?
4.    Do you meet face-to-face?
•    Who with?
•    How often?
•    Prearranged or ad hoc or both?
•    Importance of ad hoc
•    How do you get ad hoc with people elsewhere?
5.    What do you like/dislike about the media?
6.    Do you get help with technical problems from your colleagues in other locations?
7.    How do you build up a relationship with your colleagues?
•    How important is face-to-face in this?
•    How does it work in e-media?
8.    How important is it to build up this relationship?
9.    How do you develop trust with your colleagues?
10.   Would being aware that a colleague was at his/her desk be of benefit?

## Part C: Artefacts

1. Do you ever use artefacts such as shared documents in meetings?
   Co-located?
   Distributed?
2. Do you ever work on shared documents with colleagues here?
   What kind?
   What of?
   How do you develop the document?
3. Do you ever work on shared documents with colleagues in other locations?
   What kind?
   How do you communicate?
   How do you develop the document?
4. Does the artefact substitute for face-to-face at all?
5. Use of artefacts
   As:

a) Discussion document:
   Does the document serve to drive a discussion; is it a focus of discussion?

b) Collaboration catalyst
   Does working with a shared document highlight areas for further collaboration?

c) Planning
   Do you ever use a joint document for planning?
   Do you create a planning document?
   What is of most use—the process of creating the document or the actual finished product?

d) Reflection
   Does using/working on a shared document cause you to reflect (as a group) on what you are doing?

e) Demo
   Do you ever use any shared artefacts to demonstrate anything to anybody —e.g., how to do something?

f) Problem solving
   Does working on a document or going thorough a document flag up any possible problems that you then turn your minds to as a group?

g) History (minutes)
   Do you record minutes of meetings?
   How do you do this?

h) Clarification of understanding
   Do you ever use the shared document to clarify understandings?
i) Communication tool
   Do you use a shared document as a communication tool?
j) Boundary object
   Does your shared document cross any boundaries?
   What boundaries does it cross?
k) Interpretation
   Do different people get different interpretations of things that are in the document?
   Is this a good or a bad thing?
   Explain.
   How do you cope with different interpretations?
l) Representation propagation
   How does the document get created?
   What input is there?
   Vertical
   Horizontal

Can you show me any examples of artefacts and talk me through what has been done with them?
CD technique — trying to root an account in the past in context
Can I have any examples of shared artefacts?
Where are the documents kept? (intranet, shared folders)
Who has access?

*In these appendices, there are examples of the different models which are used in Contextual Design. Some of the models are very large, therefore the reduced representations shown are only intended to give an overall impression of what the model will look like. Where appropriate a small section of the model has been magnified to give the reader more detail about the type of information which might appear in the model.*

# Glossary

## 3D Audio

3D Audio is a technique that is used to provide additional depth to normal stereo sound. Conventional stereo is normally made into 3D Audio by putting stereo speakers into a room with a device which analyses the sound from the speakers. The device feeds data back to the sound system which then readjusts the sound in order to give the impression that the speakers are further apart than they actually are.

In computer systems the speakers tend to be smaller and closer together than in personal entertainment systems. 3D Audio techniques can be used to improve the sound quality. There is a range of 3D Audio devices which work with the sound card of the PC.

As well as improving the sound by giving the impression that the speakers are further apart than they really are, true 3D Audio can increase the range of sound position — normal stereo sound places a sound at any point between the two speakers (left and right). True 3D Audio can place the sound anywhere — left/right, near/far, up/down. The research group described in this book were working on an enhancement to this so the position of the sound reflected the position of the sound source. For example, in a teleconference, if the speaker in the remote location talks as (s)he is walking across the room, the sound would move in the speakers to reflect that movement. At the time, this worked through headphones and was very effective in adding an extra contextual clue.

# Artefact

An Artefact is a "thing" made by human workmanship. In the context of this book, Artefact is used to indicate objects, articles, and "things" which have been created by communities to assist them in their work and which may have some of the community's knowledge embedded in them. Examples in this book might be some of the tools which are used by seafarers to help them with navigation — these items have been created over many years by the community of seafarers and handed down. Artefacts do not have to be concrete — a process or procedure may be an Artefact.  The procedure helps newcomers to a community by providing set steps. As the newcomer becomes more of an old-timer, (s)he may develop the confidence to "break" or improve the procedure.

# Artificial Intelligence (AI)

Coined by John McCarthy at the Massachusetts Institute of Technology in 1956, the term Artificial Intelligence describes the branch of computer science which attempts to make computers act like human beings.  There have been a large number of AI languages and techniques. Two common languages are LISP and Prolog.  Current techniques include neural networks (systems which try to develop intelligence by simulating the types of connections found in animal brains), cased based reasoning and ontologies.

As well as the expert systems described in this book, AI has been (and still is) used in a number of fields:

*Games:* This is perhaps one of the areas where AI has made the most advances. Computers can now play games, like chess, against a human user.  One computer, IBM's Deep-Blue, beat a world champion (Gary Kasparov) in 1997. Chess on the PC is now available for home users.
*Natural Language Processing:* Developing computers to the point where they can understand natural, spoken, human speech has proved to be more difficult than first thought. If it were successful, it would have many advantages — users could interact with computers without any specialised skills. The user could simply give an instruction as they would to another human and the computer would obey the command.  Progress to date has resulted in some language translation programs but these programs are not as good as human translators. For example, an early system, when given the phrase "out of sight, out of mind," translated it as

"invisible, insane." Progress has also been made with speech to text systems. These are voice recognition systems and some are now proving popular for domestic PCs — but they do not *understand* what is being said. These systems are simply dictation systems and they must be "trained" by the user in order to obtain a reasonable degree of accuracy. However, they are constantly improving as the specification of domestic PCs continues to improve and can handle ever more processing demands. *Robotics:* A lot of progress has been made in this field, particularly in those applications where a machine has to do simple repetitive tasks (for example, the automotive industry). The range of applications is growing as exemplified by the solar-powered robot lawnmower which is now available for the domestic market. The processing required in robotics is to allow the robot to see, hear and react to its environment.

## Asynchronous

In IT terms, Asynchronous means not synchronised, i.e., something does not occur at pre-determined or regular intervals. For example, communication where date can be sent intermittently rather than in one single stream is said to be Asynchronous. From this perspective a telephone conversation can be described as Asynchronous because both parties can speak when they want. If it were synchronous, each communication partner would have to wait for a specified interval before (s)he could speak. However, when we talk about different communications media being Asynchronous, it is generally taken to mean that the communication partners do not have to be present at the same time — thus e-mail and voice mail would be seen as Asynchronous media.

## Autopoiesis

Autopoiesis is based in the field of biology. It is the process at the heart of Autopoietic Theory which is the collective term for a body of work developed by Humberto Maturana and Francisco Varela, two biologists from Chile. They originally used it in the field of neurobiology to characterise living systems. The process of Autopoiesis characterises living systems as living machines (Maturana was not content with listing features of the systems in order to define life). Rather he was trying to capture, in some way, the unchanging feature of a living system around which natural selection operates.

The notion of Autopoiesis has been applied to the social sciences and has developed into a theory of knowledge of a social system and has provided an opposing view to the cognitivist approach. Von Krogh and Roos (1996, pp. 2-3) describe it as proposing that the world is not a pre-given state to be represented. The world is brought forth through the creative act of cognition. From this perspective knowledge and information are developed in the brain and in social systems. Developing information is simply to "put data in form." Knowledge is developed internally in a self-referential manner. Knowledge, therefore, is private and the organisation is seen as a simultaneously open and closed system; it is open with respect to data but closed with respect to information and knowledge.

## Avatar

An Avatar is a representation of a character in a virtual environment, often taking human or beast forms. The user can change the characteristics of the Avatar, for example, hair colour, overall colour, clothes style and colour. As the user interacts in the virtual environment, the Avatar will move around the environment, e.g., walking in the direction instructed by the user. The Avatar can also interact with Avatars of other users. Avatars are becoming more sophisticated and can, for example, change facial expressions during interaction with other Avatars.

## Boundary Objects

As groups or communities from different domains work with each other or communicate with each other they develop different types of boundary objects across intersecting social worlds' through the process of creation and management.

Star (1989) and Star and Griesemer (1989) have done a lot of work with boundary objects. Star (1989) describes them as being "objects plastic enough to be adaptable across multiple viewpoints, yet maintain continuity of identity." As explained in this book she identified four types:

• Repository
• Ideal type
• Terrain with coincident boundaries
• Forms

Star and Griesemer (1989, p. 393) explained the concept as "an analytic concept of those scientific objects which both inhabit several intersecting worlds ... *and* satisfy the informational requirements of each of them. Boundary objects are objects which are both plastic enough to adapt to local needs and the constraints of several parties employing them, yet robust enough to maintain a common identity across sites. They are weakly structured in common use, and become strongly structured in individual site use. These objects may be abstract or concrete. They have different meanings in different social worlds but their structure is common enough to more than one world to make them recognisable, a means of translation. The creation and management of boundary objects is a key process in developing and maintaining coherence across intersecting social worlds."

Mambrey and Robinson (1997) studied the role of documents in a flow of work through a hierarchy and found that there were artefacts (in their case documents, folders, etc.) which strongly supported the work of Star (1989) and Star and Griesemer (1989)

## Chat Log

A Chat Log is the record of a chat session between two or more people. Chat is real-time communication between two or more people using a computer. A user can initiate a chat session with another user and they can then communicate by typing on the keyboard. The text which they enter will be visible on their partner's computer.

The Chat Log mentioned in this book stretches the definition in that it was the written record of a teleconference. As the group progressed the meeting, one of the members was making notes online. They called this their "Chat Log." This "Chat Log" also formed the minutes of the meeting.

## Cognitivism/Representationism

The development of Cognitivism in the 1960s was a reaction to the strict focus on behaviour which was demanded by the behaviourist school. Many theorists disagreed with this, thinking it must be possible to learn with no externally visible signs of changed behaviour, i.e., there were aspects of learning for which behaviourism could not account. Cognitivists therefore tried to go inside the head of the learner in order to see how learning activated (and changed) mental processes.

Cognitivists view knowledge as mental constructs (or schemas) inside the head. These schemas are representations of the outside world. The learning process is regarded as the process by which these schemas are memorised.

In Cognitivism, the acquisition of knowledge is measured by what learners *know*, unlike in behaviourism where it is measured by what they *do*. The learner is regarded as an information processor and therefore learning is seen as processing symbols.

The Cognitivist Approach is concerned with:

• Symbolic representations
• Rule manipulation
• Rule modification

At around the same time that Cognitivism was gaining ground, early research was being undertaken in Artificial Intelligence (AI). This research demonstrated computers deciphering codes and producing proofs. This, perhaps, is one of the reasons why expert systems were not totally successful — AI was perhaps restricted to the Cognitivist Approach and did not take other approaches (e.g., constructivism) into account.

## Common Ground

As explained in some detail in this book, Common Ground is a notion used by Clark (1996) in his discussion of the use of language. Clark had taken earlier discussions of Common Ground, analysed them and used the most suitable aspects for his work. He felt that Common Ground is "important to any account of language use that appeals to 'context'" (Clark, 1996, p. 92) in that, when referring to context, none of these accounts of language provide a definition of context. Clark felt that Common Ground could help with this. He notes that Common Ground is essential to coordinating joint action. More importantly for the notion of Communities of Practice is the notion of communal Common Ground: "We often categorise people by nationality, profession, hobbies, language, religion, or politics as a basis for inferring what they know, believe or assume" (Clark, 1996, p. 100). As an example, he describes a situation where he meets someone for the first time. He discovers she is a classical music enthusiast and he therefore suddenly has a much improved picture of her as he is a classical music enthusiast himself. He assumes that she would know everything that such an enthusiast would know. Having established that they are both enthusiasts they now "have a shared basis for taking all this information to be common ground" (Clark, 1997, pp. 100-101).

## Competitive Advantage

Much has been written about how to achieve Competitive Advantage. Robson (1994) suggests that Competitive Advantage is something which *might* follow if an organisation gets everything else right. Other commentators try to identify specific actions a company can take in order to generate Competitive Advantage, for example, rapid implementation of the latest technology.

Porter (1985) argues that the basis for above average performance in the long run is a sustainable Competitive Advantage. He suggests that without a sustainable Competitive Advantage, all a company can do is skim off the largest profits it can for as long as it can. He proposes that there are two types of Competitive Advantage:

• Cost leadership and
• Product differentiation

These lead to three strategies for pursuing Competitive Advantage:

(a) *Cost* — become *the* lowest cost producer. The organisation needs to seek out *every* source of potential cost advantage and be concerned with pursuing economies of scale.

(b) *Differentiation* — in this case the organisation seeks to become the best performer in the sector in some aspect of the product which is highly valued by customers (apart from cost). The organisation also seeks one particular aspect of its performance and positions itself uniquely to meet the needs of its clients in this area. Although a premium is paid for this uniqueness it is important that the organisation still maintains some sort of cost parity with its competitors.

(c) *Focus* — strategy to target a selection of a particular group or sector. The organisation will then tailor its strategy specifically to target the needs of this group or sector. This strategy may bring Competitive Advantage within the target group but will not deliver wider Competitive Advantage. In order to generate this Competitive Advantage, the organisation will need to exploit the weaknesses of its competitors which are operating on a broader basis.

Power (1985) also points out that it is not usually possible to operate cost leadership and differentiation strategies at the same time unless the company also has:

- Prime mover advantage
- Structural advantage
- Technological advantage

There is a Competitive Advantage when the organisation can deliver the same benefits as its competitors *but* at a lower cost (cost advantage) or can deliver benefits which are *greater* than those of competing products (differentiation advantage). A Competitive Advantage therefore enables the organisation to deliver superior value for its customers and greater profits for itself.

It is important to note that the aim is to deliver *sustainable* Competitive Advantage. It may be the case that an organisation implements a piece of technology which gives them an immediate Competitive Advantage but which is something that can easily be replicated by other organisations. As a result, the organisation will no longer have something unique delivering Competitive Advantage. Rather it has become the case that the "unique" piece of technology has now become standard in the field and not having it leads to competitive *disadvantage*.

## Computer Mediated Communication (CMC)

This quite simply refers to communication media which needs a computer to function. Examples are e-mail, instant messaging, text messaging, Internet forums, Internet relay chat (IRC) and video conferencing. Even though computers are now routinely used in the telephone system, the telephone is not regarded as a CMC as the use of the computer is not essential — the phone system functioned before the introduction of computers.

## Constructionism/Constructivism

These two terms are often used interchangeably and in this book perhaps I, too, am guilty of this. However, strictly speaking, Constructionism is more of an educational method based on the Constructivist Theory of learning.

Constructivism as a theory of learning is based on the notion that knowledge and meaning is *constructed* by the knower or learner based on mental activity or mental construction. People learn by taking new information and adding it to what they already know. It is said that people learn most effectively when they construct their own understanding, therefore the emphasis is on the student rather than the teacher. The student, rather than the teacher, is the one who is interacting with events and objects. As a result of this interaction the student gains an understanding of the features of such events and objects and thereby constructs conceptualisations and solutions.

The theory of Constructivism was a reaction to the notion that knowledge can be transmitted from teachers to learners — that the ideas expressed in text books or lectures are simply transmitted into the student's mind. For a Constructivist, learning means that the learner builds complex knowledge structures and must consciously think about deriving meaning. Through the effort of doing so, meaning is constructed through knowledge structures. The meaning, however, may bear no relation to the real world [consider the simple (or naïve) theories developed by younger children]. The basis of the differences between Constructivism, Cognitivism and Behaviourism is that knowledge is seen as a constructed entity rather than as a given. Therefore, according to Cognitivists, knowledge cannot be transmitted from one person to another. Rather, it has to be constructed (or re-constructed) by each person.

## Contextual Design

Contextual Design is a work analysis and redesign method based on grounded theory and ethnographic techniques. In this book, we concentrated on Contextual Inquiry for data gathering and then we used the Contextual Design models for handling the data.

Contextual Design goes through a number of stages:

*Data Gathering Using Contextual Inquiry.* This follows a form of "master-apprentice" model enhanced by the four principles of context, partnership, interpretation and focus.

Once the data has been gathered it is analysed using a number of steps:

*Interpretation Session.* Each interview is talked through by the person who did the interview. New interpretations are suggested and notes are recorded.

Models are created for each interview:

• Flow Model
• Sequence Model
• Artefact Model
• Cultural Model
• Physical Model

Once the models have been created, an affinity diagram is created from them — i.e., themes are extracted from the models and are grouped by placing together any extracted pieces of data which appear to fit together. This gives a hierarchy of themes.
The models are then consolidated, i.e., a consolidated flow model is created from the individual flow models to give a picture of the whole organisation. The same is done for each of the other types of model.
The consolidated models and the affinity are then "walked," i.e., examined for any other interpretations. The customer is involved in this stage. The idea is that the data from the models is used to drive an innovative design, ending up with a prototype which can be implemented.

## Database

A Database is an organised collection of information which can be retrieved according to specific criteria. Strictly speaking, a Database does not have to be electronic (e.g., a card index file can be regarded as a database), but current usage tends to take for granted that a Database is electronic and the data held in the Database can be retrieved by a computer. A database is made up of fields — each field is a single piece of information about an entity, e.g., name, title, address line 1, address line 2. Early databases were held in "flat files" — i.e., each entity had a row in a table. Each cell in the row held a specific piece of information. The problem with flat file databases was that data which was relevant to a number of entities had to be entered anew for each entity. Relational databases hold a number of tables which are linked by "relations." This means that if a piece of data is relevant to a number of entities it is entered only once and then linked to each of the relevant entities. Modern databases can be of immense size and can drive full information systems.

## Data Mining

Data Mining is undertaken by a type of database application which searches data to find hidden patterns. The term is often used (mistakenly) to refer to software which presents data in new ways. True Data Mining software goes further than this. Not only does it present the data in new ways but it also looks for hidden patterns and relationships. This is an immensely useful tool for marketing professionals. For example, it can help retail organisations find customers with common interests or it can help companies make use of the mass of data which they can retrieve from their websites.

## Data Warehousing

An organisation may have many different systems and databases in place across the organisation. Data Warehousing generally means the combination of many of these diverse databases across an organisation in order to give an ordered picture of the diverse data which, in turn will support management decision making. A Data Warehouse will contain a wide variety of data which is then presented in a format which will give an understandable picture of the state of the business at a particular point in time.

## Distributed Cognition

Developed in the 1980s by Edwin Hutchins and colleagues, Distributed Cognition (DC) tackles the debate as to whether cognition is primarily individual or social. DC claims that cognition takes place over both the individual and the environment thus combining aspects of Cognitivism (cognition is only in the mind) and Situationism (cognition is in the environment). It moves away from the Cognitivist view that regards the individual as an information processor.
Important parts of DC are:

• The use of artefacts and
• Representations

Artefacts can be seen to have knowledge of other people embedded in them. This is not like the attempts of knowledge engineers to replicate knowledge in a system. The artefacts of DC are more like tools which help the user do his/her job. They do not mean that the user does not need knowledge to use them — rather the user needs a different type of knowledge.

Representations can be a way of presenting a problem. The way the problem is presented and represented will make a difference as to how the problem is solved. This is then also linked to how data is presented. The example given in this book (as reported by Hutchins, 1990) describes how navigational data is presented in different artefacts — taken off a reader, on a chart, in a log book, etc. In this case the data is represented in different states and propagated across different media.

## Downsizing

In some industries, organisations are finding that they are having to make staff redundant. This may well be due to a change in the economic climate which means that the optimal size for that organisation is now smaller than was previously the case. An example might be the automotive manufacturing, as these organisations have had to reduce costs and have implemented automation on the manufacturing line. Downsizing is how managers respond to the change in circumstances.

## E-Mail

E-mail is the abbreviation for electronic mail. This is a form of messaging over computer networks. Initially restricted to internal computer networks, e-mail is now worldwide and mainstream thanks to the development of the Internet.

In order to send e-mail, the user needs:

(a) An e-mail client to read and write e-mails
(b) Access to an e-mail server. This may be in the same organisation as the user or it may be a service provided by the user's Internet Service Provider (ISP)
(c) An e-mail address
(d) An e-mail address of the message recipient

The user writes the e-mail and sends it immediately or can save it to be sent at a later stage. A written e-mail will find its way to the recipient's electronic mailbox. If the recipient is online (s)he will probably be notified by the e-mail system that there is e-mail for them. If the recipient is not online, (s)he will have to go online at intervals and check the mail to see if anything has arrived for him/her. Once (s)he has read the mail, (s)he can delete it, save it, forward to one or more people, or print it.

An e-mail can also be sent to a group of people as opposed to an individual. This can be a very useful function but should be used with care. In fact, e-mail in general should be used with care — once an e-mail has been sent it cannot be stopped and there have been many cases of people receiving e-mail which was not intended for them. In some cases this has resulted in severe financial damage to an organisation or to disciplinary proceedings being instigated against an individual. Although it is, perhaps, the most well-established of the CMCs e-mail, it is still a relatively new medium and users still make mistakes. As a result of this, e-mail etiquette and usage advice is available to help users try to avoid misunderstandings and mistakes.

## e-Meeting

An e-Meeting is a meeting which takes place using CMCs. The team in the case study used a variety of media — video conferencing, phone conferencing, and collaborative tools. They referred to all the meetings where one or more partners were in a remote location as "e-Meetings."

## Ethnography

For some people, Ethnography describes any qualitative research project which has the aim of rich description. Ethnography is much more than this. It is a research method which has its roots in anthropology but which, in recent times, has also been applied in the fields of sociology, education, psychology and business.

Ethnography is a qualitative research method which uses a broad range of data collection techniques. However, the main tools tend to be observation and semi-structured interviewing. Documentary and survey data, if used, tend to be used as supplementary material (Gill & Johnson, 1997). The main tool is probably extended participant observation. The thinking behind this approach is that the social world is best investigated in context as it cannot satisfactorily be reproduced in an artificial setting such as would be needed for an experiment. The participant observation is generally the first major undertaking in the field. As its name suggests, the researcher plays a dual role. (S)he becomes a participant in the life of the community being studied in order to gain an understanding of what that life entails. At the same time, (s)he must also act as an observer, viewing the community from the point of view of an outsider. The participant observation is supported by the open semi-structured interviews — the questions are specific but open-ended and the interview format also allows the researcher scope to extend areas of interest if necessary. Artefacts produced by the community are also collected as they embody characteristics of the community.

## Executive Information Systems (EIS)

Kaniclides (1997) notes that defining an EIS is difficult because there are many definitions available, none of which are universally accepted. (This means that there is no standard definition.) The definitions proposed differ depending on the point of view of the person making the definition and also on the context of the system itself. Additionally, the rate of technological development is quickly making the features, characteristics and capabilities of EIS constantly change.

Due to the difficulties in providing a definition, Kaniclides (1997) offers some characteristics which characterise EIS:

*"EIS are primarily designed for direct use by senior management. The computer skills required to operate them are therefore not particularly demanding ... They are often used without the need of technical assistance and are flexible to match the individual user's decision making style ... They are designed to support unstructured non-repetitive decisions associated with upper levels of management and provide features such as drill-down capabilities, and exception reporting. The support of executive decision making also requires fast access to information both internal and external to the organisation ... Information is extensively presented in a graphical format to enhance the standard textual and tabular capabilities of EIS" (Kaniclides, 1997, p. 18).*

## Expert System

An Expert System is an AI system designed to perform a task which would normally be undertaken by a human expert. A knowledge engineer creates the Expert System after studying the work of the human expert. The knowledge engineer translates the work of the human expert into rules which can be understood by the computer. Early Expert Systems were intended to replace the human expert and were, generally, unsatisfactory (Davenport & Prusak, 1998). Later versions are designed to *aid* the human expert. Some examples of Expert Systems are systems to diagnose an illness, plan and schedule delivery routes, and undertake financial forecasting.

## Global

"Global" is intended to refer to an organisational form which has developed as a result of the increased globalisation of business. Zwass (1992) described the Global organisation as a "centralised federation [where] Foreign operations are seen as pipelines for delivery of goods and services to a unified global market in search of economies of scale and scope." Karimi and Konsinski (1991) explain that in such a concern the flow of goods, information and resources is generally a one-way process from the central home base to the subsidiary, with strategic decisions being made by senior management at the central home base. The standard design of the product and manufacturing is on a global scale with the worldwide activities being centrally coordinated bring economies. The systems structure is centralised with databases and provides central planning and control to maintain tight control over subsidiaries as a high degree of coordination is necessary.

## Globalisation

The rapid development of communication and information technologies has meant that people and organisations around the globe are more connected than ever before. This has also made it more possible for money and information to travel around the world at a speed never known before. International travel and international communication are now commonplace for a larger part of the population than ever before. Boundaries are blurring as organisations establish a presence in many different locations in order to take advantage of local conditions (e.g., cheaper labour). The forces of globalisation allow businesses (and other organisations) to function to some degree as if national borders did not exist and to work on a global stage.

## Grounded Theory

More correctly called "The Discovery of Grounded Theory," this is a method for collecting and analysing qualitative data. The theory is developed inductively from the body of data which has been collected, i.e., the method is concerned with discovering theory which is grounded in social settings. After a body of data has been collected, the researcher develops themes or conceptual categories from the data. (S)he makes new observations to elaborate on or clarify these conceptions and more data can be collected to confirm (or otherwise) the initial observations. This can be an iterative process with the end result that tentative hypotheses and concepts are developed from the data itself.

Initially a social sciences research method, Grounded Theory has usefully been applied to Information Systems research as researchers have come to realise the importance of the social aspects of IS. This is particularly visible in the development of the Contextual Design method.

## Instant Messaging

This is a useful type of computer-based communication. Within the Instant Messenger, the user can create a list of contacts. The system will then alert the user when one of the contacts is online and available for communication. Using the Instant Messenger, the communication partner can swap files and chat (using the keyboard) in real time — as if they have a private chatroom. A key advantage brought by the Instant Messenger is social awareness — if you see a friend is online you are more likely to engage in ad-hoc communication.

There are several Instant Messengers, each with different standards. This means that if you want to use instant messaging with a colleague or friend, then (s)he must have the same Instant Messenger as you.

## Intelligent Agents

Intelligent Agents are software programs which are mainly used on the Web to make computing easier. They are currently used in Web browsers to help with retrieving and delivering information — the user can specify certain parameters or preferences and the agent will search the Internet and return the results to you automatically. As well as news retrieval, the agents can also act as shopping assistants.

## International

This is another new organisational structure which has been defined as a result of Globalisation. An organisation may develop from being a multinational corporation to being an international corporation. It is defined by Karimi and Konsynski (1991) as having a coordinated federation organisational structure with the subsidiaries being dependent on the home base for such things as processes and ideas. This form of organisation requires much more control and coordination than is necessary in a multinational company. Knowledge and expertise are transferred to the foreign subsidiaries, but there is nevertheless still some scope for the local development of new products, strategies and ideas. Zwass (1992) added that the foreign subsidiaries are seen as "appendages to the domestic corporation where core competencies are honed."

## Internet

Quite simply, the Internet is an international computer network connecting millions of computers and smaller networks, decentralised by design and owned by no one.

The Internet originally comes from work funded by the U.S. Government who developed the ARPANET (ARPA = Advanced Research Projects Agency) thinking it was useful in a military sense — it was intended to be resilient in the case of attack. A lot of defence data was transmitted over this network but in 1983 it was split into ARPANET and MILNET as security was not felt to be good enough and too many people had access. ARPANET gradually became the Internet which is now accessible to anyone with a PC, a modem and a phone line. Internet usage has grown spectacularly in recent years. In 1987, there were 20,000 computers with numbers growing at 15% per month. In 1994, there were 3 million and in 1997 it was expected that there would be more than 1 billion computers connected. It is very rare now to find an organisation, no matter how small, without access to the Internet. Schools have connected to the Internet to take advantage of the wealth of information which is available.

## Internet Relay Chat (IRC)

Developed in Finland in 1988, IRC has become a very popular facet of the Internet. It is beginning to gain acceptance as a popular and cheap alternative to long distance telephone calls. IRC is a chat system and it allows users anywhere on the Internet to join in live discussions.

To join a discussion you will need an IRC client and access to the Internet. The client sits on the user PC and sends messages to the IRC server and receives messages back from the server. The IRC server broadcasts messages to all users who are logged on to the same channel — there can

be many discussions going on at once, each in its own channel.
In IRC, discussions happen in real time and the conversation is live — as soon as you log on, other users can see you there and when you enter some text, everyone else on your channel immediately see it. IRC is a medium which can cause newcomers some difficulties, therefore it is worthwhile reading the instructions and getting to grips with the IRC client before entering a discussion.

## Intranet

An Intranet functions like an organisation's private Internet in that it uses the same protocols and hosts websites and web pages. These look just like any other website and web page, and function in the same way except that access is restricted to authorised users. An Intranet will generally be situated behind a firewall to minimise the risk of unauthorised access.
Intranets are used to share information and are now being used for collaborative work. This means that they are attracting attention from the Knowledge Management field.

## Knowledge Base

Earlier definitions of a Knowledge Base were restricted to Knowledge-Based or Expert Systems. They referred to the part of the system which held facts and rules which were needed to solve problems and which were expressed using some type of formal knowledge representation.
More recently, the term has come to be used to refer to a central repository of information, e.g., a database of related information about a specific subject. It is a computer-based resource which can be easily disseminated (often on the Internet) and is often part of a Knowledge Management system. The aim of having a Knowledge Base is that it can facilitate the collection of information, its organisation, retrieval and dissemination.
Having a well-organised Knowledge Base can save money for an organisation by reducing the amount of time people spend trying to find information.
If a Knowledge Base is implemented as part of an AI project, it will often have the capability to "learn" built into it.
In this book, a number of Knowledge Bases were discussed in the case studies. These tended to be well-structured databases which were

available, for example, to both technicians and end users. The value derived from the Knowledge Bases in these cases was dependent upon the domain knowledge of the person using the knowledge base.

## Legitimate Peripheral Participation

This is the process by which a newcomer to a community will gradually work his or her way to full participation in the community (Lave & Wenger, 1991). Lave and Wenger's (1991) examples were based around the apprenticeship model where a newcomer (the apprentice) was allowed to undertake basic tasks (i.e., in the case of tailors, cutting basic shapes out of cloth). As they became more experienced, they were given more complicated tasks until finally they became old-timers and could participate fully.

## Lotus Notes

Lotus Notes is a suite of groupware programs developed by the Lotus Development Corporation. Groupware is software which helps groups to work with the members connected via a computer network. Organisations can share documents, work on documents together and collaborate even though the communication partners might be in different locations.

## Marginals

Marginals are community members who are members of different communities (Star & Griesemer, 1989). Wenger (1998) also recognised the importance of these people but he referred to them as "brokers." As they are members of different communities they will have experience of the customs, languages and relationships in the different communities of which they are members. This brings a number of benefits, for example, it means that marginals are in a position to help with mutual understanding. It also means that they bring a different perspective to a problem which might help with its solution.

## MS Exchange

MS Exchange is the mail server developed by the Microsoft Corporation. A mail server is software which handles files, e-mails and information in response to an e-mail client. An e-mail sent to an e-mail address will arrive at a user's mailbox on a mail server from where it can be retrieved by the user's e-mail client.

## Multimedia

Multimedia refers to the ability of computers to present information in a variety of ways — text, graphics, images, video, animation and sound. In most cases, this is integrated, meaning that the presentation of information can be presented using many different ways at once.

Due to the rapid increases in PC performance, coupled with decreases in price, multimedia PCs are now mainstream whereas only a few years ago multimedia on a PC was uncommon. It is not unusual now for a PC to be able to edit and play video film.

Multimedia applications are very large and therefore the most effective media are CD-ROM and DVD.

## Multinational

The Multinational Organisation is a development of a domestic exporter which has further developed its international operations. In the multinational operation, production, sales and marketing are decentralised to foreign locations whereas general administration and financial management are controlled from the home base (Laudon & Laudon, 1995). In such a company, the foreign subsidiaries may have a substantial degree of operating independence as products are adapted to suit local demands and conditions (Karimi & Konsynski, 1991).

## Multi-User Dungeons (MUDs)

A Multi-User Dungeon (also called a Multi-User Dimension) is a virtual space where users can set up an Avatar to represent themselves and, through which, they can interact with other users. Originally a MUD was a fantasy game played out in medieval scenarios with castles, dragons, other beasts and magic items. Now the term MUD tends to refer to any cyberspace environment where multiple users can communicate in real time, often in a text based format

## NetMeeting

NetMeeting is an application that was developed by the Microsoft Corporation to help users work collaboratively. It is incorporated into Internet Explorer (Microsoft's Web browser) and supports chat sessions, whiteboard, application sharing and document sharing.

At the time of the case study, the respondents felt that it was not a particularly intuitive application. It was used because the members of the CoP were highly IT literate and were therefore well placed to make best use of the potential offered by the application. At the time, they did not recommend it to other users in the organisation because they felt users would struggle to use the application and would have an unsuccessful meeting.

# NT

Windows NT is one of the Windows family of operating systems developed by the Microsoft Corporation. It is a 32-bit operating system designed for network environments and is therefore targeted at the business market. Windows NT Server is designed to run the server in a network environment and NT Workstation is intended to run on the client machines in the network.

## Object Oriented Multi-User Dungeons (MOOs)

A MOO is an object oriented development of a MUD system.

## Ontologies

An Ontology is a form of knowledge representation and is a vehicle for knowledge sharing and reuse. The term "ontology" comes from metaphysics and the philosophical sciences where it means a systematic account of existence and is used to explain the nature of reality. Artificial Intelligence assumes that if something exists it can be represented and the field of AI has absorbed the term where it is used to mean an explicit and formal representation (or specification of the representation) of all the entities, objects and concepts of the area of interest. It also covers the relationships between all these entities so is intended to be a high level formal specification of a specific knowledge domain.

## Optical Character Recognition (OCR)

OCR is a system that reads text from a printed sheet and converts it into a form which can be read by a computer. Even scanners in the domestic user market now come with OCR software.

If a piece of text is scanned using the scanner's normal settings, then the scanner will take an image of the text. If it is scanned using the OCR program, the text will be scanned directly into a file which can be edited using a word processor. Text scanned using the OCR application can be likened to a Scrabble board — the words and letters can be manipulated. A piece of text scanned using the scanner's normal settings will be akin to a photograph of the Scrabble board — it will look the same but nothing can be manipulated.

OCR systems become ever more powerful and can now cope with many different fonts. However, they still have difficulty with handwriting.

## Outsourcing

Outsourcing is similar to downsizing in that it is a way in which an organisation might seek to reduce costs by cutting the number of staff employed. In this case, the organisation will pay another company to provide services which were previously performed in-house, for example, IT support.

## PowerPoint

PowerPoint is presentation software developed by Microsoft. Using PowerPoint (or other similar packages), the presenter can show slides, notes, graphics, animations, etc., to accompany the presentation.

## Qualitative Data

Qualitative Data are data that have been gathered using qualitative methods such as participant observation and open semi-structured interviews. In this case data is gathered from observing the community being studied. It returns a mass of data in the form of notes and observations as opposed to data which are returned from *quantitative* methods (e.g., surveys and questionnaires) which lend themselves to statistical analysis. Qualitative data need analysing in a very different way, for example the extraction of themes leading to the inductive development of theory. *(See also Grounded Theory.)*

## Reification

Reification means taking something from your experience and giving it a concrete form. For example, all communities have their practice (i.e., what they *do*) and will create tools, stories, procedures and artefacts which reflect that practice. In these cases the practice has been reified.

## Representation Propagation

This refers to the occasions in Distributed Cognition where a representation is transferred (i.e., propagated) over or between different states or media. *(See Distributed Cognition.)*

## Representationism/Cognitivism

*(See Cognitivism.)*

## Rightsizing

"Rightsizing" is simply a euphemism for downsizing. *(See Downsizing.)*

## Search Engines

A search engine is a program which searches documents for keywords and returns a list to the user of all the documents where the keywords were found. The most common application for this technology is the Internet where users can choose from a range of search engines (e.g., Altavista [http://www.altavista.com]; dogpile [http://www.dogpile.com]) to search for pages on the World Wide Web. When a user enters a search term, the search engine does not go and search the World Wide Web. Behind the scenes, part of the search engine ("spider") is permanently trawling the World Wide Web and fetching as many documents as possible. Another part of the search engine (the indexer) then indexes the words in the document. It is this index that is searched when a user enters a keyword search.

## Smartboard

Also called an Interactive Whiteboard, this is a whiteboard that acts like a gigantic computer screen. It can show exactly the same as a computer screen (applications, video, multimedia, video conferencing images). Using special pens it can also be directly written on. This input can then be sent directly to the printer. In the case study in this book, the Smartboard was used in an E-meeting. It was showing the images from two desktop video conferencing cameras and Mike was making notes from the meeting. At the end of the meeting he sent the notes to be printed on the printer which was situated in the same room as the American partners. This technology is now starting to make its mark in schools.

## SSADM — Structured Systems Analysis and Design Method

SSADM is a set of standards which were developed for systems analysis and design in the 1980s. It was primarily aimed at large projects and was intended to reduce the failure rate.

It covers the life cycle of a system design and uses three main techniques to look at:

- Data structures
- Data access requirements
- Processing (updating) of data
- Permitted sequences of events which change data
- User interaction with the system

The three techniques are:

*Logical Data Modelling:* in this stage the data requirements of the proposed system are identified, modelled and documented. The main purpose of this stage is to divide the data into:

(a) entities — things or people about which data will need to be held
(b) relationships between the entities

Having identified these two parts, further steps are taken to create the optimum data model.

*Data Flow Modelling:* a technique for analysing processing. In this stage, the interest is in how data moves around an information system and how it is accessed and changed. This is also identified, modelled and documented. The models are decomposed into different levels and identify primarily:
(a) Processes — activities or actions which change data from one form to another
(b) Data stores — where data is held

(c) External entities — which send data to the system or receive data from the system

(d) Data flows — routes which the data can take

*Entity Behaviour Modelling:* events which can affect an entity and the order in which they occur. They are identified, modelled and documented for each entity in the form of entity life histories and entity event matrices.

Each of these techniques provide a different view of the system and must be checked and cross-referenced against each other to provide a complete view or model of the system which is being designed.

The above techniques fall into one of the following stages. SSADM has five separate stages (listed below) which are each further sub-divided into step and tasks:

(a) Feasibility Study: step to ascertain whether a system would adequately support the business processes and whether it is worth proceeding further, i.e., it assesses the economic justification for the system.

(b) Requirements Analysis: Assuming the findings of Stage 1 are positive, the next step is to identify the requirements of the new system. The main step to achieving this is to model the processes of the existing (probably manual) system.

(c) Requirements Specification: This stage goes beyond the requirements and creates a detailed specification. New techniques will be identified for some stages of the processing.

(d) Logical System Specification: In this stage the logical specification of the system is produced.

(e) Physical Design: An actual database design and a set of programming specifications are created from the logical design.

SSADM is not a parallel process — each step builds on the steps which have gone before. It is too large and complicated for most projects and is best suited to any system which has:

• A complex, static data structure
• Largely straightforward processing
• Potential evolution in processing but not in data

## Synchronous

In computer terms, synchronous means that something happens at regular intervals. Communication between a computer and a device is asynchronous as it can take place at any time and the interval is likely to be irregular. However, communication within the computer itself is generally synchronous because it is governed by the clock of the Central Processing Unit (CPU).

In terms of communication media, synchronous means taking place at the same time, i.e., the telephone is a synchronous medium.

*(See also Asynchronous.)*

## Tele-Conferencing

A Tele-Conference is a multi-party conversation held via telephone or some other telecommunications connection. In the examples in this case study, the participants were in two locations with a group in each location being gathered around a polycom. (A polycom is a central speaker with a keyboard and three microphones.) Modern telephones often have the function built in to allow the user to set up a conference call with a number of other users.

## Transnational

This is the direction for which many international companies appear to be aiming. It is an organisational form which appeared in the late 80s to early 90s. Zwass (1992) describes it as an "integrated network" where all units contribute on an equal basis to integrated worldwide activities. They are not regarded as having to merely execute a centralised strategy as "each … is viewed as a source of ideas, skills, capabilities and knowledge that can be beneficial to the company as a whole" (Karimi & Konsynski, 1991).

The national subsidiaries are coordinated but the firm is still able to respond to local needs by virtue of the fact that subsidiaries are not totally subordinate to headquarters. They have the opportunity to contribute as equals. The nature of such a company enables it to coordinate facilities and for people to respond quickly to circumstances anywhere. In many cases, the firm can appear to be stateless and probably not have national headquarters. Rather, it has regional headquarters with possibly a world headquarters.

Developments in IT and telecommunications have enabled the development of this kind of concern as the speed of communication enables the concern to consider the whole world to be one market. Problems of distance and time are greatly reduced.

## UNIX

UNIX is a multi-user, multi-tasking operating system which was designed specifically for use in a networked environment. Created at Bell Labs in the early 1970s, it was designed to be powerful, stable and flexible. It has become a very mature operating system. Its origins can still be seen in the command line operation and the cryptic commands it uses.

UNIX has become very popular in large organisations and universities.

## Video-Conferencing

This is a meeting or discussion carried out between communication partners who are in different locations but who can see and hear each other using electronic media such as video. The images and audio data are transmitted by a telecommunication network. The conference can take place anywhere in the world.

A high quality video image will need a lot of bandwidth so high fidelity video conferences tend to take place in specialist suites over high bandwidth networks. Desktop video conferencing is more popular because it is more affordable — both in terms of the cameras and the required bandwidth. The video image is of a much lower quality but it gives the communication partners some context. A user can be at his or her PC with a camera on top of it, speaking on the telephone and seeing images of his/her communication partners on the PC screen.

## Virtual Environment (VE)

"A collaborative computer mediated social environment that enables geographically dispersed participants to make contact through an artificially generate sense of proximity known as 'tele-presence.' This is manifested through the various communication devices that are employed by the participants" (Conkar, 1999, p. 9).

## Virtual Reality (VR)

VR is an artificial environment created by computers to represent a virtual world. It appears to the user as though (s)he is immersed in the world as it reacts to the user's actions. The user may well be wearing a VR suit with sensors in gloves and other parts of the suit. A helmet will have goggles or a screen which shows the image to the user. It may also track the movement of the eyes and show different images depending the direction in which the user is looking. As the user turns, a different image will be presented; the user may stoop to pick up and object and, because of the sensors in the gloves, will feel as though (s)he is actually touching the object — so at least three of the senses are catered for (touch, hearing, sight).

Great advances are being made in VR systems but they still need very powerful processing and therefore have not yet become mainstream.

## Virtual Team

Lipnack and Stamps (1997) define a virtual team as follows:

*"A virtual team, like every team, is a group of people who interact through interdependent tasks guided by a common purpose.*
*The image of face-to-face interactions among people from the same organisation typifies our older models of teamwork. What sets virtual teams apart is that they routinely cross boundaries. What makes virtual teams historically new is the awesome array of inter-active technologies at their disposal" (Lipnack & Stamps, 1997, pp. 6-7).*

## Voice Mail

Voice Mail is much more than an answering machine. It is more like e-mail for voice messages in that a full voice mail system will allow a spoken message to be saved, forwarded or replied to.

## War Stories

These are stories told based on the teller's experience and which are told to illustrate a point, perhaps as a contribution to problem solving. The teller's colleagues may learn something from the story. It may make them think of something else or lead them to come up with something new and innovative. War stories can be part of the creative process.

## World Wide Web (WWW)

The WWW is a system of servers on the Internet which hold documents formatted in html (hypertext mark-up language). Html documents can hold links to other documents and can include images, animations, sound and video. This means that a user can start with one document and follow a trail of discovery as (s)he follows links to other documents. These documents can be held on servers all over the world but this is totally invisible to the user. In order to read these pages, the user will need a program which can read pages written in html. These programs are called web browsers. Two of the most popular web browsers are Microsoft's Internet Explorer and Netscape's Navigator.

It is important to remember that the WWW is *not* synonymous with the Internet — not all servers on the Internet are part of the WWW.

## Web Form

Early web pages could only *present* information. Later developments meant that could then also *collect* information. A Web Form is a form on a web page which can take input from a user. Once the form is filled in, the data is then passed back to the organisation for processing. The data might be a survey, user details for subscription, a purchase, a booking, a CV submission, or anything else where an organisation is collecting data from its users via the Web.

## Yellow Pages

These take their name from the telephone directories with listings according to service. In terms of Knowledge Management, Yellow Pages are directories of experts within the organisation.

## Y2K

Also known as the Millennium Bug, the Millennium problem and the Y2K problem, Y2K was a major computer problem as the end of the 20$^{th}$ century approached. It was found that a number of computer systems written at a time when memory was at a premium could only represent a year in two digits (e.g., is 03, 1903 or 2003?). This problem mainly affected "legacy" systems which were written in the 1970s and 1980s — the writers of these systems were probably astounded that they were still in use at the end of the century, long after the end of their life expectancy. The problem also affected some personal computers because the BIOS systems were found to be at risk. This meant that organisations were checking every PC and millions of lines of programming code.

Predictions were made of worldwide computer meltdowns at midnight on December 31, 1999, but predictions of disaster were wide of the mark. The question still remains — was the problem as serious as predicted after all or was it hyped by people earning a lot of money working on the problem? Or was the lack of disaster due to the planning and all the work which had been put in, in advance, to tackle the problem?

# About the Author

After 11 years teaching Modern Languages, **Paul Hildreth** went back to university, in York, UK, to "convert" to IT. Having completed his MSc, he stayed on to do a DPhil exploring the field of Knowledge Management. This work convinced him that Knowledge Management is not about technology but about people and led him to explore the emerging and fascinating field of Communities of Practice. Recognizing the pressures imposed on organizations by globalization, he concentrated on researching how Communities of Practice can function in a distributed international environment. The work produced a number of well-received journal and conference papers.

Having completed his DPhil, Paul now runs his own independent Knowledge Management and computer consultancies. He lives in rural North Yorkshire with Maggie, Tom, and Buzz the cat, and when he manages to find a little spare time likes to indulge his hobbies of kit and classic cars, and guitar.

# Index

## Symbols

3-D audio 87

## A

acit-explicit pairing 24
active cores 150
ad hoc communication 107
American Core 116
apprentice 36
apprenticeship 18
artefact 26, 138
artificial intelligence (AI) 5, 8
asynchronous 69
autopoiesis theory 21, 62

## B

boundary object 30, 113, 154, 159

## C

case-based reasoning (CBR) 9
co-located group 159
co-located phenomenon 55
co-location 73, 79, 150
coffee-talk 123
cognition 27
cognitivist view 20
cognitivist/representational approach 22
coincident boundaries 31
collaboration 68, 105, 128, 160
comfort zone 168
common ground 25, 33, 41, 73, 159

common purpose 42, 79
communication 104, 128, 168
communications media 142
community 160
community e-mail 142
community identity 147
community members 95
community of practice (CoP) 1, 25,
    35, 158, 167
competitive advantage 4
computer-mediated communications
    (CMCs) 68
computer-supported co-operative work
    (CSCW) 26
confidence 73
constructionist 20
constructionist view 20, 26
CoP characteristics 124
copyrights 9
core-competency 20
cross-team collaboration 87
cultural barriers 12
cultural community 34
cultural differences 3
cultural issues 130
culture 11, 21, 35, 68, 108, 130
culture-based approach 14

## D

data reasoning 21
data warehousing 9
databases 9
development of the relationship 116

learning 8
learning and knowledge creation 15
legitimate peripheral participation (LPP)
    36, 42, 98
legitimation 37, 72, 99, 126, 147
local area network (LAN) 122

## M

marginals 95
measurement 16
media 29, 105, 151
mental model 8, 11
motivation 79, 131, 146, 161

## N

narration 39, 43
national community 34
NetMeeting 82
network enterprise 4, 68
networked communication media 4
new knowledge 43
newcomers 125
newsletter list 142

## O

occupational community 34
ontologies 9
opportunistic communication 107
optical character recognition (OCR) 85
outsourcing 1, 7, 25, 44
overhead projector (OHP) 122

## P

participation 36, 135, 148, 160
participation duality 98, 159
participation in communities 22
patents 5, 9
perceptual copresence 73
peripherality 38, 148
personal computer (PC) 82
physical artefacts 26
physically distributed environment 108

## R

real virtuality 12
regeneration 42, 44
reification 50, 74, 98, 160
reification duality 159
relationship decay 132
relationships 42
repositories 31
representation propagation 155
representational artefacts 29
representational view 20, 26
representations 27
resource knowledge 19
resourcing 86

## S

self-knowledge 19
shared artefact 116, 141, 154, 159
shared background 98
shared domain language 73
shared language 98
sharing 168
shoptalk 34
social aspect 164
social awareness 107
social barriers 12
social issues 98, 151
social participation 50
socialization 35
sociology 66
soft knowledge 24, 26, 158
stories 19, 145, 160
strong relationships 160

## T

tacit knowledge 2, 17
task focus 136
technical terminology 34
tele-conferencing 68
temporal peripherality 167
trademarks 5, 9
transactive knowledge 19
trust 73, 162

# U

undirected research  144
unspoken conventions of the community
        45

# V

vertical team meeting  84
vertical teams  113
video or audio conference  144
video-conferencing  48,  68
virtual CoP  72
Virtual Environments (VEs)  66,  74,
        167
virtual teams  66
voice mail  68

# W

war stories  39,  124,  162
wizards  96
working relationship  71
WWITMan  105

# Y

Y2K  90
Yellow Pages  10

# *NEW* from Idea Group Publishing

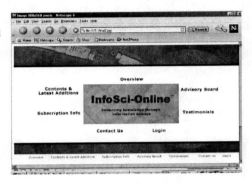